АЛЕКСАНДР

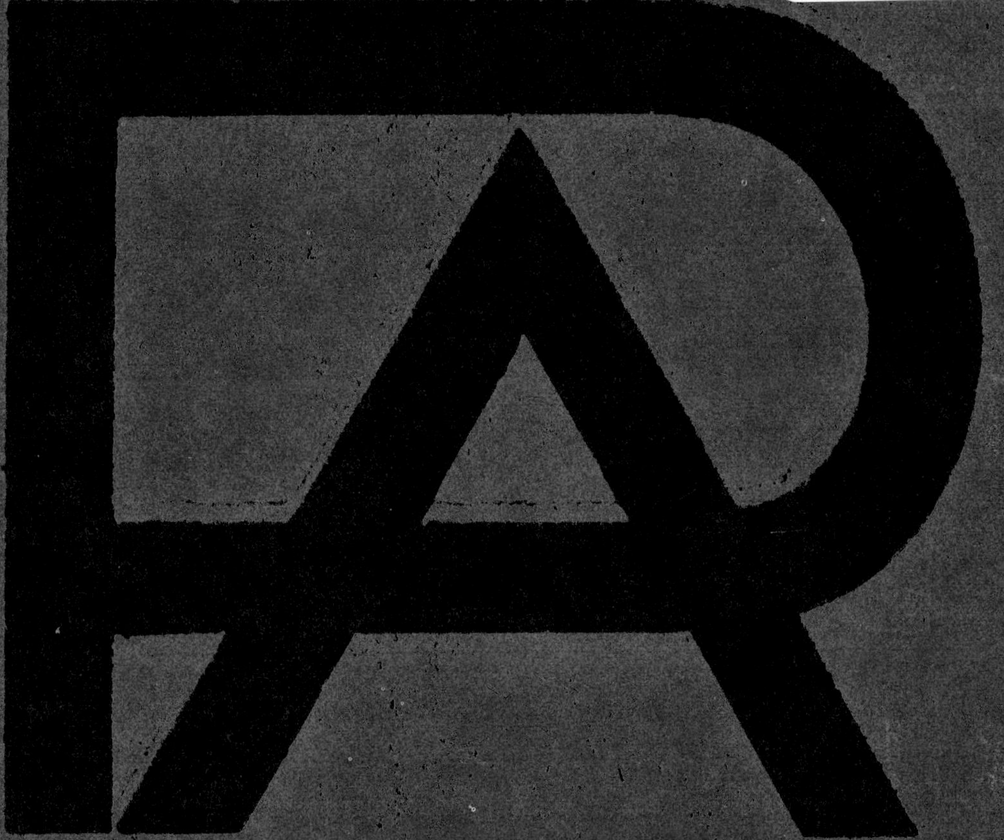

РОДЧЕНКО

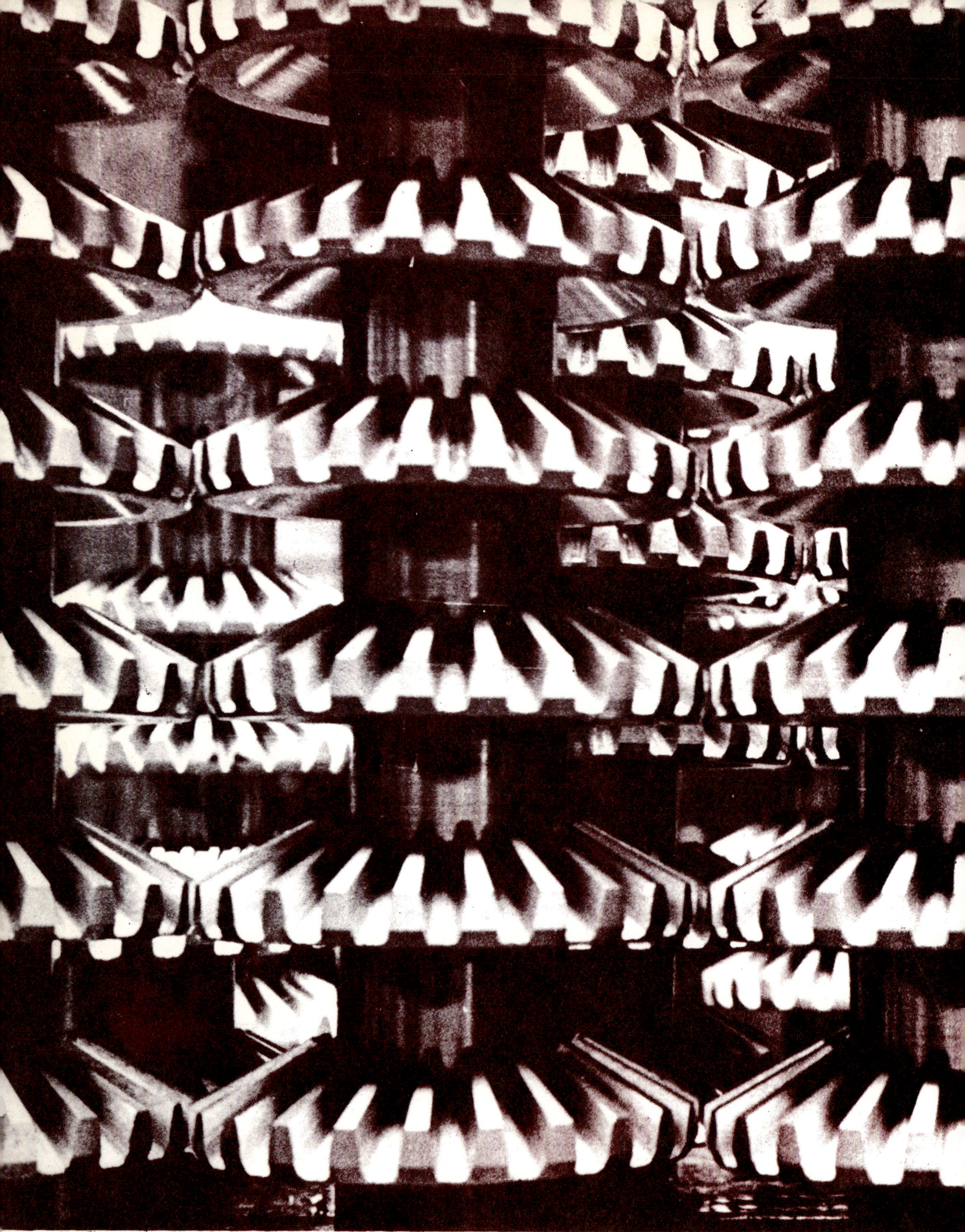

RODCHENKO

AND THE ARTS OF REVOLUTIONARY RUSSIA

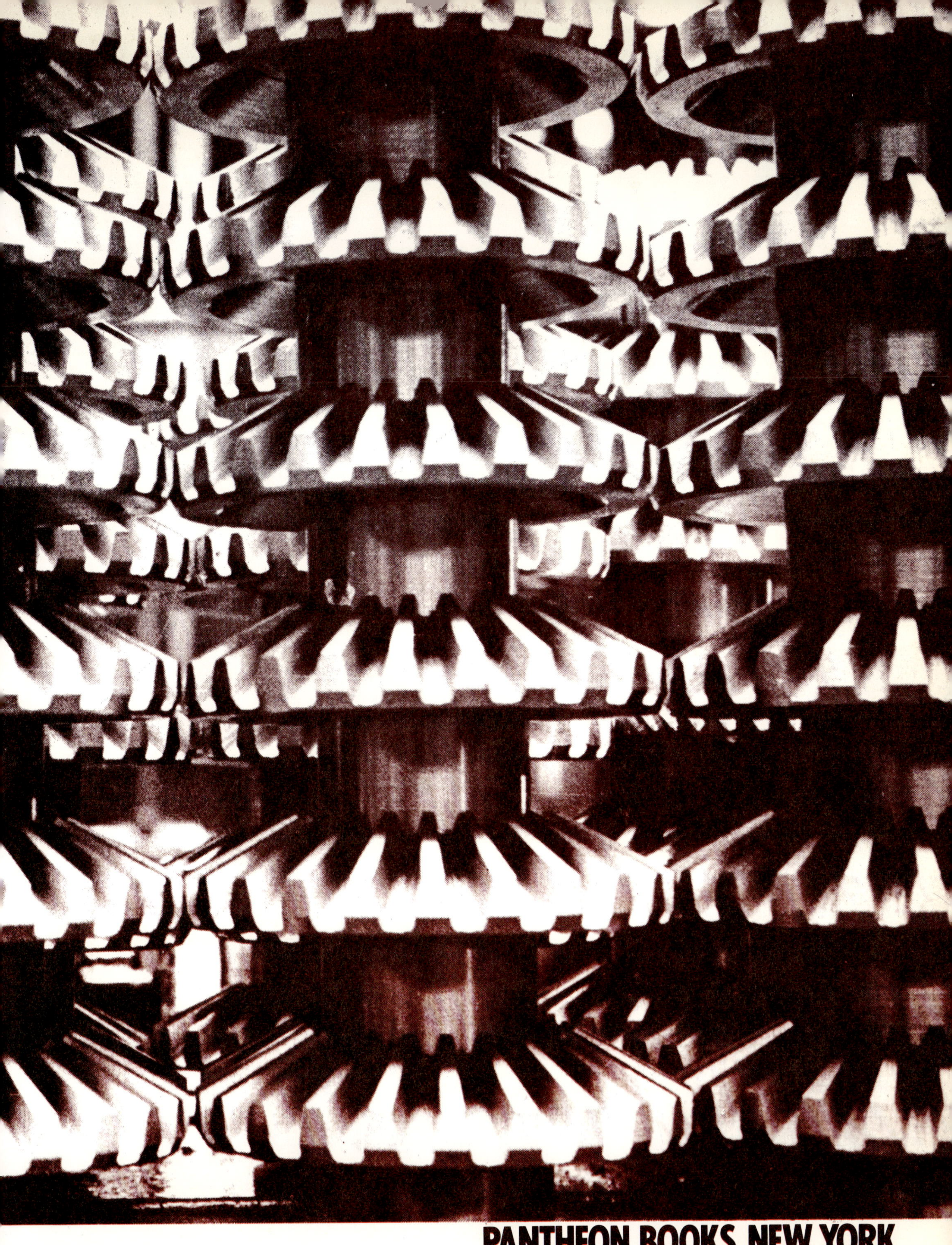

PANTHEON BOOKS, NEW YORK

EDITED BY DAVID ELLIOTT

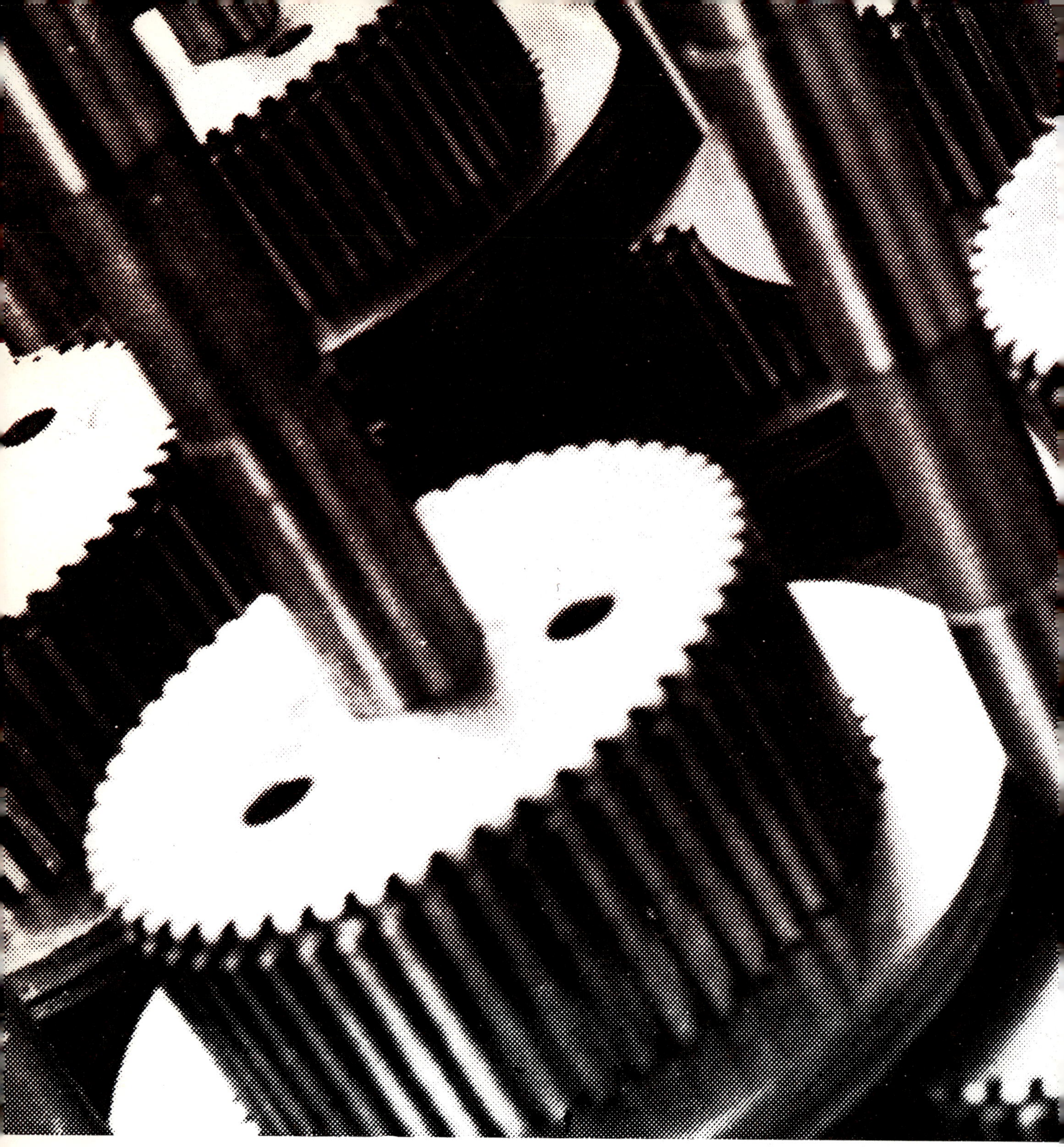

 Published in the United States by Pantheon Books, a division of Random House, Inc., New York, and simultaneously in Canada by Random House of Canada Limited, Toronto. Originally published in Great Britain as *Alexander Rodchenko* by A. Zwemmer Ltd. in association with Museum of Modern Art, Oxford.

Library of Congress Cataloging in Publication Data

Main entry under title:

Rodchenko and the arts of revolutionary Russia.

Reprint of the 1979 ed. published by A. Zwemmer, London, in association with Museum of Modern Art, Oxford, issued under title: Alexander Rodchenko.
1. Rodchenko, Aleksandr Mikhailovich, 1891-1956—Addresses, essays, lectures. 2. Art, Russian—Addresses, essays, lectures. 3. Art and revolutions—Russia—Addresses, essays, lectures. 4. Art, Modern—20th century—Russia—Addresses, essays, lectures. I. Elliott, David, 1949-
N6999.R62A88 1979 709′-2′4 79-2305
ISBN 0-394-50854-8
ISBN 0-394-73756-3 pbk.

Manufactured in the United States of America
First American Edition

Grateful acknowledgment is made to the following for permission to reproduce artwork on the pages indicated: the Albright-Knox Art Gallery, Buffalo, New York, General Purchase Fund, 1978: p. 12 (Rodchenko, Alexander, "Untitled" c. 1918–20, oil on canvas, 46 cm. x 36 cm.); Mr. George Costakis: pp. 15, 16, 35; the Galerie Jean Chauvelin, Paris: p. 39; the Museum of Modern Art, New York: pp. 36, 38, 52 (center); the Rodchenko Archive. Moscow: pp. 10, 11, 14, 17, 18, 32, 33, 34. 40.

Cog wheels, 1930

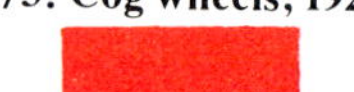

Pages 2/3: Cog wheels, 1927

Page 1: Rodchenko's studio stamp

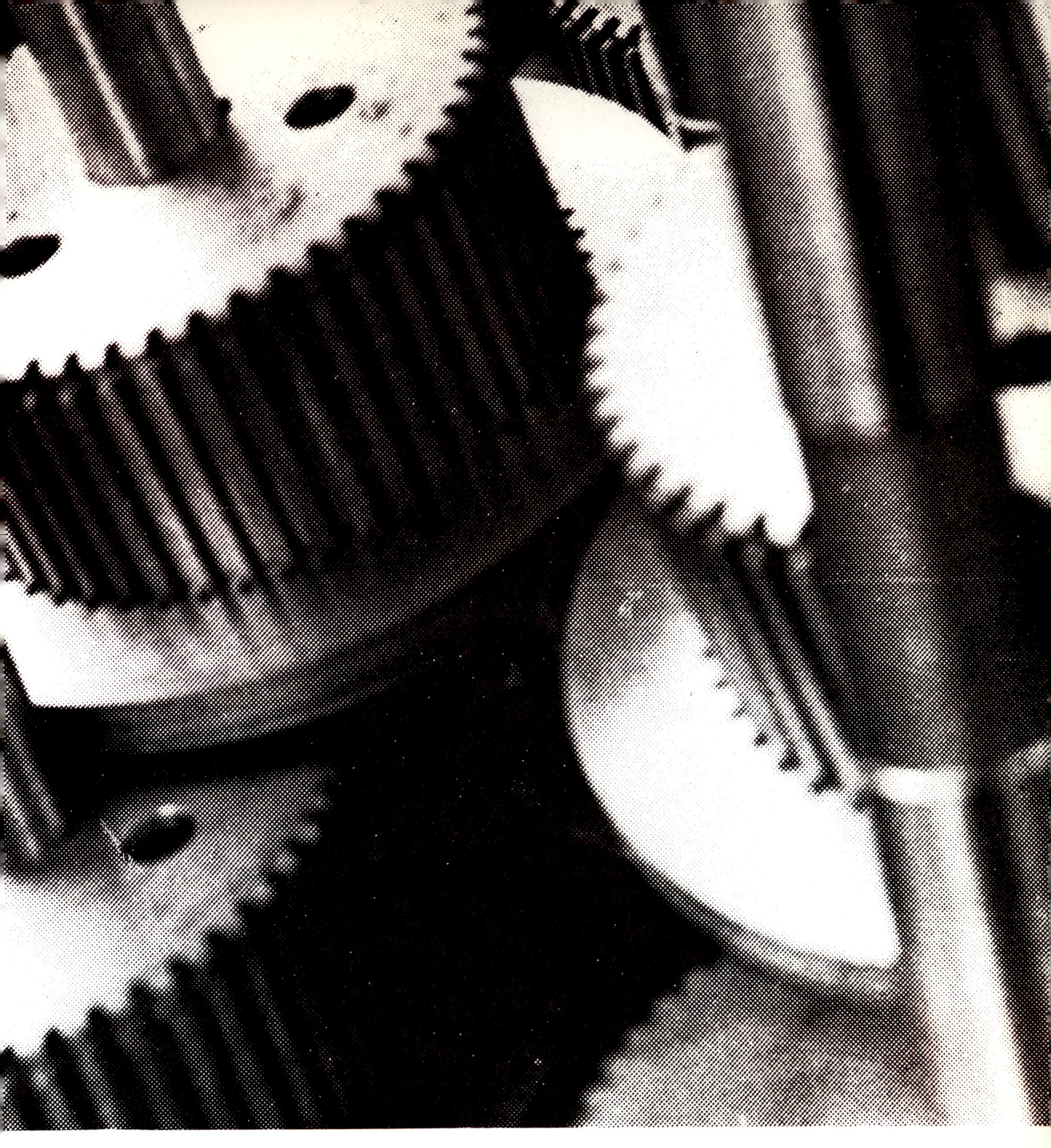

CONTENTS

INTRODUCTION

Opposite page: Rodchenko in the worker's suit of his own design. Photograph by Mikhail Kaufman, 1921

by David Elliott

It is not usual that twenty-two years should pass after the death of a well known and respected artist before a complete retrospective exhibition of his work is organised. Such however has been the case with Alexander Rodchenko.

In making this book we have tried to provide not only a factual breakdown of what Rodchenko did and when, with some opinions on his theories and works, but also to give a sense of the feeling of the time — what it was like to be a student (or teacher) at Vkhutemas, or the sense of loss that must have been widely felt on hearing of the suicide of Mayakovsky.

Rodchenko was a revolutionary artist in both the political and aesthetic sense. From the time of his arrival in Moscow from Kazan in 1915, through to the end of his life, he believed that it was the role of the artist to act as a catalyst for social change. In new forms and new means of expression Rodchenko hoped to transform man's perception of ordinary objects — to show things as they really were, to suggest how things could and might be. He totally rejected the metaphysical and the mystical in his work — although these ideas were current in the works of such advanced artists as Vasilii Kandinsky and Kazimir Malevich. Such tendencies seemed to be illusionistic, an escape to the past, an avoidance of reality. Rodchenko wished to express in forms which had no reference beyond themselves the specific properties of the elements he had employed. Each painting became a experiment in which the raw elements of colour, form, space, facture and line became the protagonists. These paintings and the constructions which resulted out of them were always full of energy, rich in their associations: under the at first inscrutable cover of non-objective forms Rodchenko enacted dramas that are known to us all.

Rodchenko continued his systematic work in both painting and three dimensional construction until, in 1921, he was led to what for him was the ultimate statement in painting: a construction of three monochrome canvases in red, yellow and blue. The reductive tendencies of the dissolution of surface which had assumed an increasingly important role in his non-objective painting, had been taken to their ultimate conclusion. A desire to make a painting which was complete in itself without any reference to outside influences had led him to distill subject matter to a single element — colour within the co-ordinates of the painted canvas. As well as being the "last painting" this work marked his severance with the last remnants of a "fine art" painterly tradition. Along with others in a similar position such as L. Popova, A. Vesnin and V. Stepanova, he had decided that the artist should make art not out of inner compulsion but out of a feeling of responsibility towards his fellow citizens; he should serve the community in the same way as a doctor or scientist.

The nature of Russian society had been transformed by the Revolution and these changes had to be communicated to everyone through graphic and industrial design. The old forms implicitly expressed the old ideologies; new opportunities were available to all and a new, enthusiastic way of expressing man's relation to the world had to be found. The solution lay in Production Art.

As the decade progressed the innate visual conservatism of the population at large led to the criticism of work which expressed itself as much through formal innovation as through subject matter. In the late 1920s such work was denounced for its "formalism".

To Rodchenko the visual quality of his work always remained paramount, and his statement of 1915 that he wished to show usual things in an unusual way held true throughout his life. In his photography in the late 1920s his devotion to the unusual in the usual, his rejection of the "fetishisation of fact", led to much criticism. It was claimed that the dynamic close-ups and oblique viewpoints with which he constructed his photographs were a parody rather than an epitome of a new Soviet reality.

From the beginning of the 1930s the advanced art of Rodchenko and his contemporaries did not receive official support. The climate had changed, and at a time when the Soviet Union was struggling with a series of Five Year Plans to modernise industry and agriculture to establish economic viability it was felt that the simple rhetoric of Socialist Realism provided a more easily intelligible framework for communicating the changes that were taking place. Like many of his colleagues Rodchenko was not able to comply with this prevailing aesthetic and as a result he was thrown more and more in upon himself with few outlets for his work. A reconciliation was effected when in 1935 his photographs began to appear in newspapers and magazines again and even before then, with his wife Varvara Stepanova, he had made a number of designs for books, periodicals and photo-albums.

These years were difficult, yet Rodchenko continued to work. The groups of artists, his friends, who had previously worked together had become fragmented; some had died, those that continued worked in isolation. Rodchenko continued and in 1941, when writing his memoirs of his friend and master, Vladimir Tatlin, he could easily have been referring to his own life and work: "He was truly a great Russian painter who, although he would have liked recognition, waited... and was prepared to wait. And I am sure that recognition will still come to him. Only true Russian painters can work like this in the shade over the years without their true worth being recognised. They have a great love of work and faith in the future, even whilst remaining unknown, sometimes until death..."

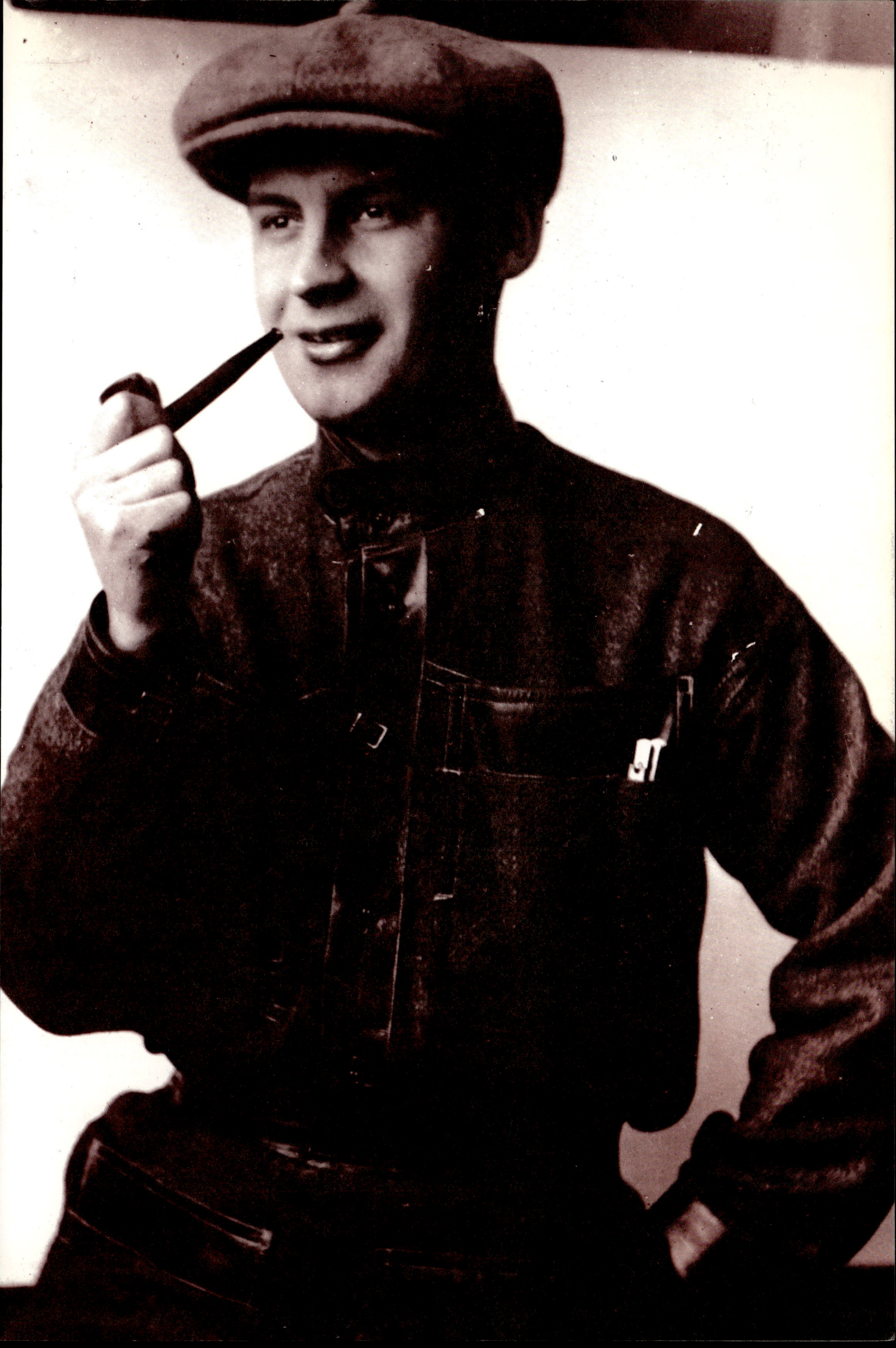

FROM THE EASEL TO THE MACHINE

Rodchenko's manifesto from the catalogue for the X State Exhibition Moscow, 1919

As a basis for my work I have put nothing.
—M. Stirner, "The Sole One"

Colours disappear — everything merges into black.
— A. Kruchenykh, "Gly-Gly"

Muscle and pluck forever!
What invigorates life invigorates death,
And the dead advance as much as the living advance.
— Walt Whitman, "Leaves of Grass"

Murder serves as a self-justification for the murderer; for thereby he tries to prove that nothing exists.
— Otto Weininger, "Aphorisms"

I devour it the moment I advance the thesis, and I am the "I" only when I devour it.
...The fact that I devour myself shows merely that I exist.
— M. Stirner

Gliding o'er all, through all,
Through Nature, Time and Space,
As a ship on the waters advancing,
The voyage of the soul — not life alone,
Death, many deaths I'll sing.
— Walt Whitman, "Leaves of Grass"

The crushing of all "isms" in painting was for me the beginning of my resurrection. With the funeral bells of colour painting, the last "ism" was accompanied to its grave, the lingering last hopes of love are destroyed, and I leave the house of dead truths.

Not synthesis but analysis is creation. Painting is the body, and creation is the soul. My work is to create new painting, and I have to look at things as they are. Literature and philosophy are for specialists in those subjects, I am the inventor of new discoveries in painting.

Christopher Columbus was neither a writer nor a philosopher — he was merely the discoverer of new countries.

Rodchenko's Statement at XIX State Exhibition Moscow, 1920

Non-objective painting has left the Museums; non-objective painting is the street itself, the squares, the towns and the whole world. The art of the future will not be the cosy decoration of family homes. It will be just as indispensable as 48-storey skyscrapers, mighty bridges, wireless, aeronautics and submarines which will be transformed into art.

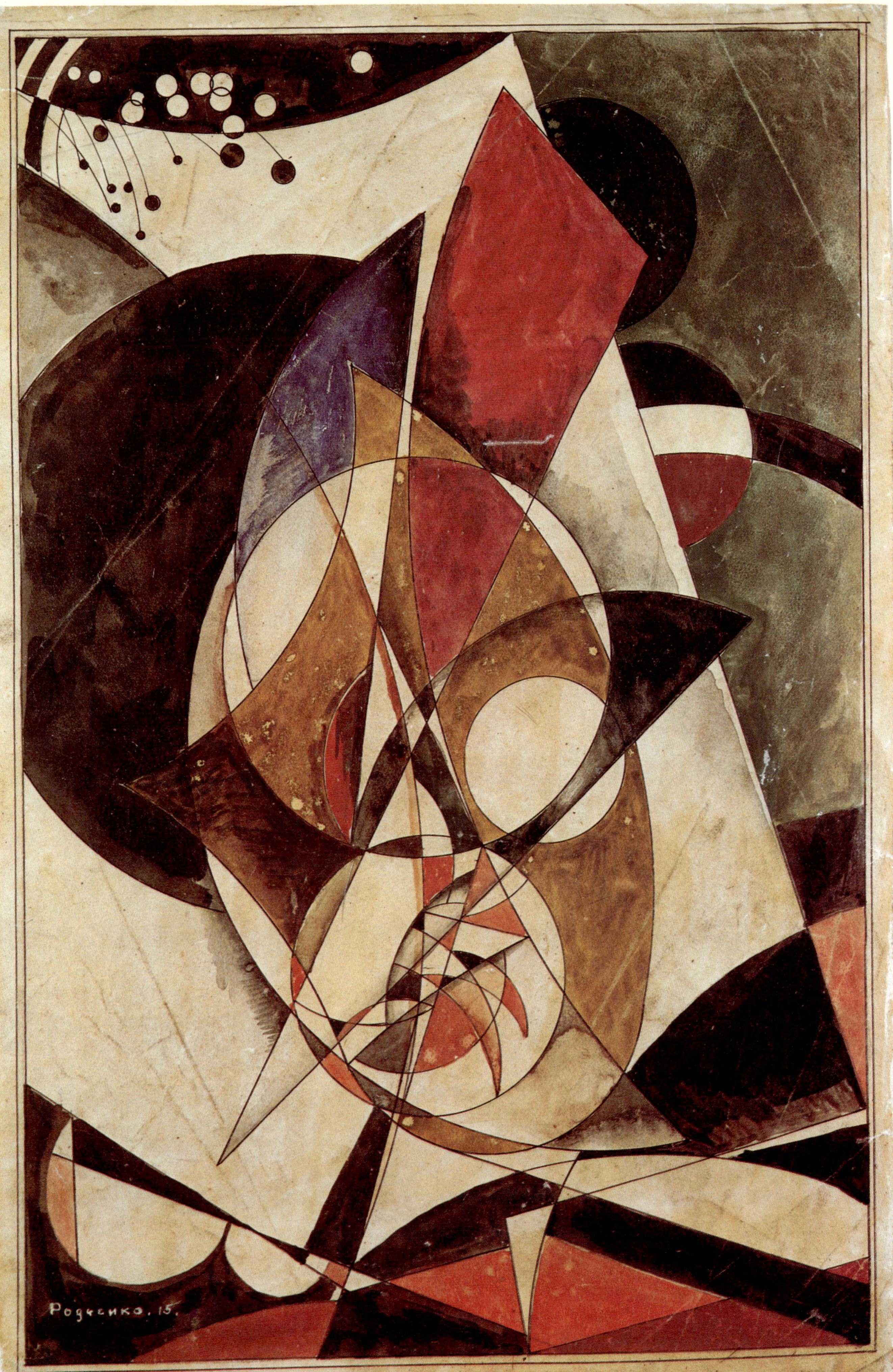
Родченко. 15.

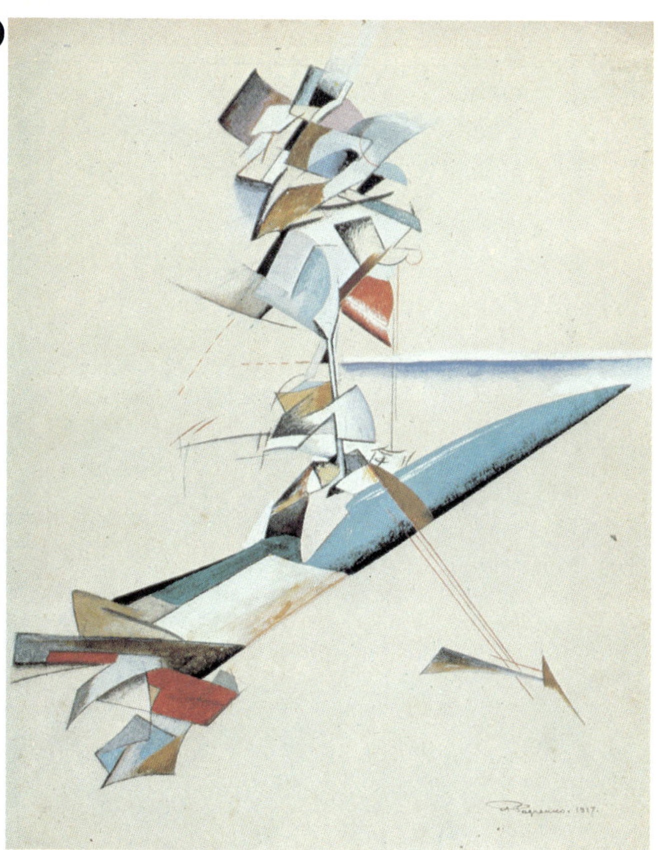

Untitled composition, tempera, 1917

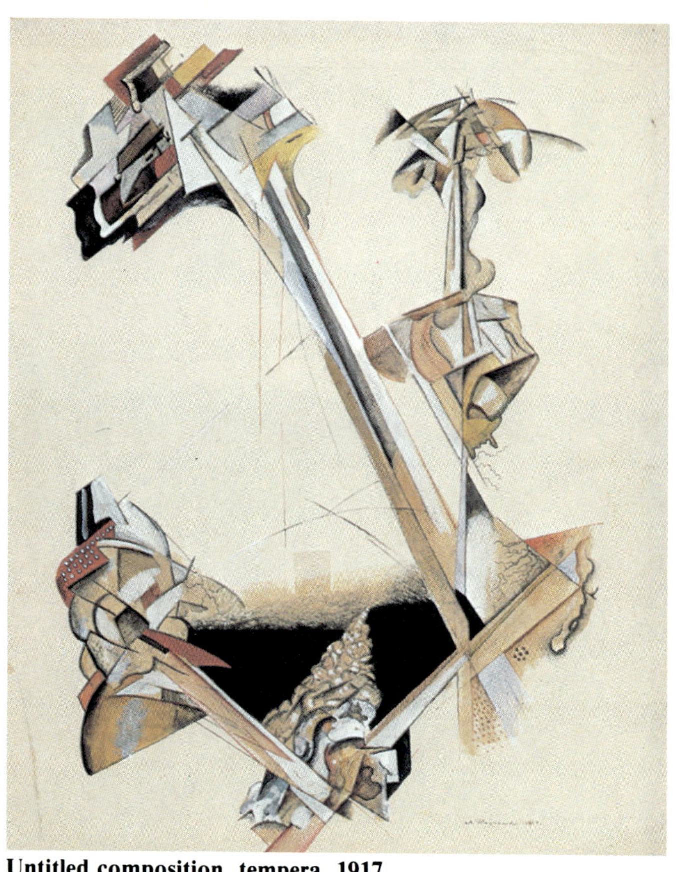

Untitled composition, tempera, 1917

Opposite page: Untitled composition, watercolour and ink, 1919

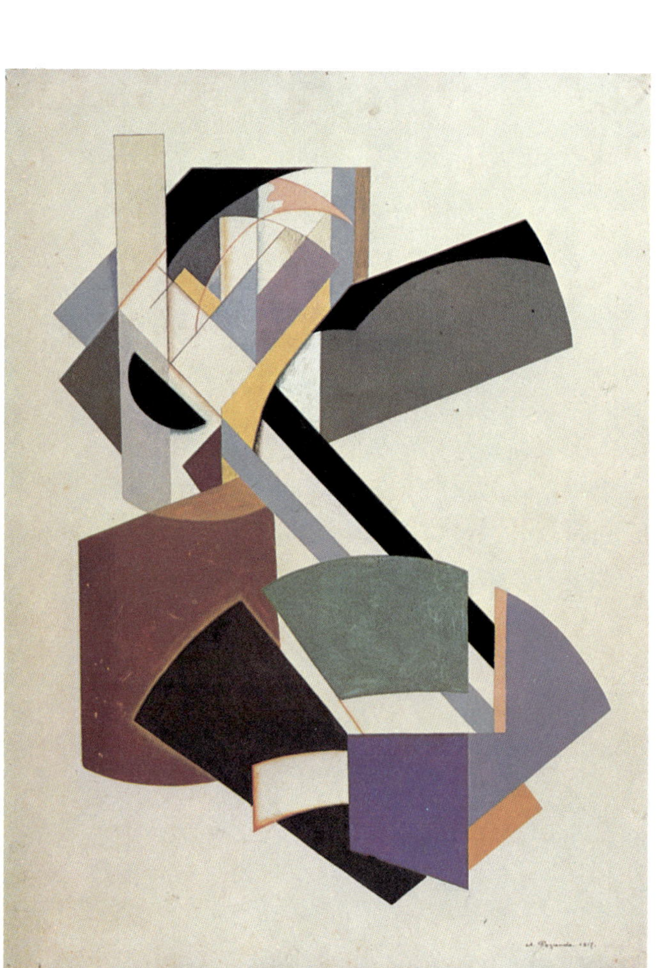

Untitled composition, tempera, 1917

Right: ''Biziaks'' project for a kiosk, gouache and ink, 1919

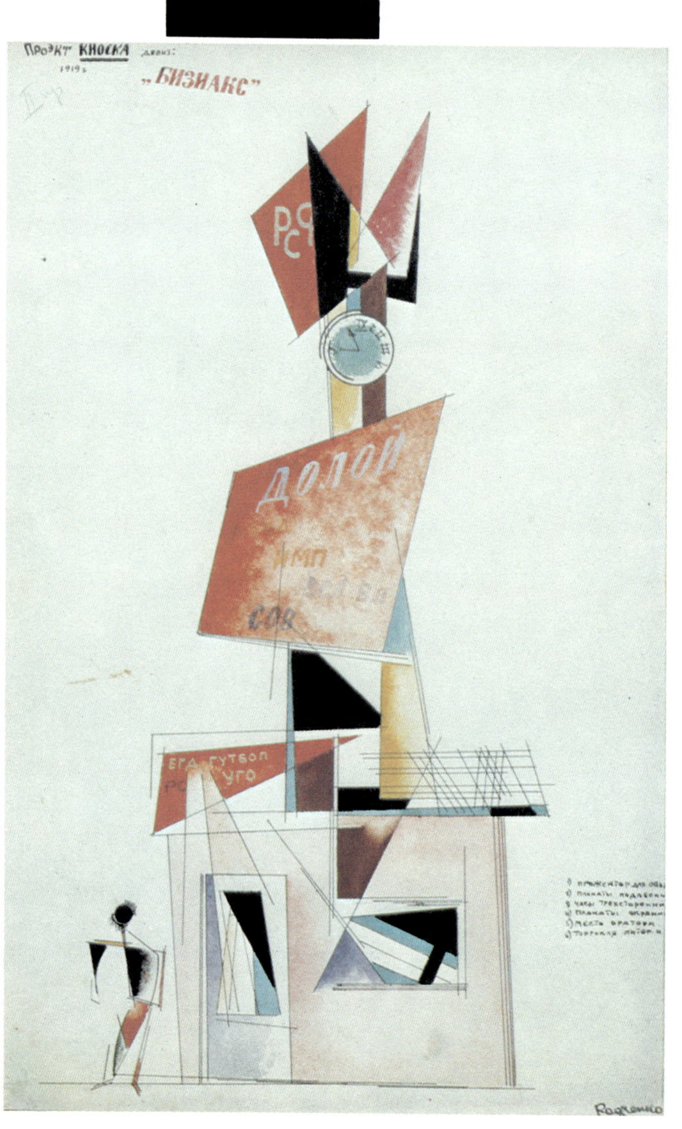

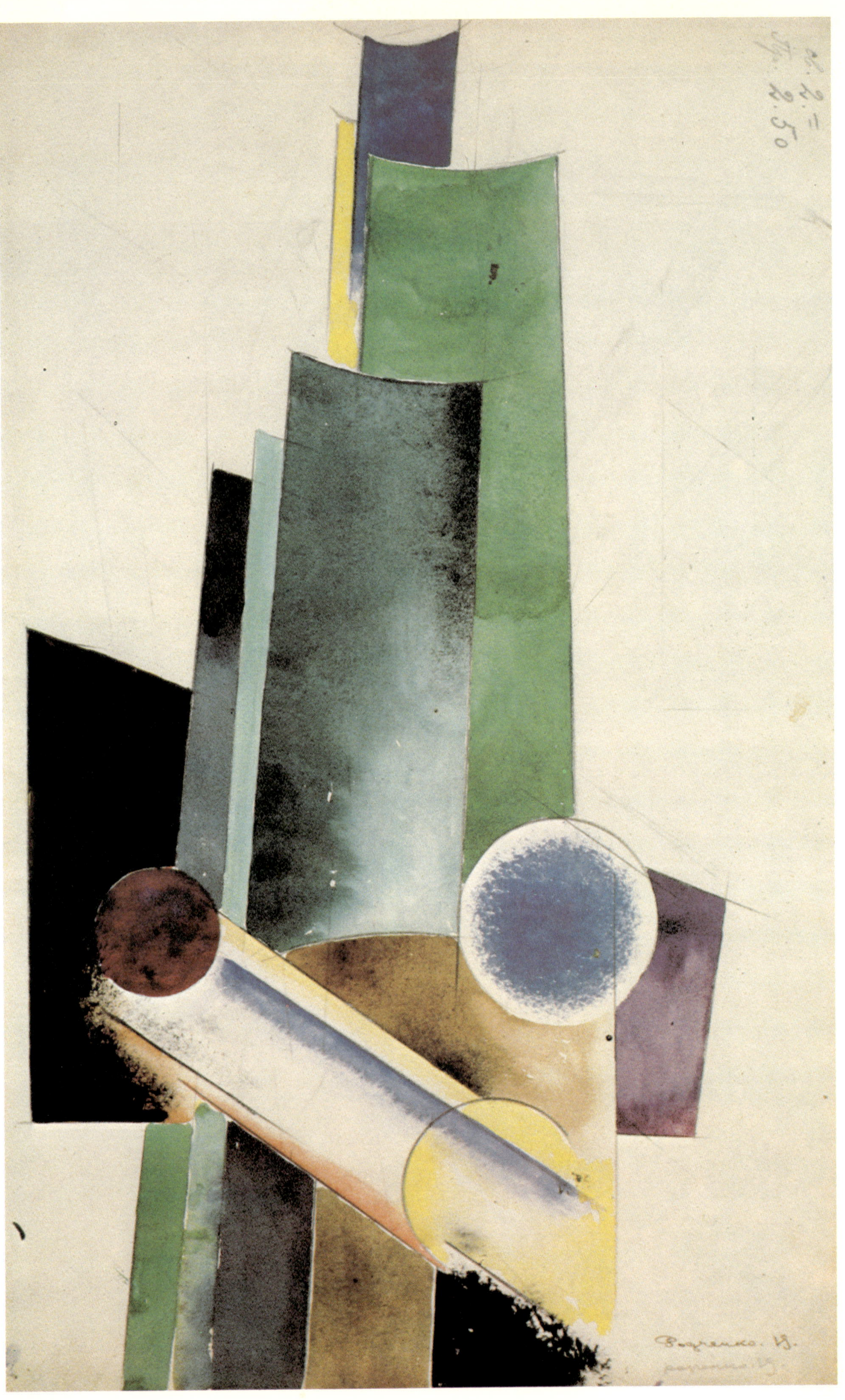

Non-objective composition, oil on board, 1919-20

12

Non-objective composition, oil on wood, 1920

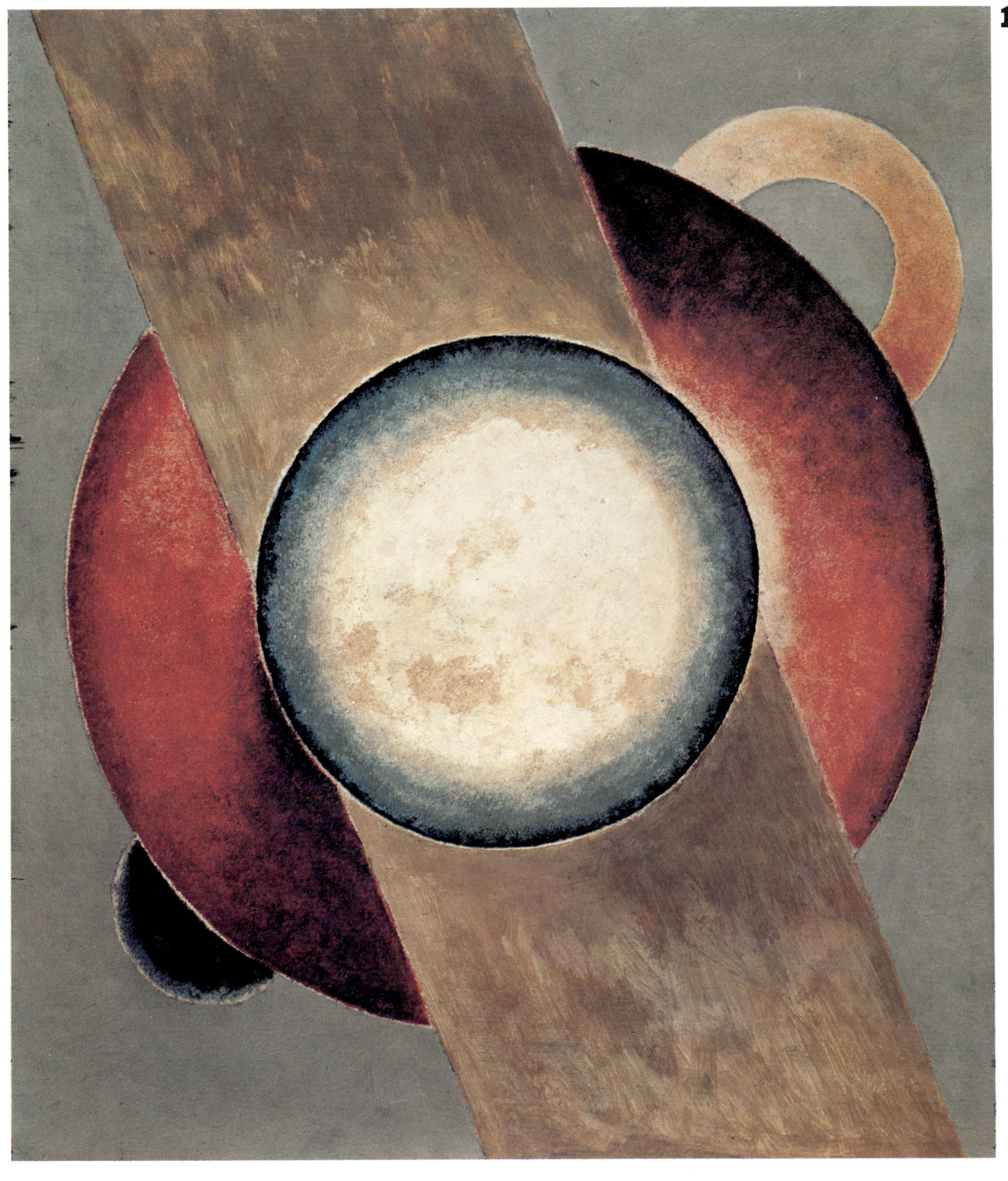

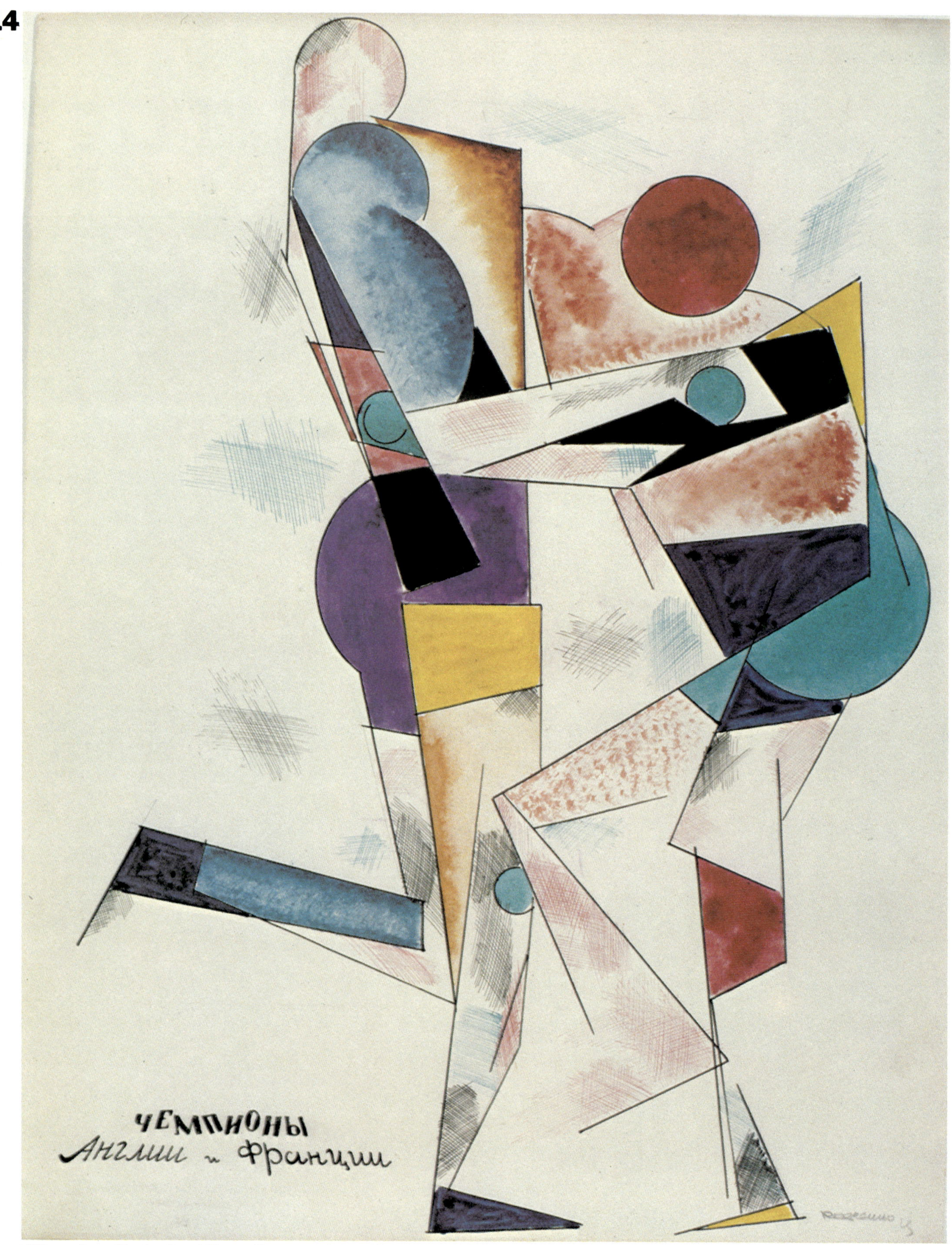

"Champions, England and France", watercolour and coloured ink, 1919

Opposite page: Figurative abstraction, oil on wood, 1919

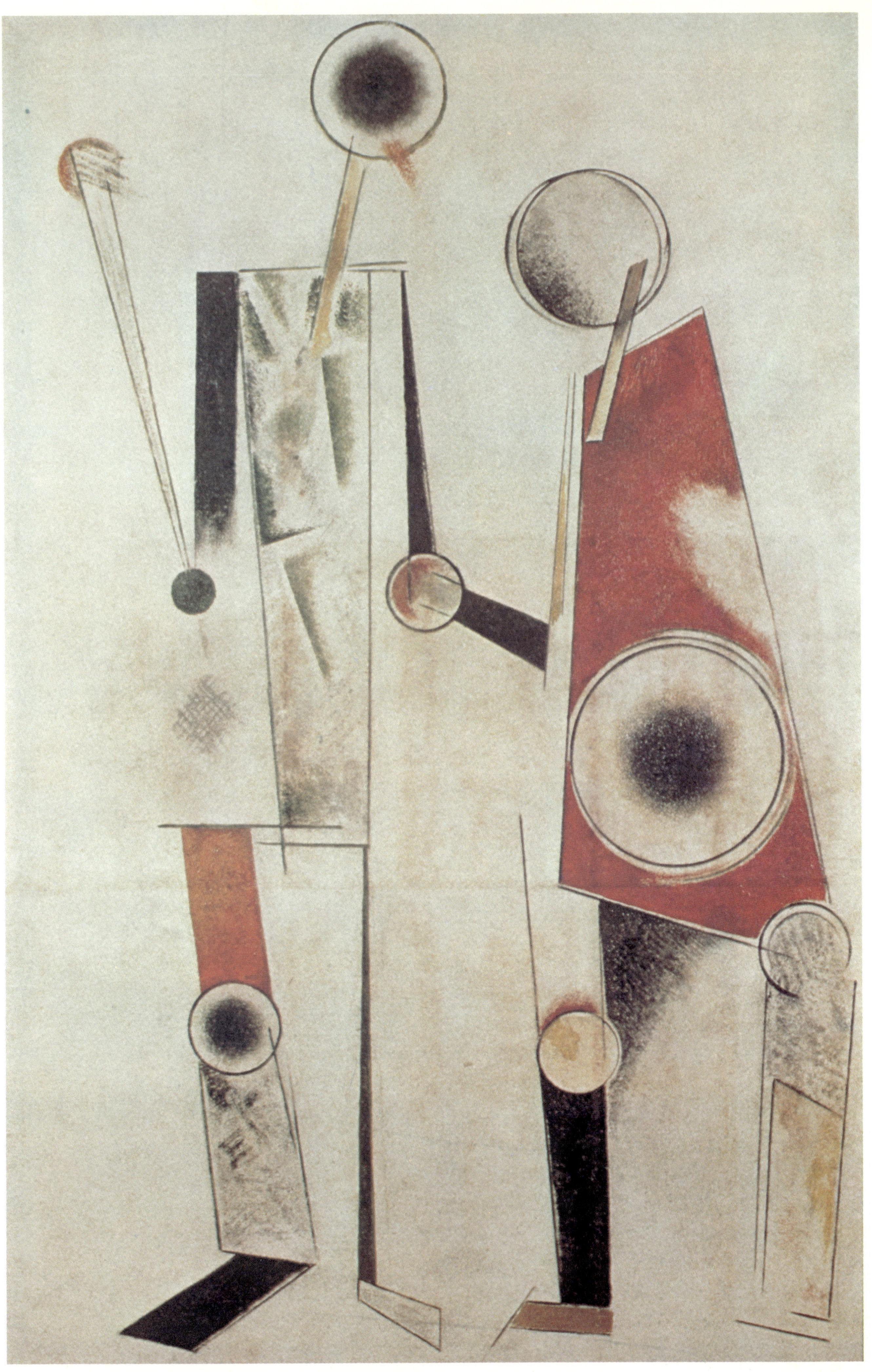

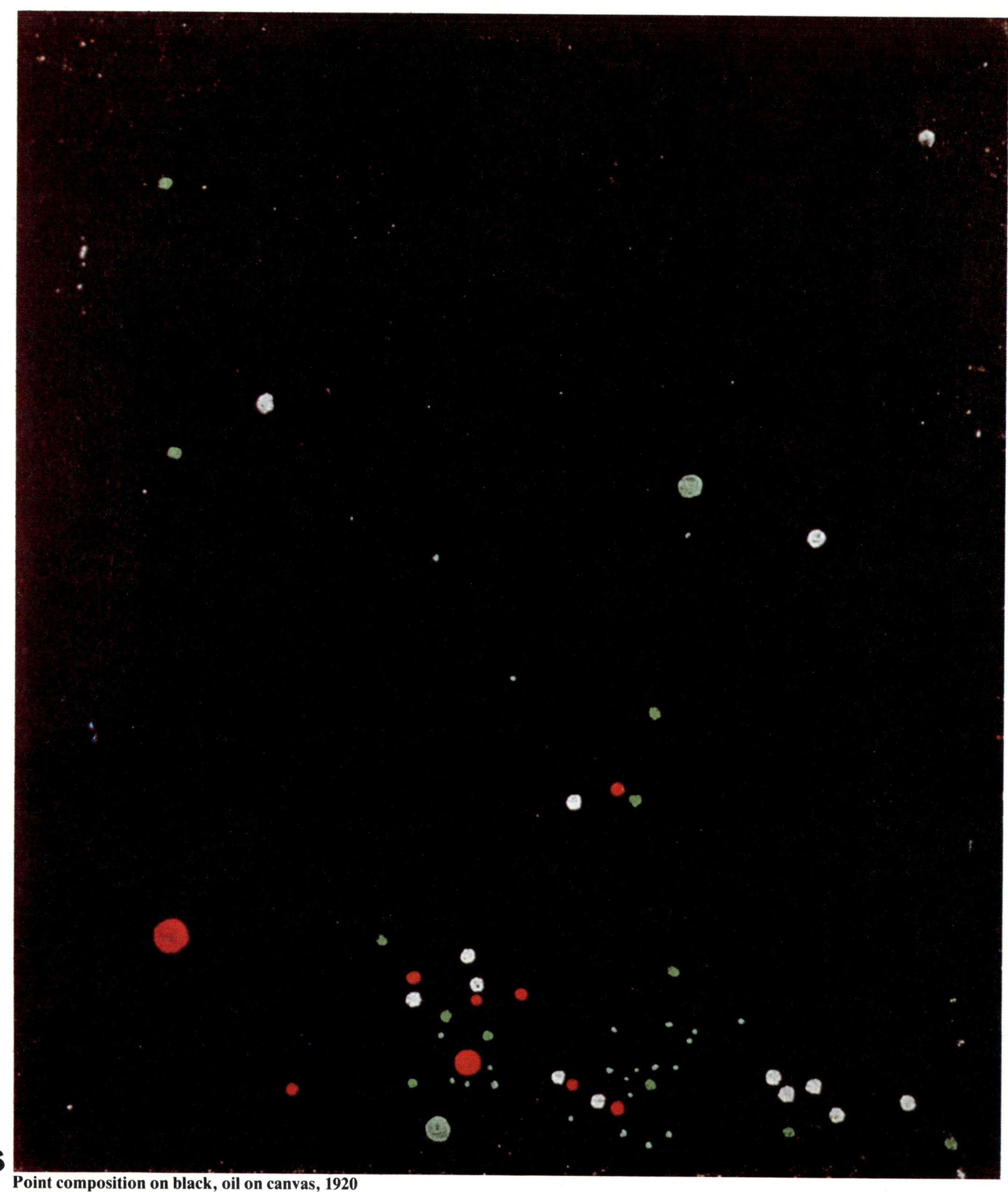

16

Point composition on black, oil on canvas, 1920

Opposite page: Untitled composition, oil on wood, 1920

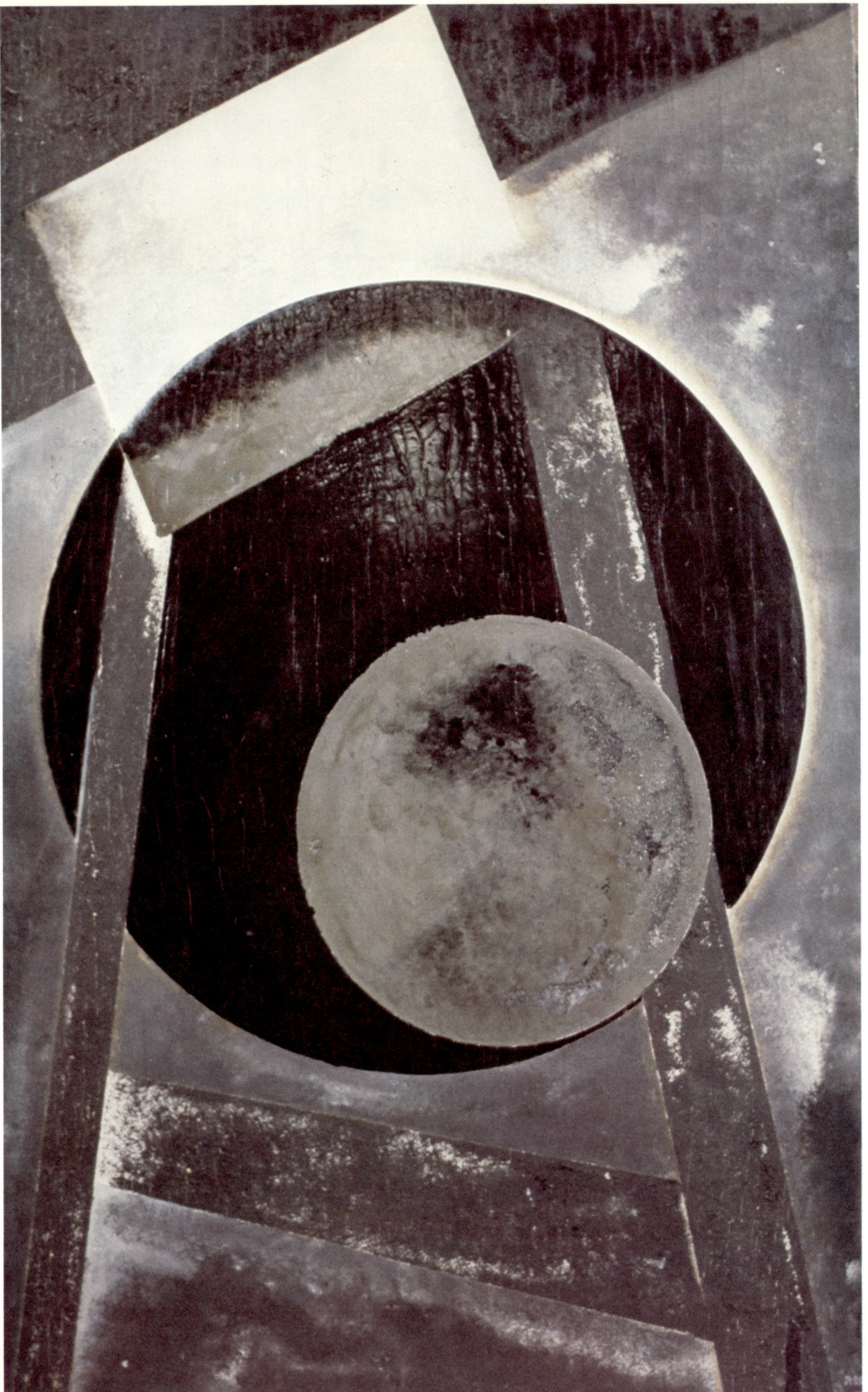

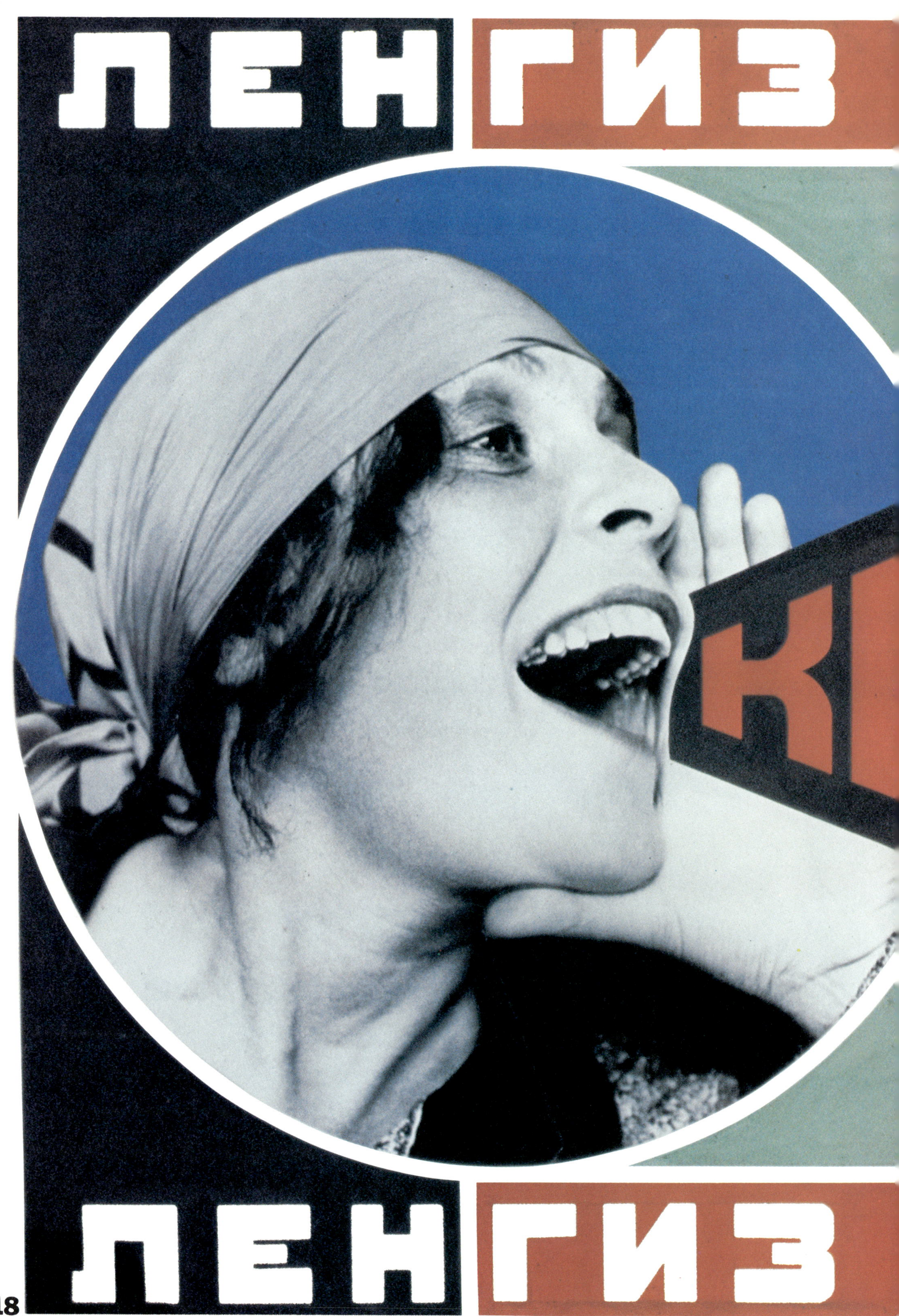

"Knigi" (Books), window poster, 1925

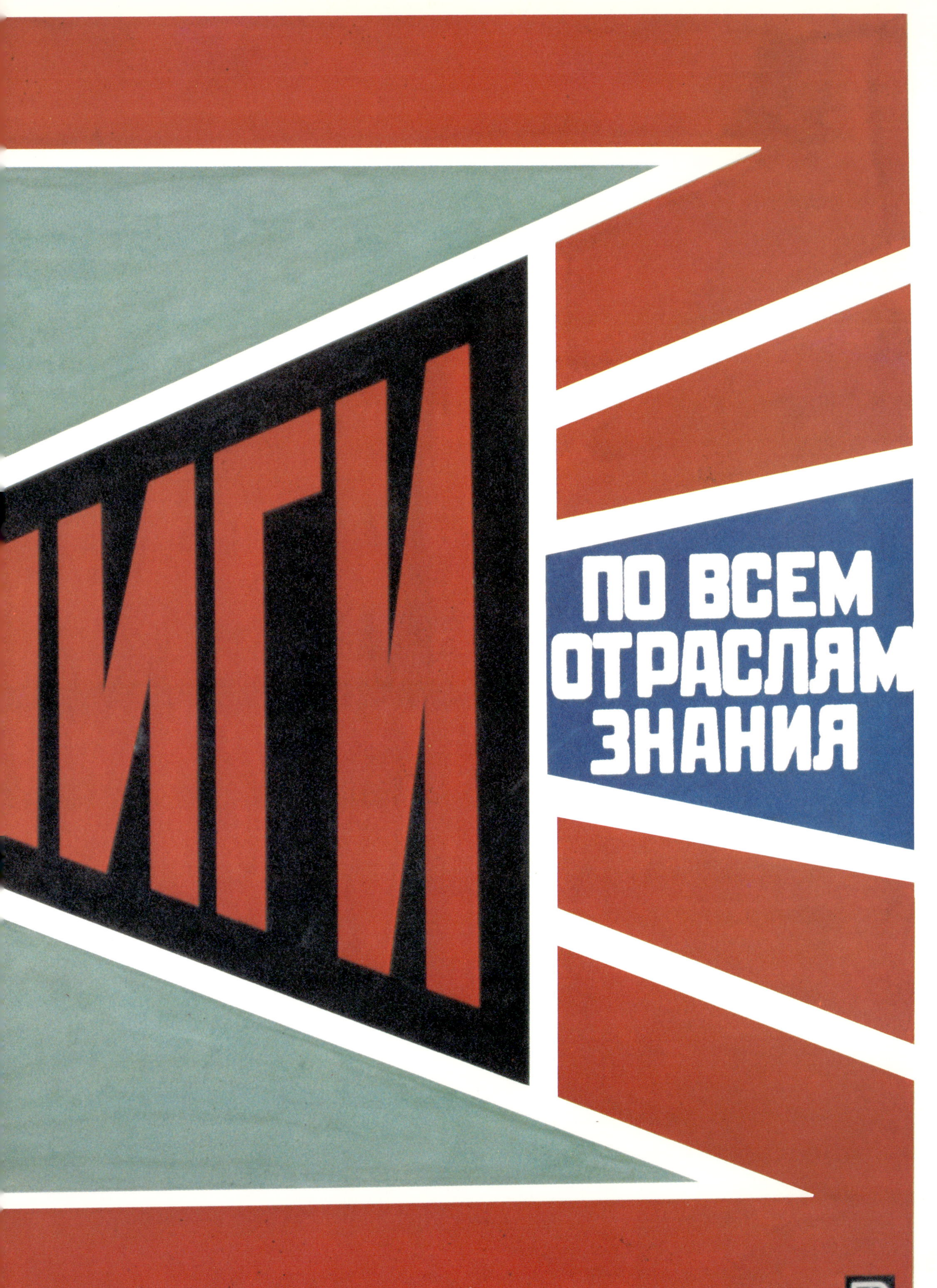
ИГИ
ПО ВСЕМ
ОТРАСЛЯМ
ЗНАНИЯ

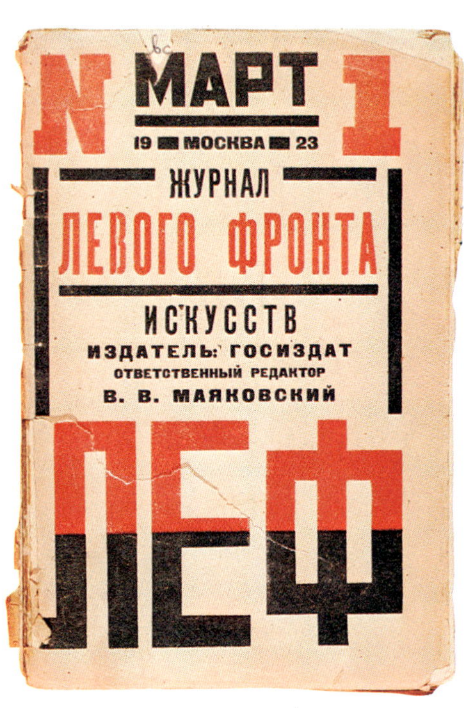
N
МАРТ
1
19 МОСКВА 23
ЖУРНАЛ
ЛЕВОГО ФРОНТА
ИСКУССТВ
ИЗДАТЕЛЬ: ГОСИЗДАТ
ОТВЕТСТВЕННЫЙ РЕДАКТОР
В. В. МАЯКОВСКИЙ
ЛЕФ
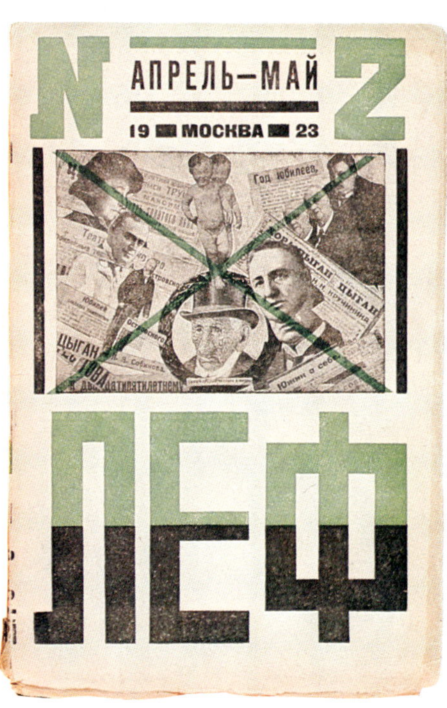
N
АПРЕЛЬ—МАЙ
2
19 МОСКВА 23
ЛЕФ
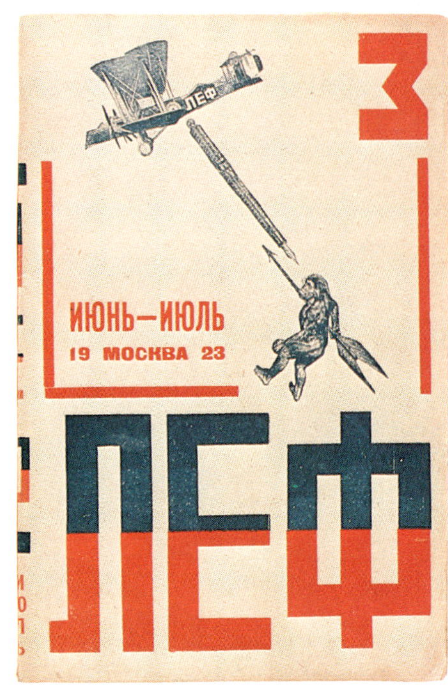
3
ЛЕФ
ИЮНЬ—ИЮЛЬ
19 МОСКВА 23
ЛЕФ
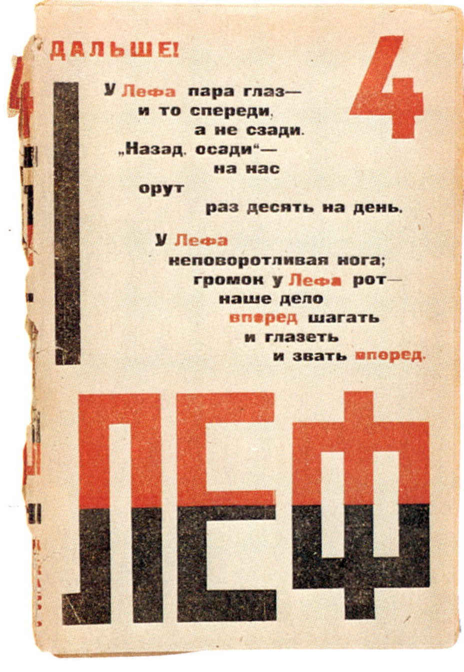
ДАЛЬШЕ!
4
У Лефа пара глаз—
и то спереди,
а не сзади.
„Назад, осади"—
на нас
орут
раз десять на день.
У Лефа
неповоротливая нога;
громок у Лефа рот—
наше дело
вперед шагать
и глазеть
и звать вперед.
ЛЕФ
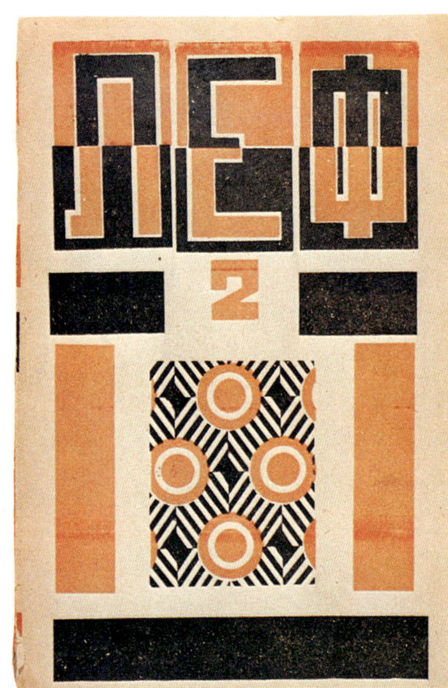
ЛЕФ
2
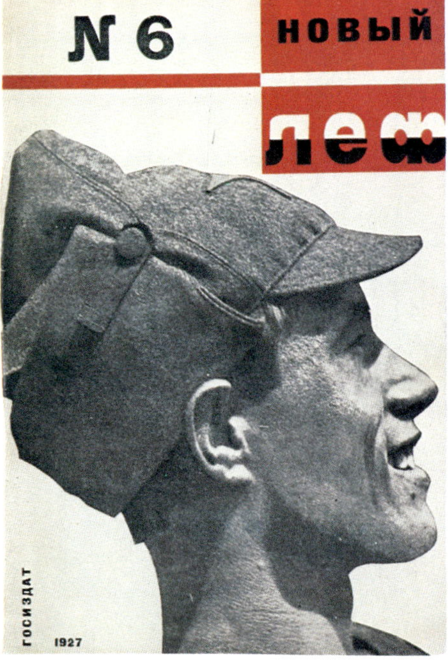
N 6
НОВЫЙ
леф
ГОСИЗДАТ
1927
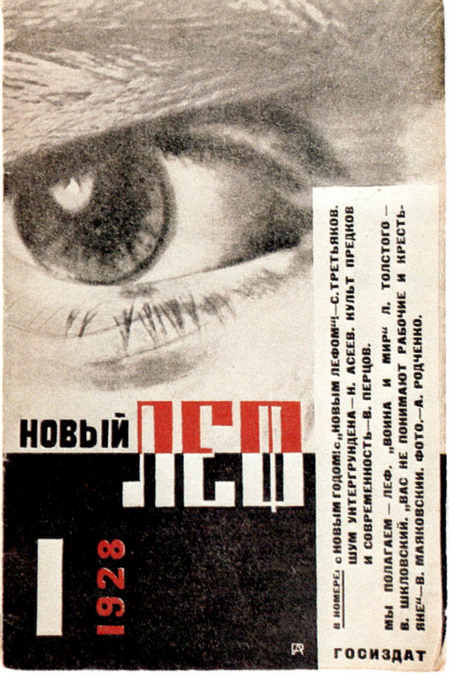
НОВЫЙ
ЛЕФ
1
1928
В НОМЕРЕ: С НОВЫМ ГОДОМ! С „НОВЫМ ЛЕФОМ"!—С. ТРЕТЬЯКОВ. ШУМ УИТЕРГРУНДЕНА—Н. АСЕЕВ. КУЛЬТ ПРЕДКОВ И СОВРЕМЕННОСТЬ—В. ПЕРЦОВ.
МЫ ПОЛАГАЕМ—ЛЕФ. „ВОЙНА И МИР" Л. ТОЛСТОГО—В. ШКЛОВСКИЙ. „ВАС НЕ ПОНИМАЮТ РАБОЧИЕ И КРЕСТЬЯНЕ"—В. МАЯКОВСКИЙ. ФОТО—А. РОДЧЕНКО.
ГОСИЗДАТ
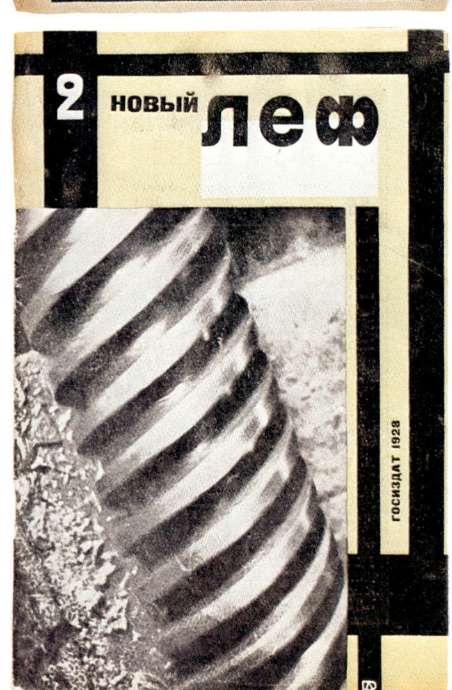
2
НОВЫЙ
леф
ГОСИЗДАТ 1928
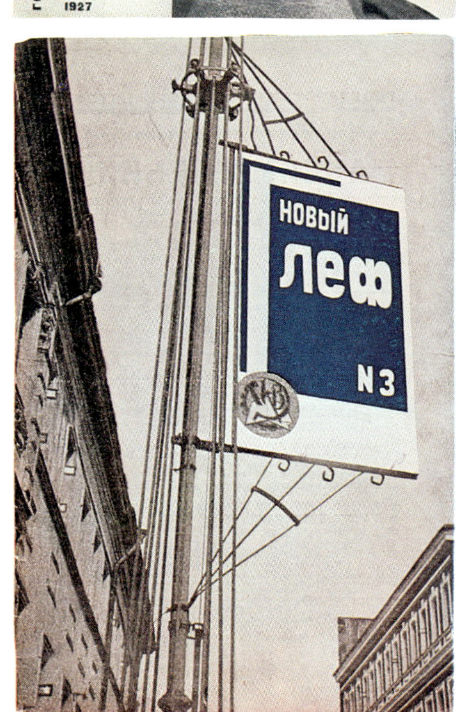
НОВЫЙ
леф
N 3

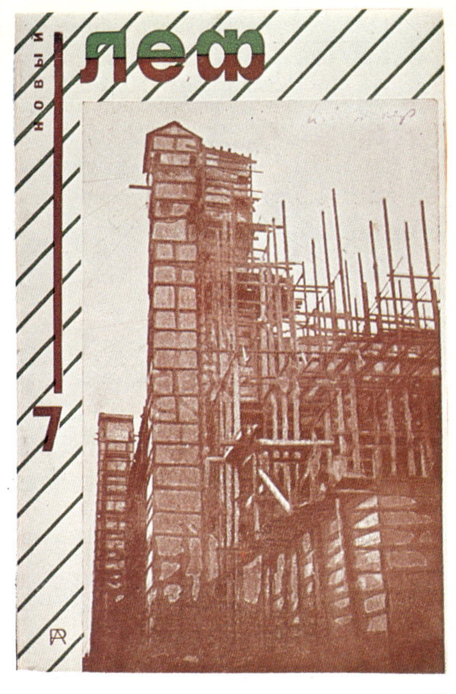

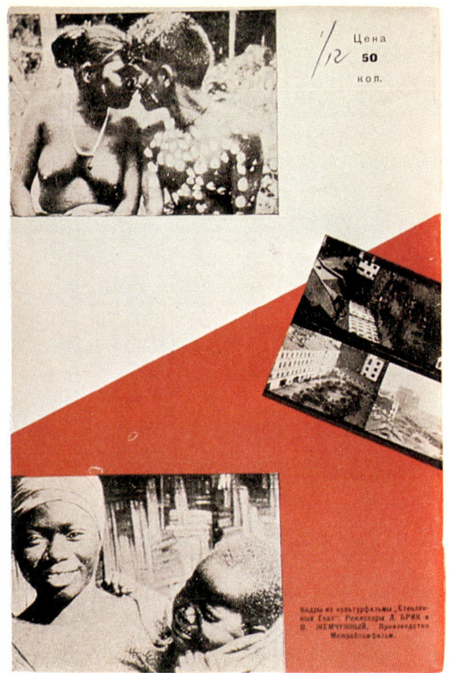

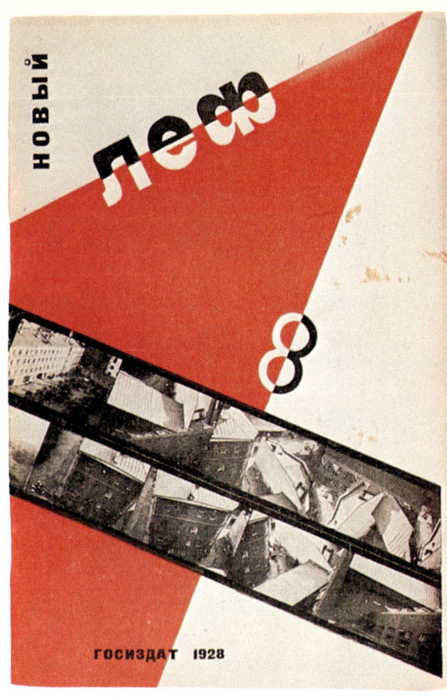

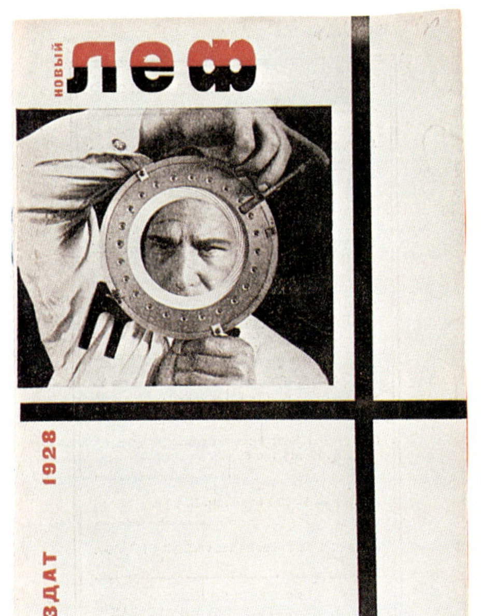

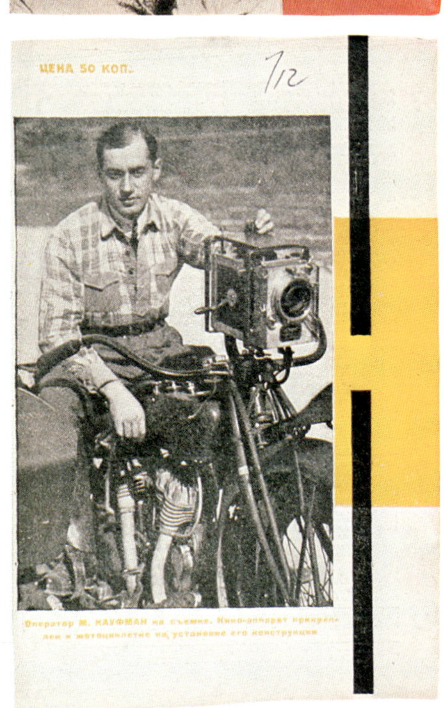

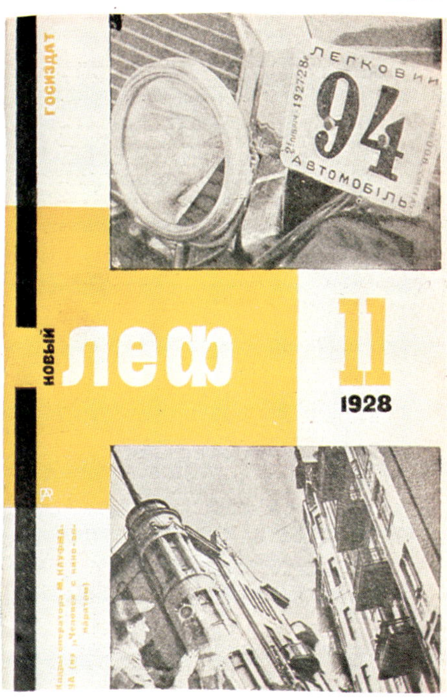

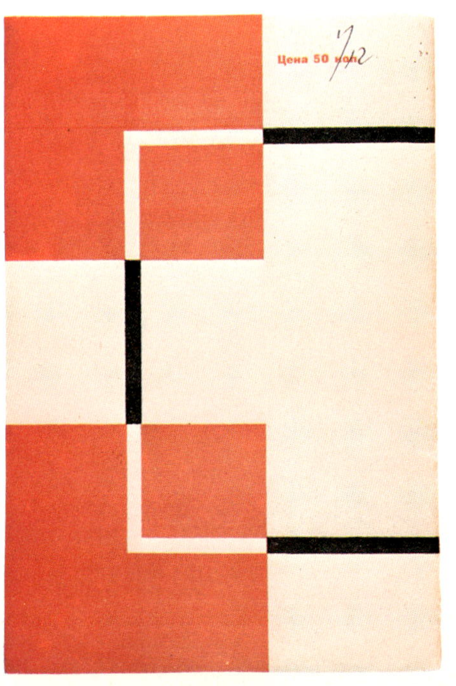

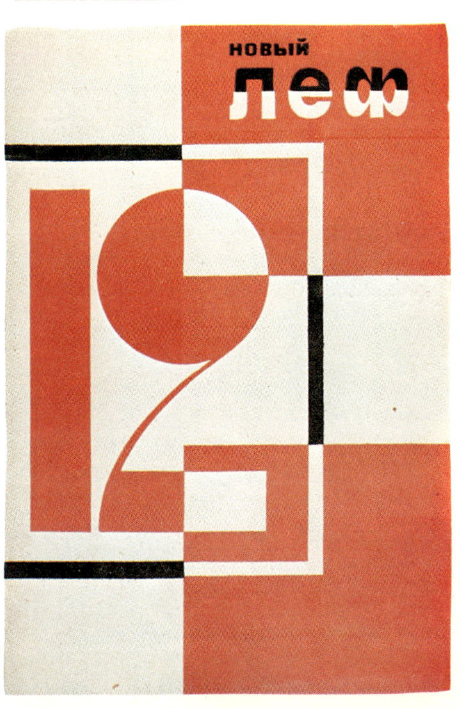

Covers for the magazine "LEF" (Levyi Front Iskusstv— Left Front of the Arts). Editor-in-chief: V. Mayakovsky, 1923-5. Covers for "Novyi LEF"

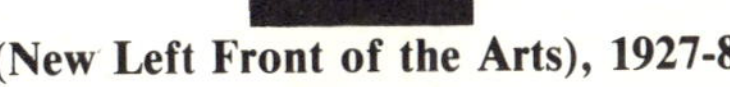

(New Left Front of the Arts), 1927-8

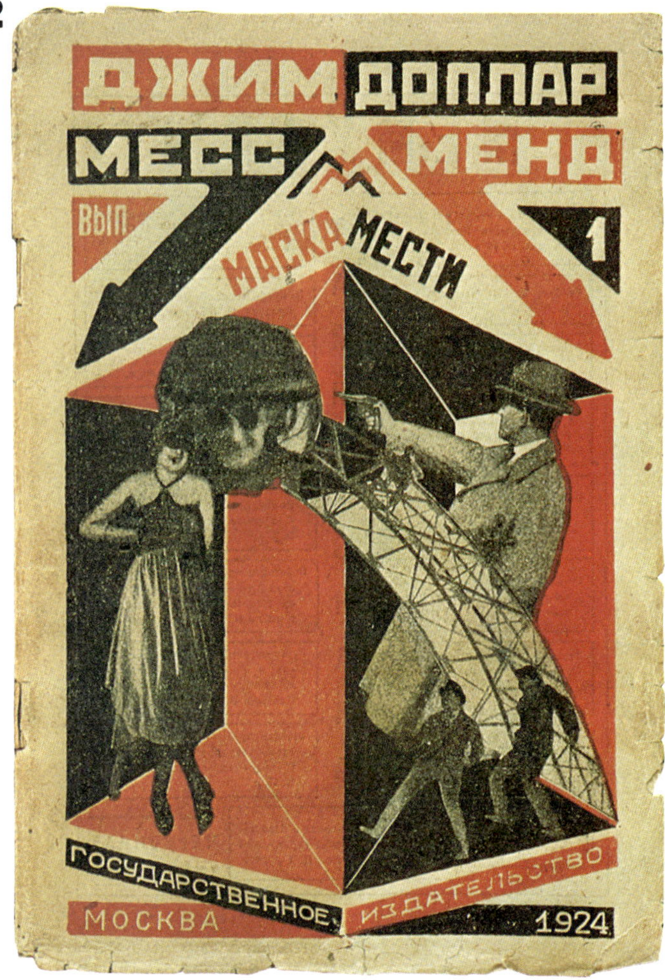

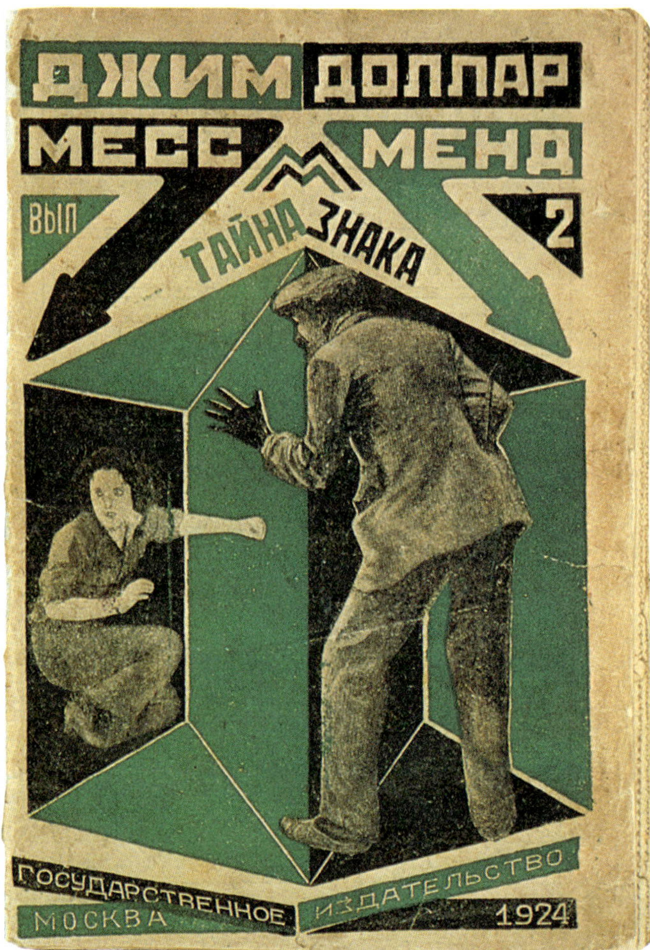

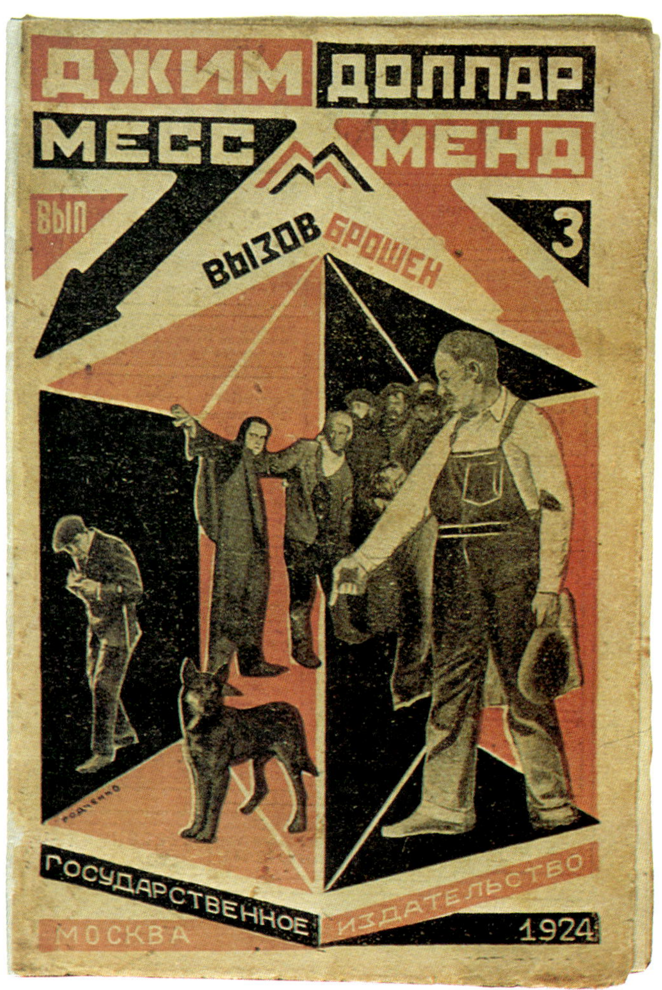

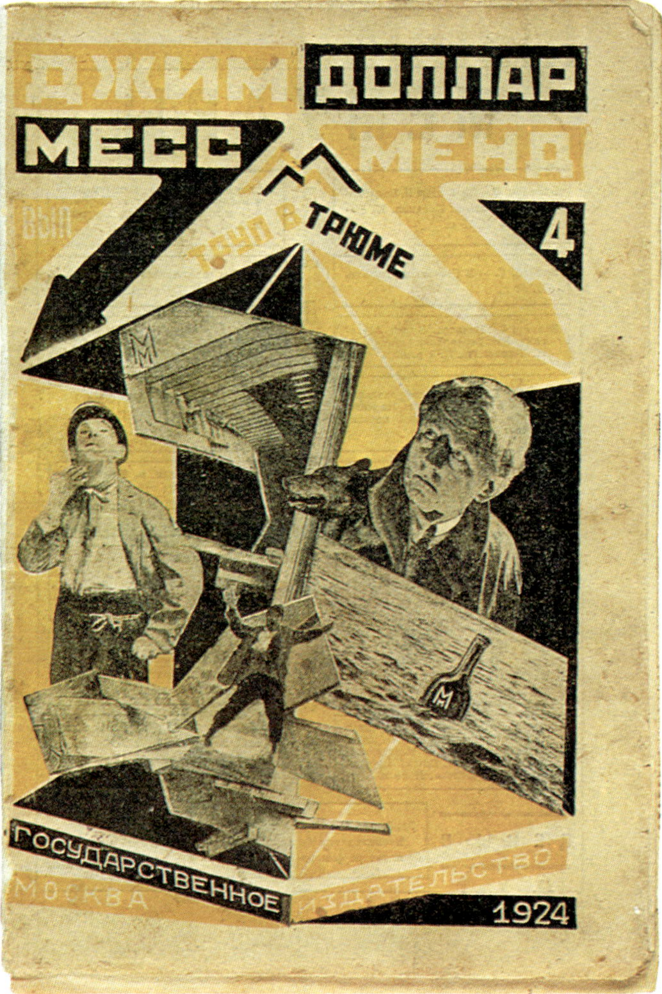

Eight covers from a series of ten for Jim Dollar (M. Shaginian), "Mess Mend", 1924.

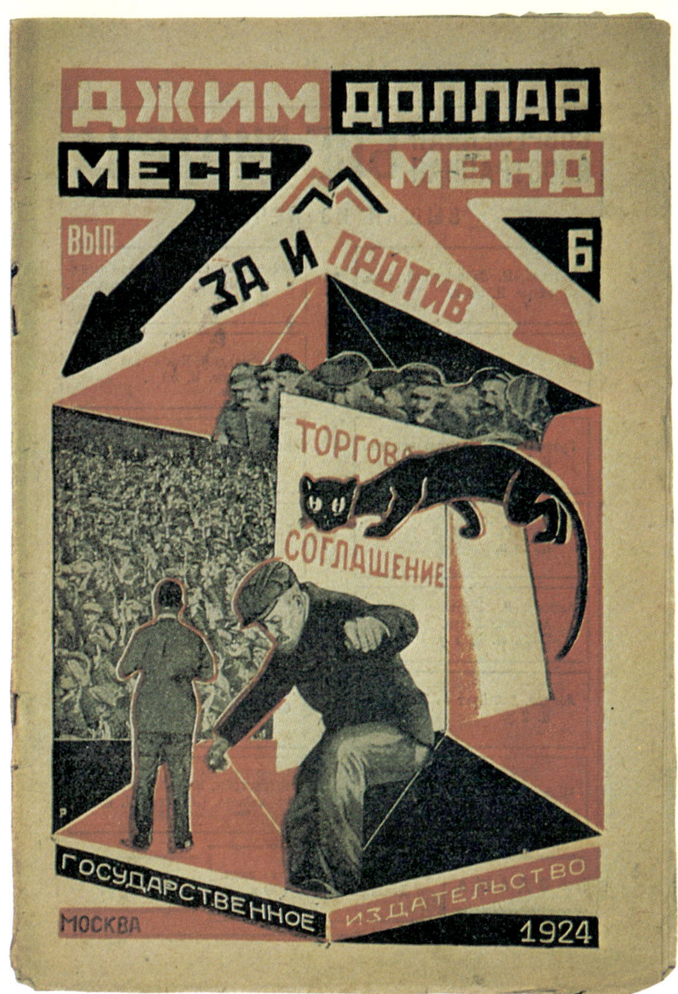
ДЖИМ ДОЛЛАР
МЕСС МЕНД
ВЫП 6
ЗА И ПРОТИВ
ТОРГОВ
СОГЛАШЕНИЕ
ГОСУДАРСТВЕННОЕ ИЗДАТЕЛЬСТВО
МОСКВА 1924

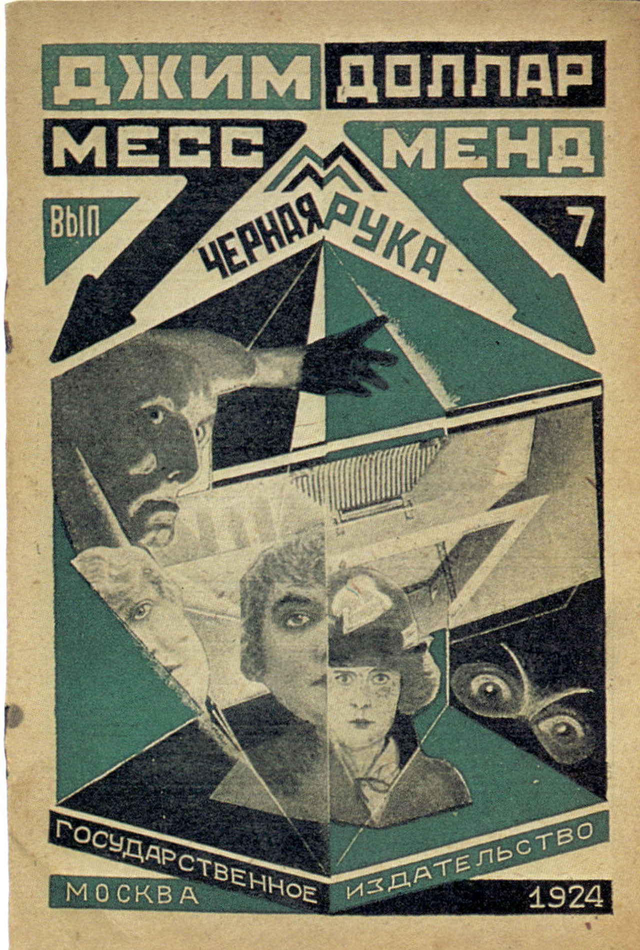
ДЖИМ ДОЛЛАР
МЕСС МЕНД
ВЫП 7
ЧЕРНАЯ РУКА
ГОСУДАРСТВЕННОЕ ИЗДАТЕЛЬСТВО
МОСКВА 1924

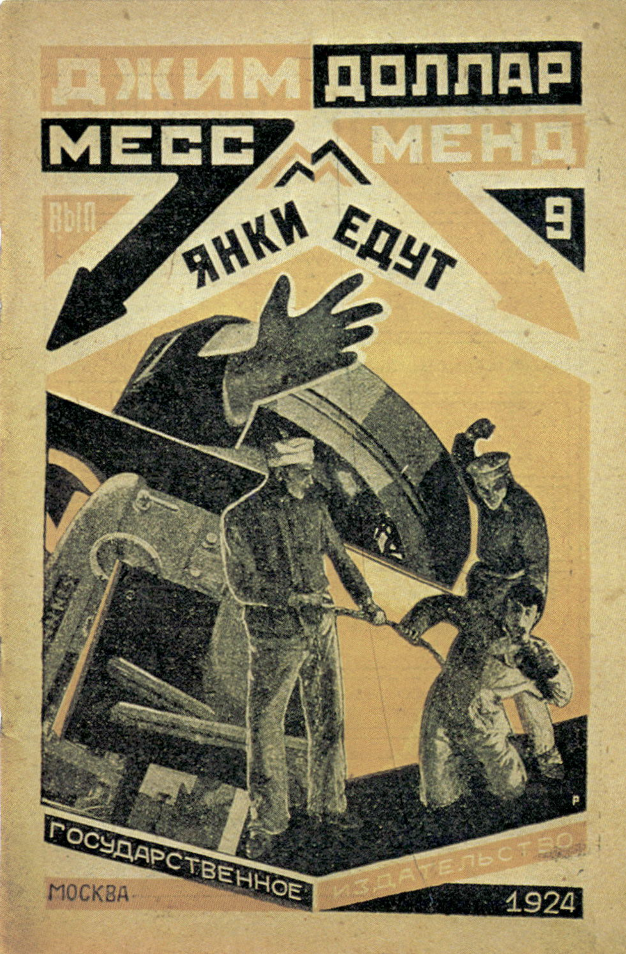
ДЖИМ ДОЛЛАР
МЕСС МЕНД
ВЫП 9
ЯНКИ ЕДУТ
ГОСУДАРСТВЕННОЕ ИЗДАТЕЛЬСТВО
МОСКВА 1924

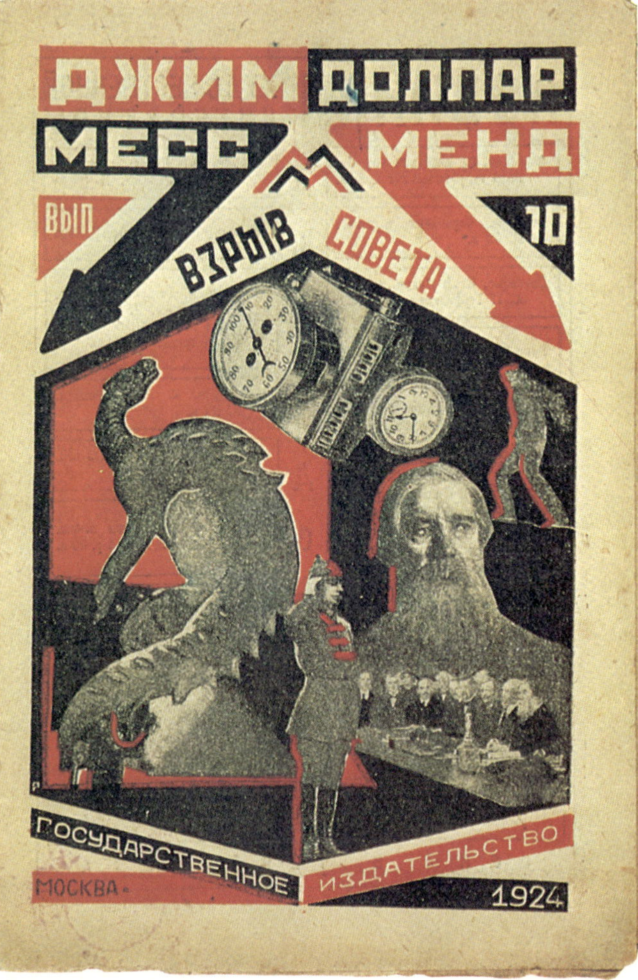
ДЖИМ ДОЛЛАР
МЕСС МЕНД
ВЫП 10
ВЗРЫВ СОВЕТА
ГОСУДАРСТВЕННОЕ ИЗДАТЕЛЬСТВО
МОСКВА 1924

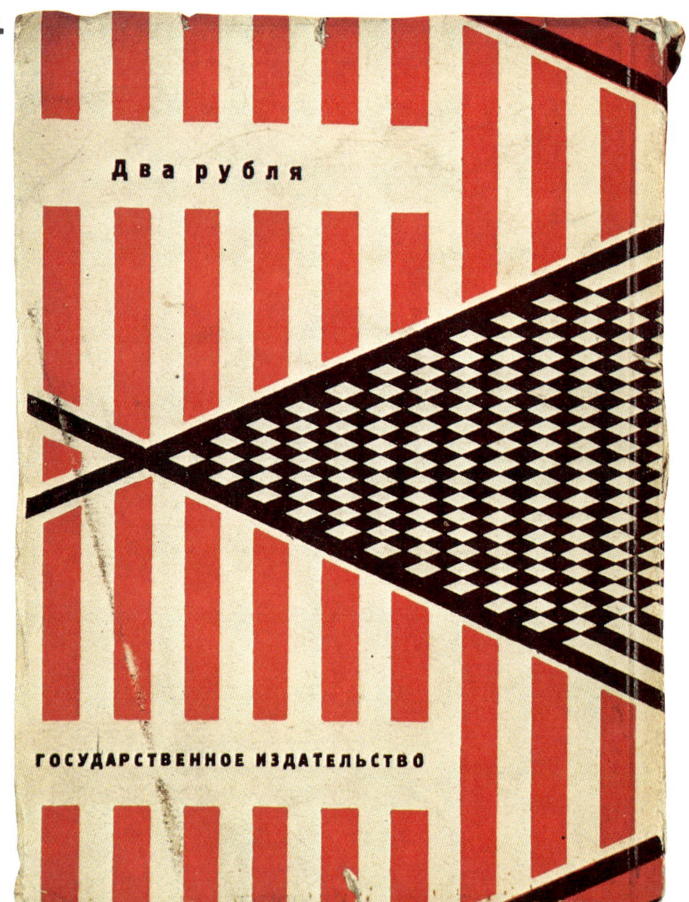

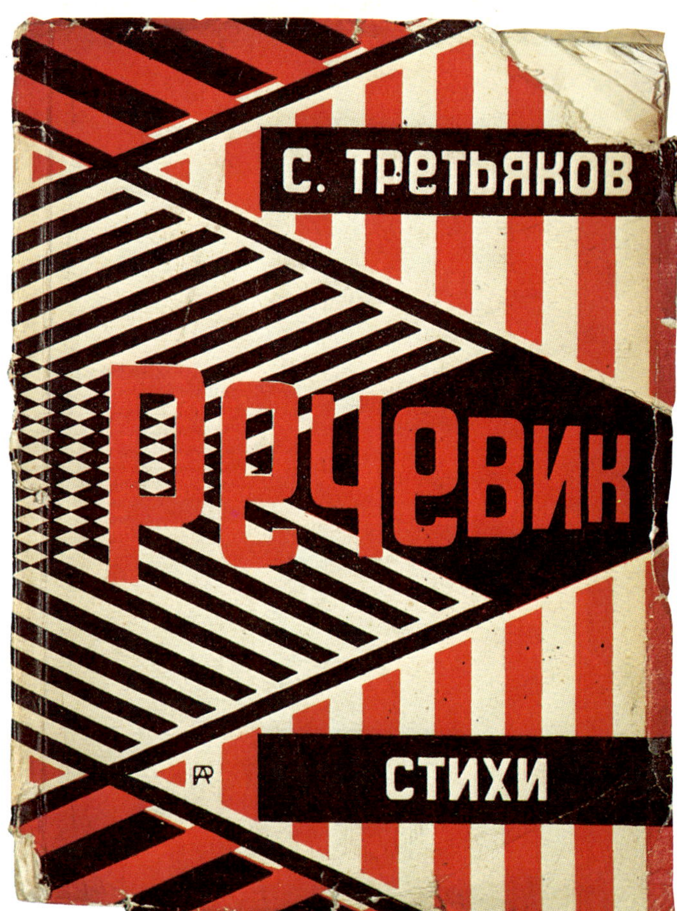

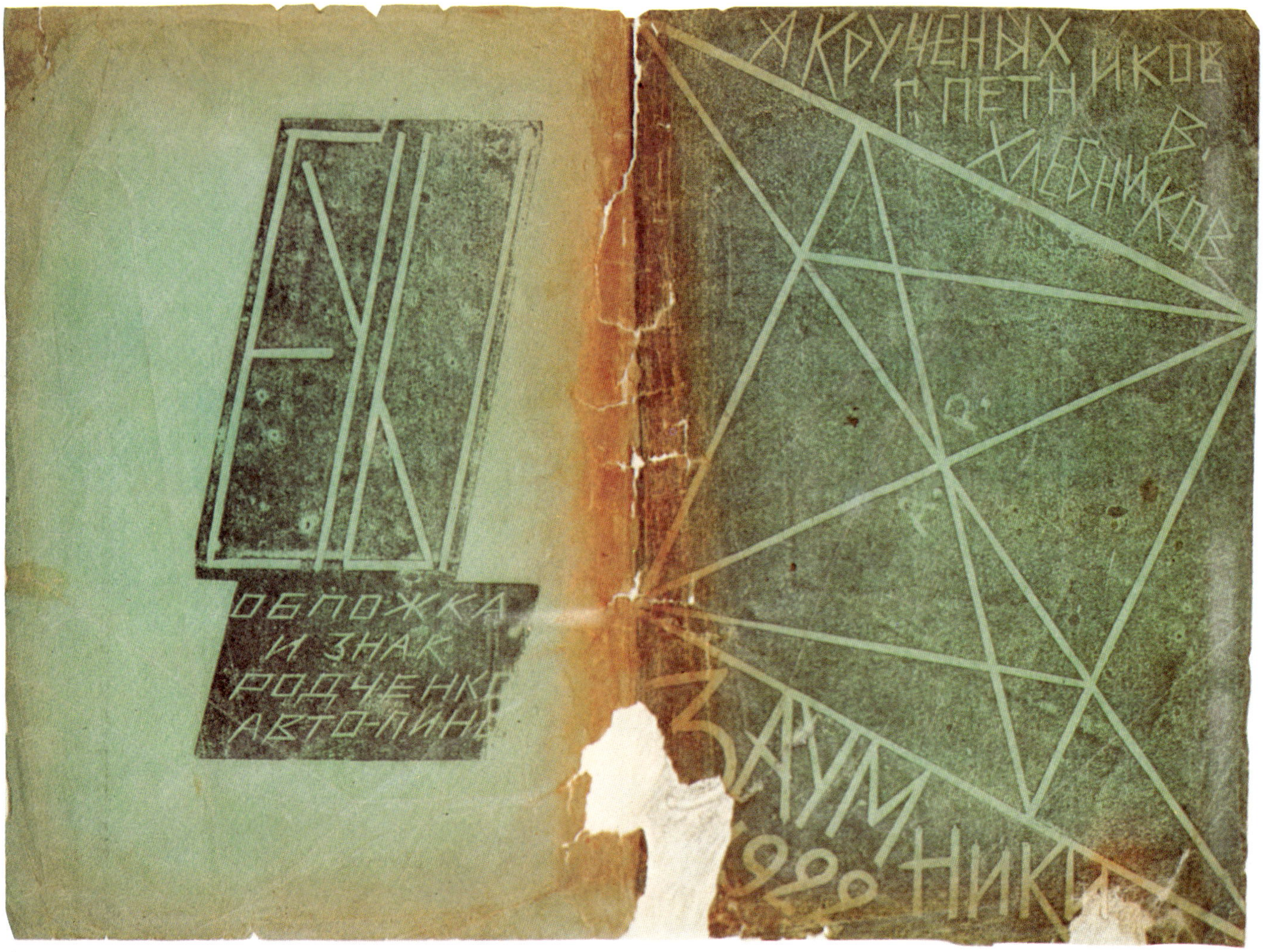

Cover for "Zaumniki" (Collection of "zaum" poems), 1922. Top: Cover for S. Tret'iakov, "Rechevik Stikhi" (Speech verses), 1929.

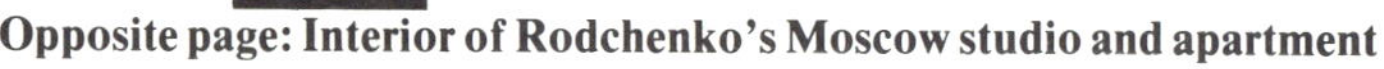

Opposite page: Interior of Rodchenko's Moscow studio and apartment

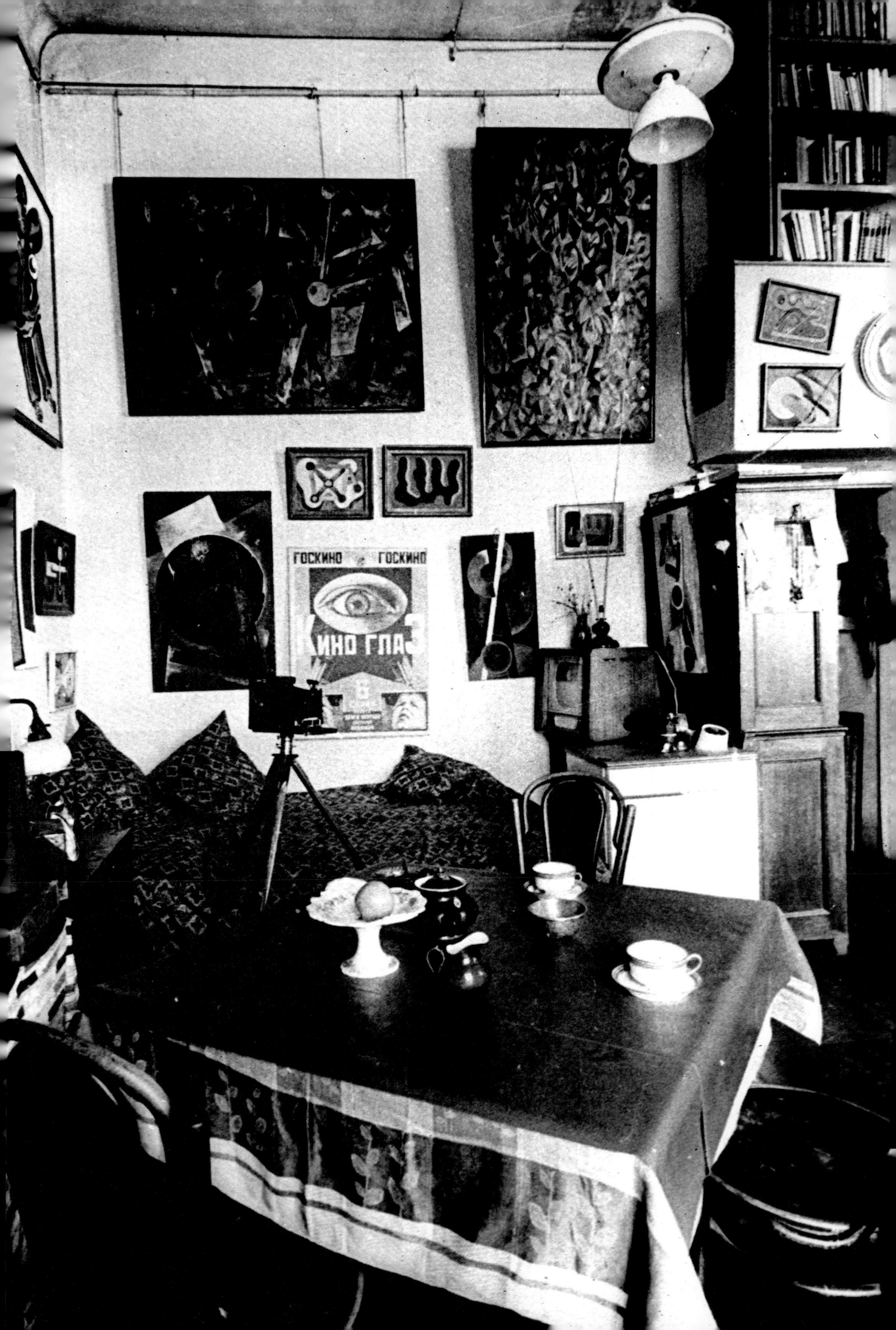
ГОСКИНО ГОСКИНО
КИНО ГЛАЗ

ALEXANDER RODCHENKO

An introduction to his work by Alexander Lavrentiev

"Not synthesis but analysis is creation. Painting is the body and creation is the soul. My work is to create new painting and I have to look at things as they are." A. Rodchenko, 1919.[1]

"The art of the future will not be the cosy decoration of family homes. It will be just as indispensable as 48-storey skyscrapers, giant bridges, wireless, aeronautics, submarines, etc."
A. Rodchenko, 1920.[2]

At first glance the relationship of an artist to himself, to his work and to its development is only a matter for the history of art, but more important is the appraisal of the past according to the needs of contemporary culture. Only some aesthetic values of the past are now accepted, others are rejected. Both the personal and the functional are important and when they meet art can be born. But what conditions or problems lead the artist to do one thing and not another? What compels him to work?

Evidently this is the area where personal, biographical facts and impressions of events in the world around him intertwine and compel him to be what he is and experience contemporary reality in one way and no other.

In art there are a multitude of professions which create visually beautiful images: painter, sculptor, architect, photographer.... At the beginning of the century they were joined by the designer....

It is difficult to imagine a man who could master all of these things at once. One may doubt the competency of one man in so many fields. But the reason why Rodchenko could work successfully in different aspects and genres of art lies in his creative method — in his extension of the range of activities governed by artistic criteria. Artistic considerations were applied in all areas of life. This approach has always existed in opposition to a narrowly professional outlook. But it depends on there always being a new area of activity, in this case design, which attempts to embrace and explain everything — including the development of our consciousness towards nature and ourselves.

For Alexander Rodchenko art alone could not possess such magical qualities, and it was only when he employed scientific methods to make facts and practical representations combine that he began to move forward boldly into new areas. Science seems infallible in its representation of man, it strives towards the objective reflection of people's lives, of nature. Science and art for Rodchenko merge into one single process of cognition, characteristic of a period when man was researching increasingly complex phenomena to gain a complete mastery of their laws.

Rodchenko's library bears witness to his undying interest in fields that seem far removed from art: mathematics, physics, astronomy, philosophy. For Rodchenko, an artist by education, painting became a scientific and creative method of apprehending reality. This method, which allowed him to work in different media, became confirmed through his practice. The transference of these essentially isolated representations of the world into the sphere of human life allowed Rodchenko to combine unexpected professions — artist and radio-engineer for example.

In "Novyi LEF" Rodchenko ironically reconciled these two activities: "It is interesting to be doing experimental photography but aesthetics only makes up about 90% of a photograph. That is why I am working with radios at the same time — for discipline. There is no more than 10% art in radios."[3] In the same notebook he also wrote than he wanted "art to be invention and training", and that he wanted "to see something new even in ordinary and usual things".

During his period of study at the Kazan School of Art, 1910-1914, Rodchenko studied history of art exhaustively and then began to experiment with many different kinds of subject matter and media. It would be a mistake to say that he worked only from nature, as in the Kazan School of Art students were taught to draw from memory. Students had to concentrate on the most important feature of a subject — the structure of the object/still life/portrait — and if they could not record it from memory, then nothing could be reconstructed later. The perception and recollection of the structural features of this or that composition of colours or volumes becomes almost a process of invention. After all, invention is a process of creation based on what has been remembered.

On the reverse side of some drawings by Rodchenko of 1920 are sketches in

Alexander Nikolaevich Lavrentiev (grandson of A.M. Rodchenko). Born 1954. Trained as a designer. Now works in the Department of History and Theory of Design at the Institute of Industrial Design in Moscow.

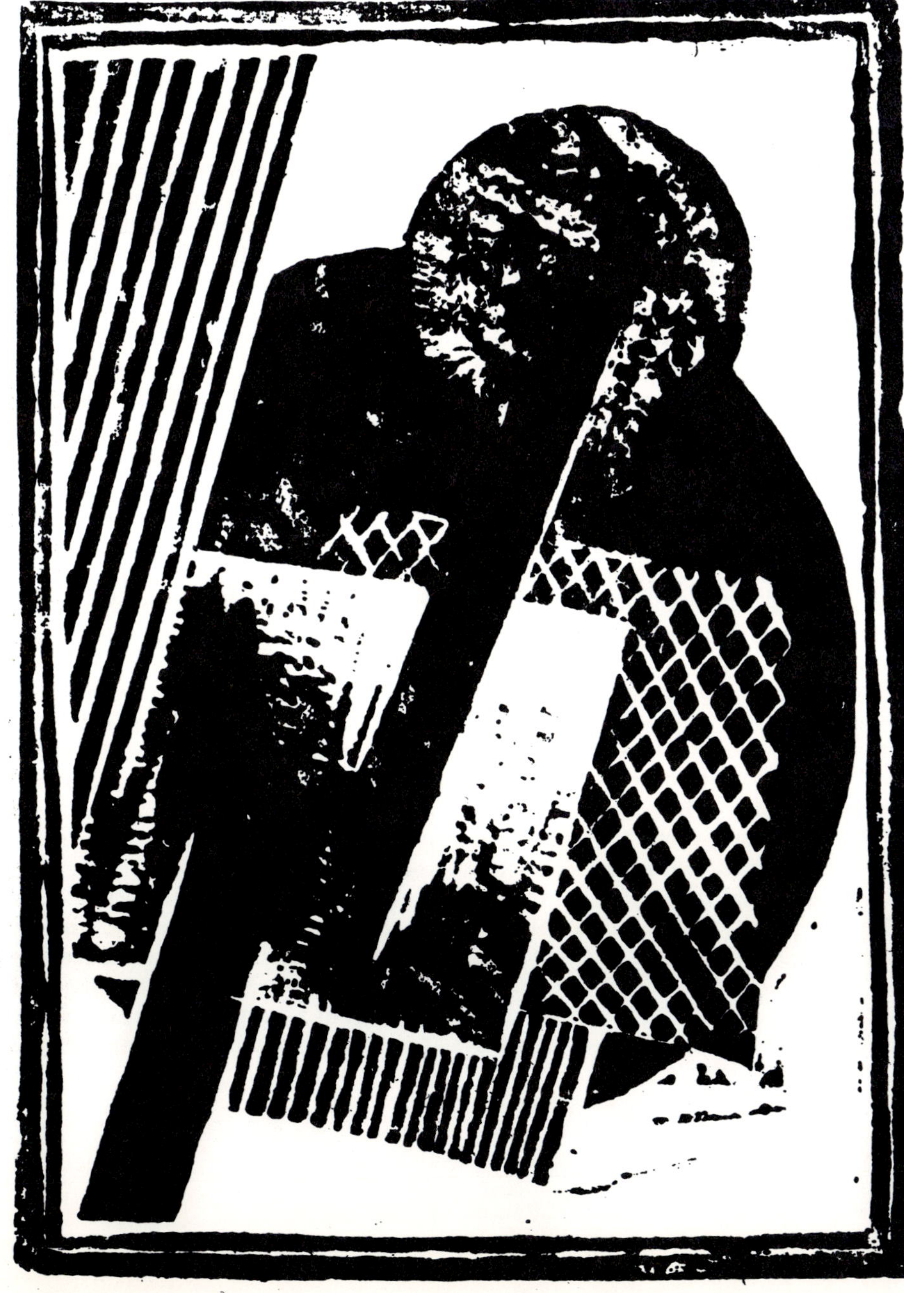

Untitled composition, linocut, 1918

descriptive geometry made earlier in Kazan which bear witness to this important subject which influenced him in the earliest stages of his work. Descriptive geometry developed his analytic, volumetric-spatial way of thinking and also the precision, accuracy and definition of his graphic design.

Each exercise was done very precisely with compasses, drawing-pen and ruler. Now we no longer need wonder why Rodchenko, the artist, had technical drawing instruments. It seems that since his time at the Kazan School of Art he had always had them on hand to draw the finest of lines.

This brings us to another important question: how did line first appear in Rodchenko's early graphic designs? It was first used in an auxiliary role for frames, accents and then in the actual material of the drawing.

By the beginning of 1914, having taken part in several art exhibitions, Rodchenko had already begun to work as an independent artist. His favourite themes were human figures and his attitude towards them was chiefly conveyed by decorative means. The background, whether architecture or nature, was brushed in by large broad marks. At times the development of the background interested him more than that of the figures and he would go on to make this the subject of independent compositions, working on them from memory.

The background gives dimension and foundation to a composition; its details are always larger so that they will contrast better with the smaller figures of people. It is therefore natural that Rodchenko was interested in the rich colours and decorative style of Medieval and Eastern motifs, which he collected in scrapbooks. His reading and passion for the work of Aubrey Beardsley also contributed to his invention of fantastic forms of architecture, clothes and poses.

Because of the techniques and materials he used these are extremely diverse works: watercolour, varnish, oil paint, tempera, charcoal are all employed, often together.

Rodchenko used these materials to treat the surfaces of his paintings; these ranged from works with a thick, raised uneven surface to those with delicate dabs of paint on "levkas" with the most subtle tonal transitions in watercolour.[4] Rodchenko is however distinguished from other artists of this period by the use to which he puts this range of media and compositional techniques. Technique and material are closely connected, the manner of execution emerges as the outer manifestation of the material (and for painting this is fundamental).

In 1915 Rodchenko single-mindedly and acutely directed his work towards the portrayal of everyday things. This was his very first and earliest "designer's programme".

"Yes, I have found something to paint and think that it will be new and daring. I shall free painting, even Futurists' painting from what it has up until now clung slavishly to.
I prefer to see usual things unusually... I have found an entirely original path."[5]

The date of that statement corresponds approximately to the period when Rodchenko was working on a series of abstract black and white graphic designs and collages made of multi-coloured pieces of wallpaper. These collages, called "still lives", apparently preceded the graphic designs. One of them was shown in 1916 at the Futurists' exhibition "The Store". At the same exhibition Malevich exhibited his "alogisms" of 1913, for which he also used collage. Rodchenko also showed his graphic designs, which were drawn with compasses, drawing-pen and ruler.

In 1915, Rodchenko named these works "Compositions". Today we see in them his attempts to create a complete organism neither drawn nor painted from nature but constructed according to her laws. We should see them as the realisation of certain formulas of construction which are appropriate to each particular type of composition.

It was in these works that construction was born; born because it developed organically and not from fragments brought mechanically together. Parts of the works pulsate and move. However the forms in them are still only linked compositionally and not constructively. They do not yet have a deliberate spatial quality, but line — the future element of construction — does appear here, in 1915, for the first time.

In 1922 Rodchenko was preparing the monograph in which he intended to explain the evolution of his work. By that time his pictorial method had been brought to a peak in the works, "Smooth Colour", which consist of three canvases evenly painted in red, blue and yellow (1921).[6] "the Last Picture has been painted" was the title of N. Tarabukin's paper on these works, which he read at Inkhuk. The implications were clear to Rodchenko as well, when in his monograph he included as his latest works the titles to Dziga Vertov's films and the cover lay-out of the magazine "LEF". This was production art and his works from this point can be seen extending in a logical progression through the years...

Following on from his discoveries in painting it is important to see in these works how his attitude to the subject, and its form, construction and appearance changes.

In 1917, Rodchenko was, at first on canvas, investigating the possibilities of using planes to make forms. He discovered that "a given plane of a given size can only be defined in space by the existence of another plane on it or crossing it." (Rodchenko, 1922). This law was discovered by Rodchenko and put into practice in the two-dimensional space of a painting.

But this also appears to have been the principle governing the construction of the lamps for Filipov's "Café Pittoresque". In these designs bright, concave planes intersect one another and are held firm at their points of intersection. There is no linear construction here. The fundamental and sole element defining form is the plane. Naturally the concept of a design is different from its realisation. Unfortunately, photographs of the lamps no longer exist. One can only guess how the planes were fastened together, how the lamp was placed inside, how the light was in fact reflected....

Installed these would have been fantastic structures about half a metre high, the metal lampshades reflecting light onto the cabaret tables. Rodchenko instinctively twisted the planes so that they screened the glare from the lamp at eye level. These lamps spread a comfortable light around them. The numerous gaps between the planes, which were not all joined together into a single casing, ensured a constant stream of air for ventilation.

If we examine the work of 1917-1918 then we can see an "obvious constructive connection of forms" which "not only have a pictorial unity but an almost constructional one. The whole system of forms folds away like a folding chair but does not come apart. It is like a complete disciplined organism only within the space of a board, Here is a linear approach to the depiction of forms on a simple plane, a rendering of solid forms in paint, mechanical colouring and a sharp, linear definition of the edges." (Rodchenko, 1922).

In the paintings of this period colour dissolves and curves the planes but does not disturb their equilibrium.

The same structure can be seen in his architectural designs of 1918-1919. The composition of a design for a newspaper kiosk is built on planes and lines. The aim and purpose of each detail is absolutely clear: the construction here lies in the correlation and distribution of the supporting and supported parts. However the spatial "folding and dismantling" constructions of 1918-1919 were even more important as prototypes for these works.

It is characteristic of Rodchenko to conceive of works as part of a series in groups. Even if he only managed to realise one it was, all the same, thought of as part of a group — as one in a series of works conforming to some general

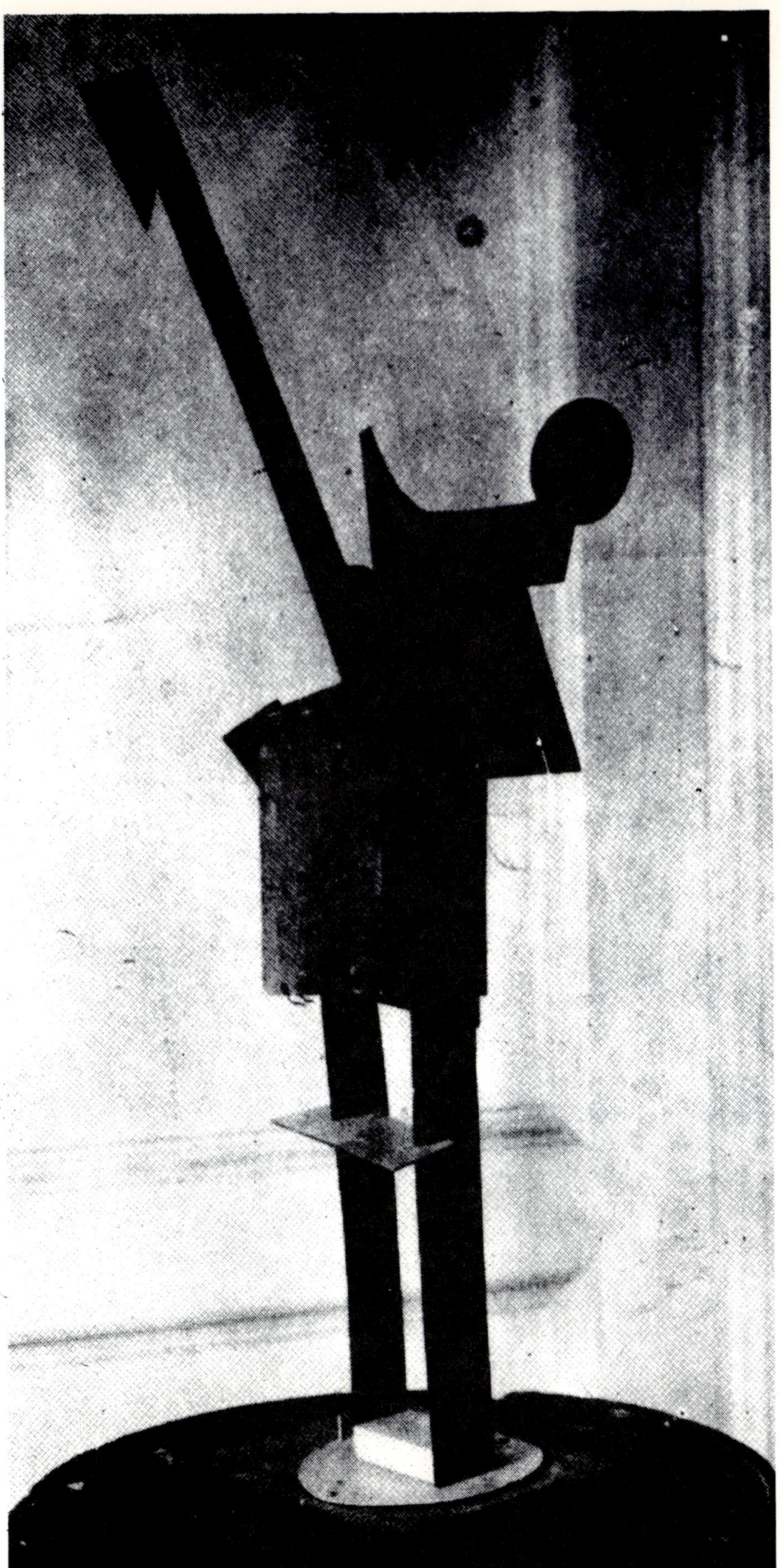

theme. Here too the sense and beauty of a work is not to be found in each separate piece but in the logic of the progression from one composition to another.

Each sculpture of 1918-1919 was an invention. All of them had symmetrical frontal projections, as is the case with many natural and technological forms. There was always a pillar at the centre carrying the load and at the foot a stand. But each time the form of the whole work and the means of fastening the parts were entirely new.

Pivoted constructions will appear later in Rodchenko's architectural projects: a kiosk, Hall of Soviet Deputies and others.

When he began work on this series of sculptures Rodchenko used various materials: wood, veneers, tin-plate, cardboard, nails. From work to work each piece became simpler and visually more distinct. The visual noisiness seen in the nailed joints and coarse textures of the early experiments diminished and died out in the later works. Once instead of using nails he had a better idea of making a collapsible sculpture of cardboard that could be taken to pieces and was held together in its slots by friction. He also discovered that planes placed perpendicularly to one another create a strong and distinctive sensation of space. He had discovered one of the most powerful resources of art: Visual Logic. We can now see how each work stands, balances and how one form flows out of another.

The concept of serial paintings and graphic designs encourages the artist to try to see in one design all possible modifications for future works. It is possible that the plastic source of later kinetic forms lies here.

Rodchenko was able to realise these ideas when he designed and saw made the furniture and interior for the Workers Club in 1925, which was shown at the international Exhibition of Decorative Art in Paris. It was an oblong room designed to accommodate 30 people and to be used as a reading room, lecture hall, theatre and also for various other occupations and games.

In order to make all these changes of function possible, he proposed a special type of furniture. At the centre of the room was a platform. For lectures with diagrams or posters a part of the

Standing construction, 1918

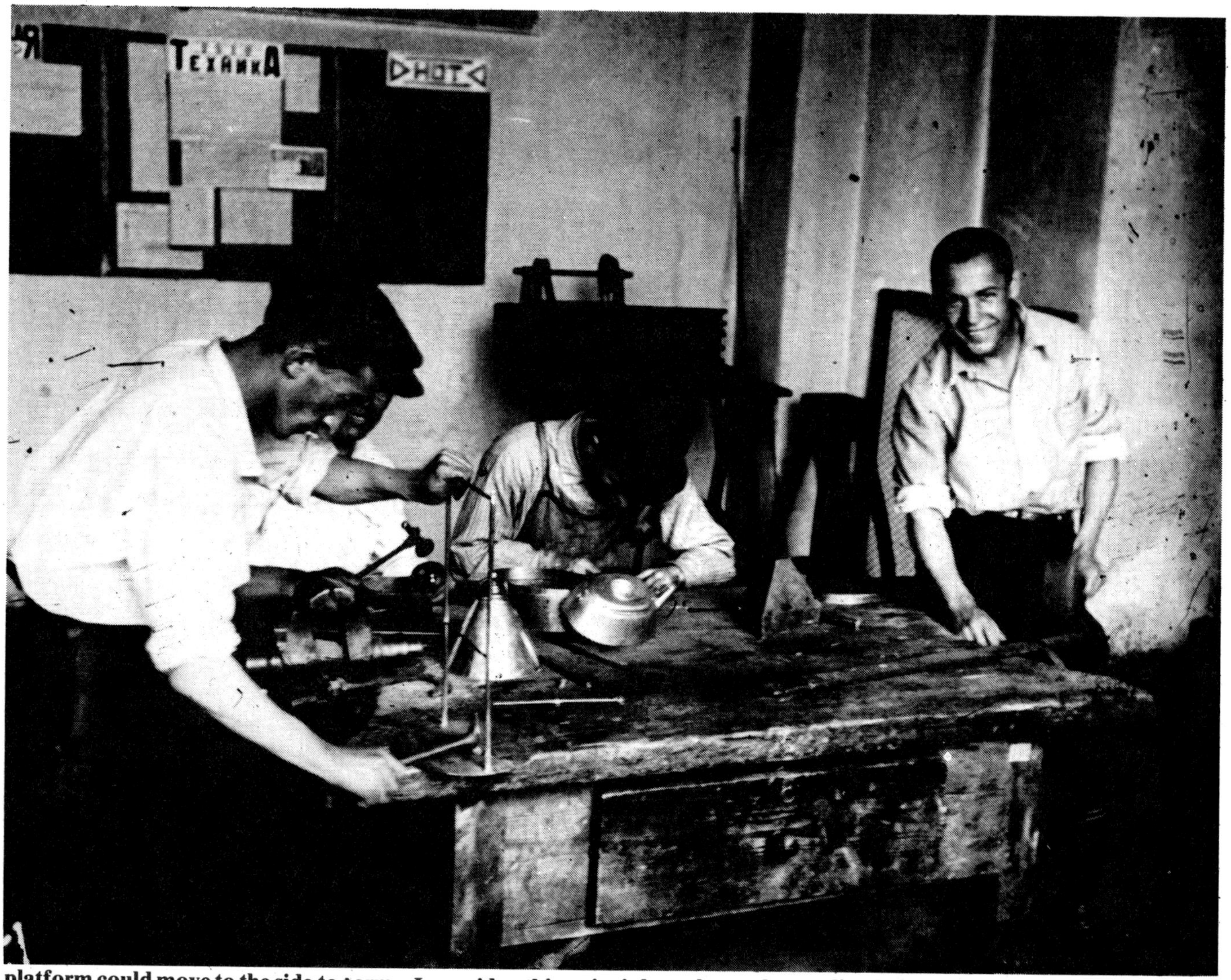

platform could move to the side to form a vertical plane. A long podium could be moved out from underneath to be used for exhibits and as a stage for theatrical productions. A folding screen could, if needed, be used as a curtain for the theatre. As a whole the construction looked light and graceful. The basic moving and working parts were painted red. The supporting construction was neutral grey. In this way by simply changing one central object the whole room could be converted to a specialised use. The visual information could also be changed on hand-operated rolling bands and advertisements for books were displayed on a set of revolving six-sided drums.

There was a chess table in an area specially marked off for play. The two armchairs and chess board were one functional piece and even this could be made to move without disturbing the players — the colour of the pieces could be changed without standing up, as the board could be turned and fixed in a new position. Rodchenko explained the principle which had governed his direction of the building of the Workers' Club when he wrote that, "almost all the pieces are built on a dynamic principle so that you can open out an object in a small space to work and put it back compactly afterwards. I consider this principle to be a characteristic typical of and inherent in contemporary work."

For ten years Rodchenko directed work at the metal-working faculty of Vkhutemas according to this principle. This was a period in his life of intensive work and also simultaneously he began to work in photography.

Rodchenko did not become involved with photography by chance. He had the same attitude to the process of taking photographs, processing, printing, as he had to technology in general. The laboratory, the chemicals — these were all a part of something new and progressive. He designed and built his photographic workshop himself. Photography for him was not simply a functional process; he saw it as a modern way of recording the world distinct from the old, traditional way using brush and paint.

According to his own words he also took up photography because he lacked photographs to use in photomontages. Since 1923 photomontage had been one of his most favourite methods of working; he took up photography in 1924. And almost immediately in the spring of the same year he exposed 9 photographic plates 9 x 12, which he used as visiting cards for the rest of his life. The portraits of Vladimir Mayakovsky taken on the same day have been seen by the whole world and we still continue to look at them and marvel at the expression of the poet's face, marvel that such a sculptured expression can be conveyed on a two-dimensional plane, marvel at the way in which the innermost character of the man is shown before our eyes.

This small group of photographs, including portraits of Rodchenko's contemporaries and the portrait of his

Below: Design for chess board and chairs for the Workers' Club, 1925

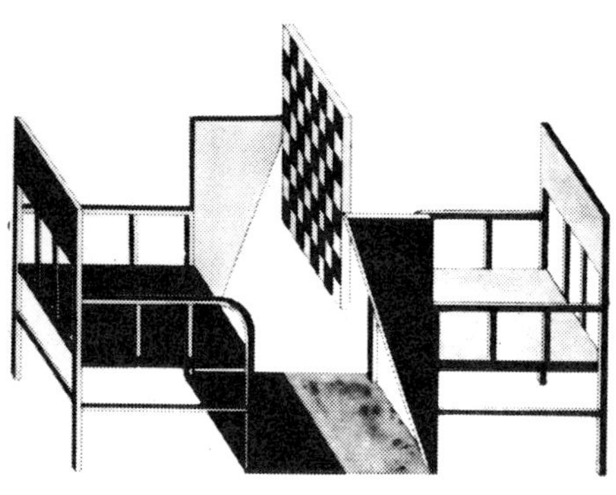

mother, use the whole range of expressive means open to photography in 1924 to the full. They are taken at eye level directly in front of the seated or standing subject. The light is diffuse coming from the north-facing windows of the workshop. The plywood wall of the workshop forms the background.

All Rodchenko's photographs of the '20s are worked out intellectually in order that the essence of the world should be conveyed. Rodchenko advised photographers that "One must take several different photographs of an object, from different places and positions as though looking it over". For him photography was a means of apprehending things — their life.

Depth is created by a juxtaposition of planes. Side-scenes project into the close-up of an object and arrest the eye, marking off the space. Foreshortening allows an unexpected sweep into depth from the foreground back into infinity. Even then Rodchenko used sky as the background to his photographs. It is light like the white surface of a piece of paper. What emerges is a silhouette and photography becomes an original drawing seen by a "mechanical eye".

The series of still-lives "Samozveri" 1926 and "Glass" of 1928 on the other hand are set on a black background. "Glass", it turns out, is surprisingly versatile: it is interesting both tonally and graphically, for its smoothness and textures, transparency and opaqueness.

Of course this compositional system has its roots in Rodchenko's paintings and this is one of the reasons why he came to photography with a strong feeling for the composition of a print. Until the last moment of his life brush and camera lay on his work table like symbols of the two sources of his creativity — art and science.

... And man is left as the measure of everything.

The people he photographed walking barefoot in shorts on asphalt. ("The Road for a Woman", 1925), are beautiful and young, like the new world. Such perhaps is the future of people who are disciplined, clever, physically well-developed.

And the future was to be found in people, in their faces. If they had been photographed from a usual point of view, they would not have seemed at all remarkable but here the angle propels them into the future, towards us in the present day and past us towards tomorrow.

Workers' Club designed by Rodchenko for the "Exposition internationale des Arts décoratifs", Paris 1925.

Opposite page: Metalworking Faculty (Metfak) of Vkhutemas, 1926. Left to right: P.K. Zhigunov, N.A. Sobolev, Z.N. Bykov.

1. Statement from catalogue of X State Exhibition, Moscow, January, 1919.
2. Statement at XIX State Exhibition, Moscow, 1920.
3. Published in "Novyi LEF", No. 6, 1927
4. "Levkas" is a plaster of paris ground (like gesso) traditionally used in the preparation of boards for ikons.
5. From an unpublished letter to Stepanova, 1915.
6. These paintings were also called "Pure colour".

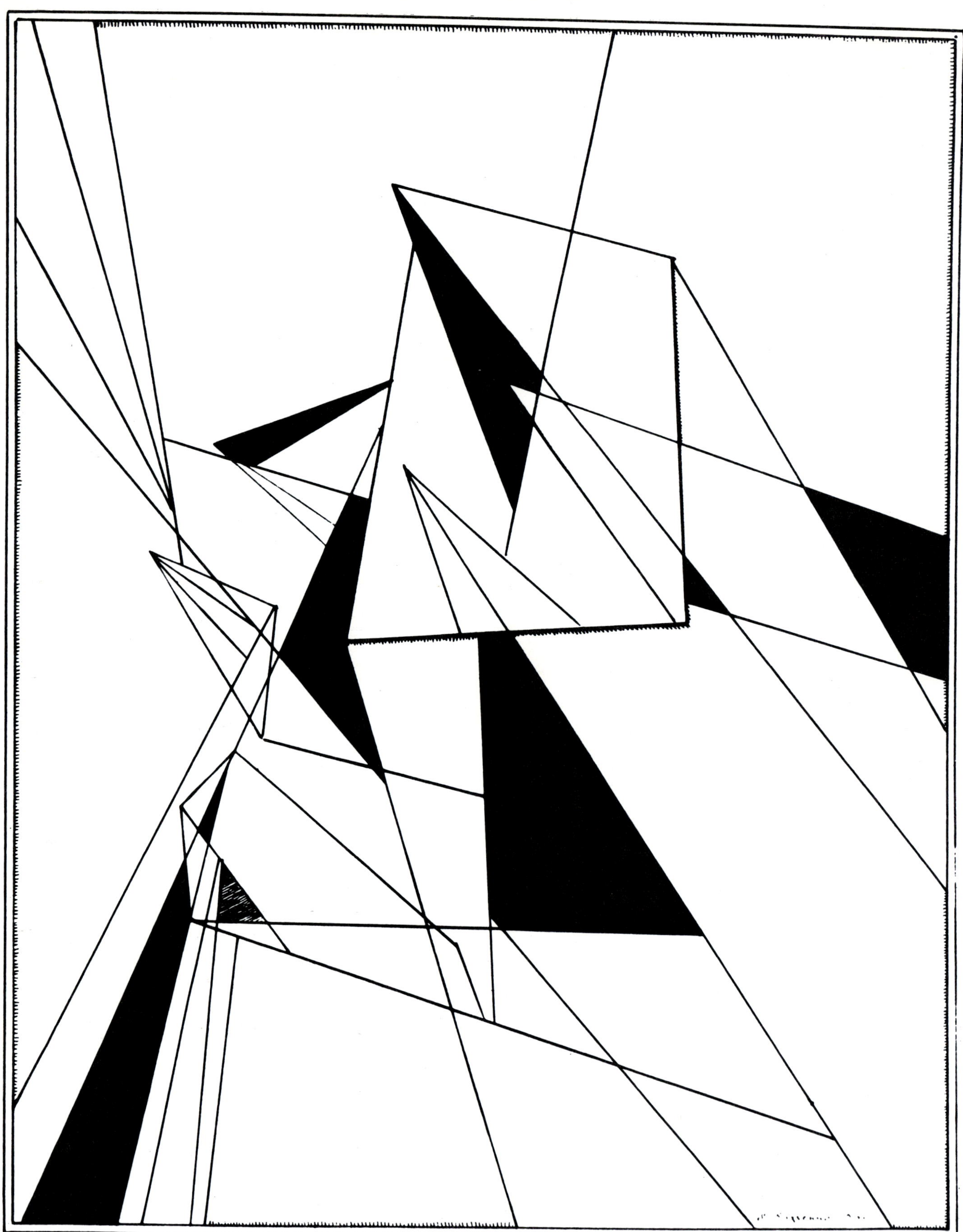

Untitled composition, ink on paper, 1915

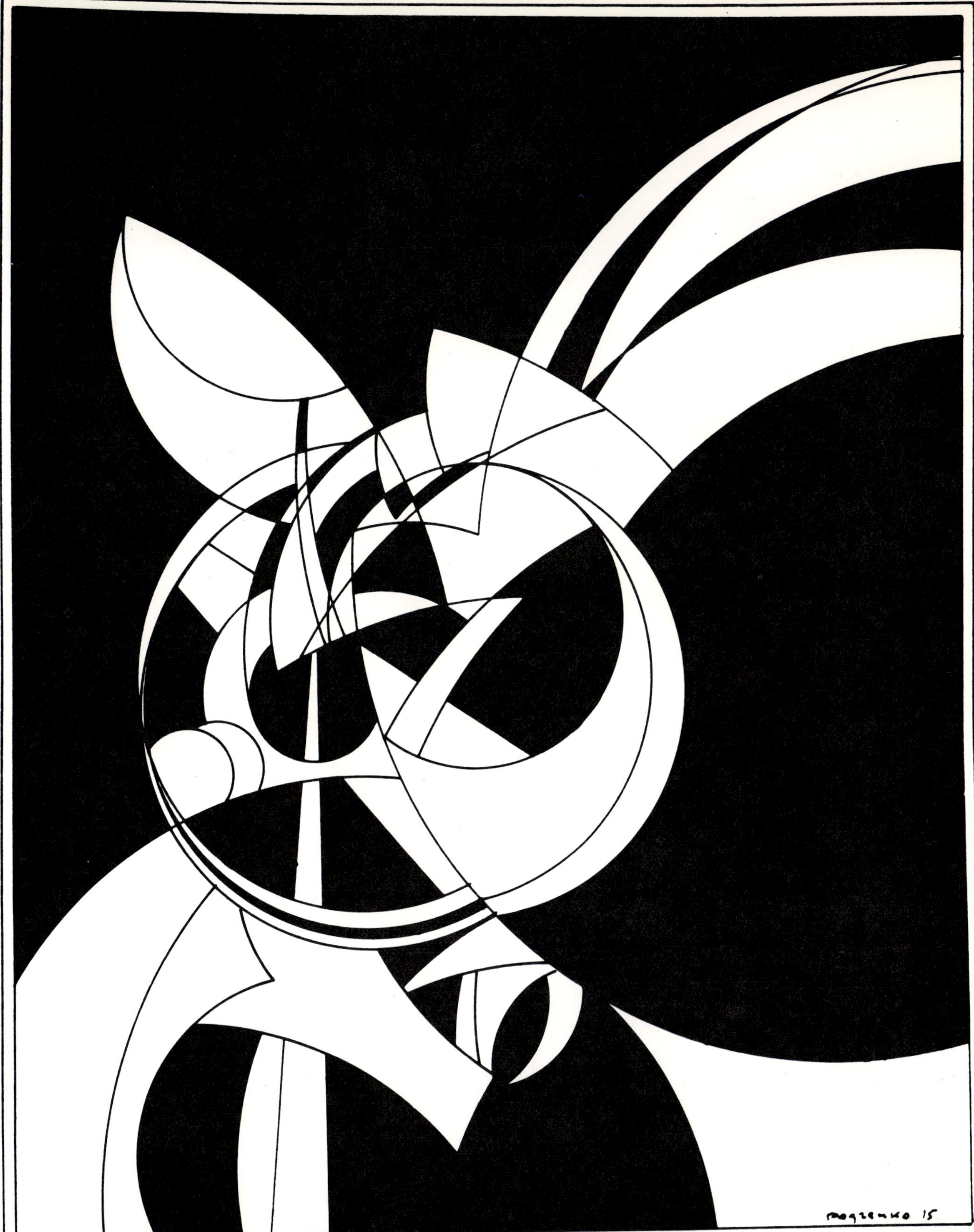

Untitled composition, ink on paper, 1915

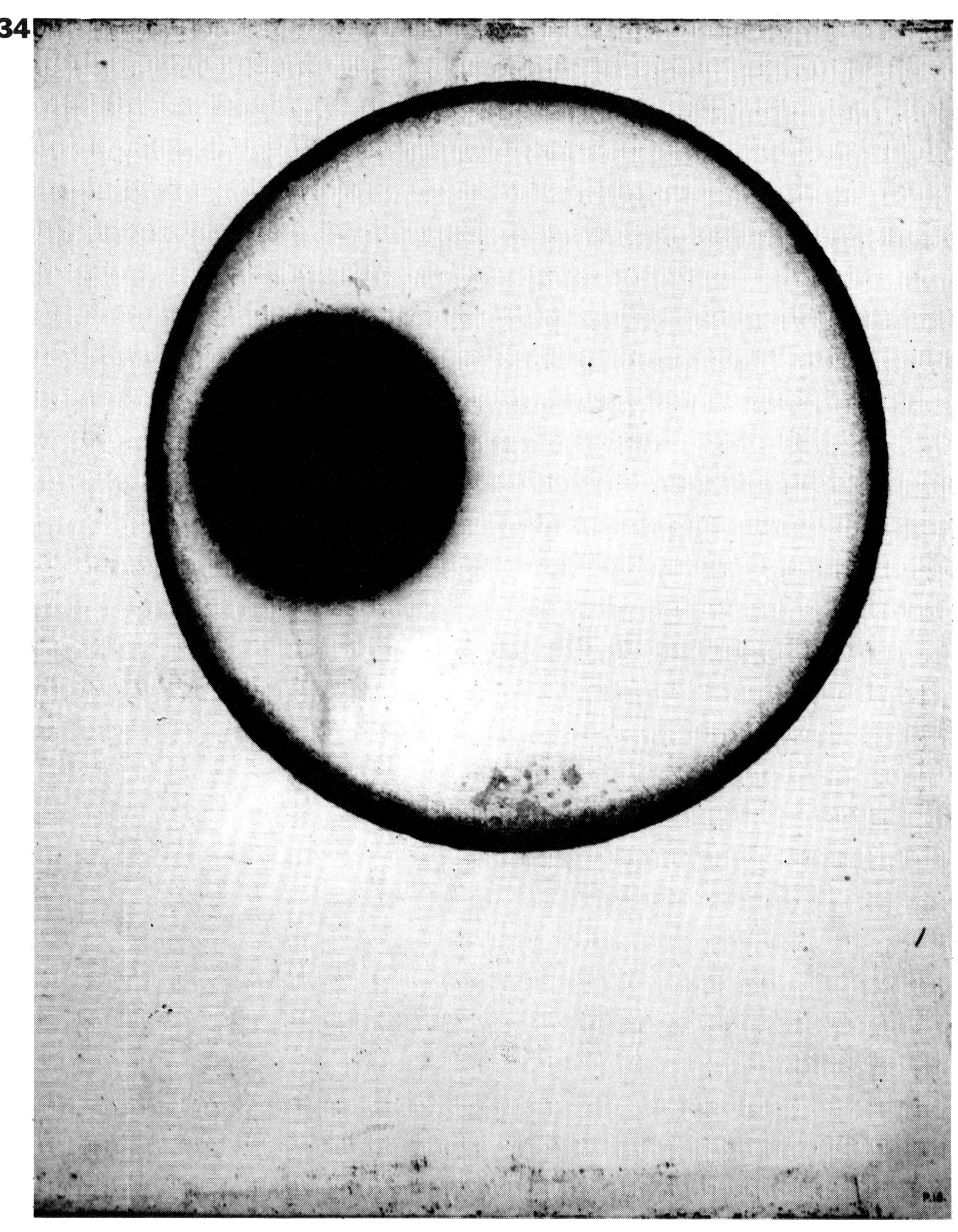

"Concentration of Colour", oil on canvas, 1918

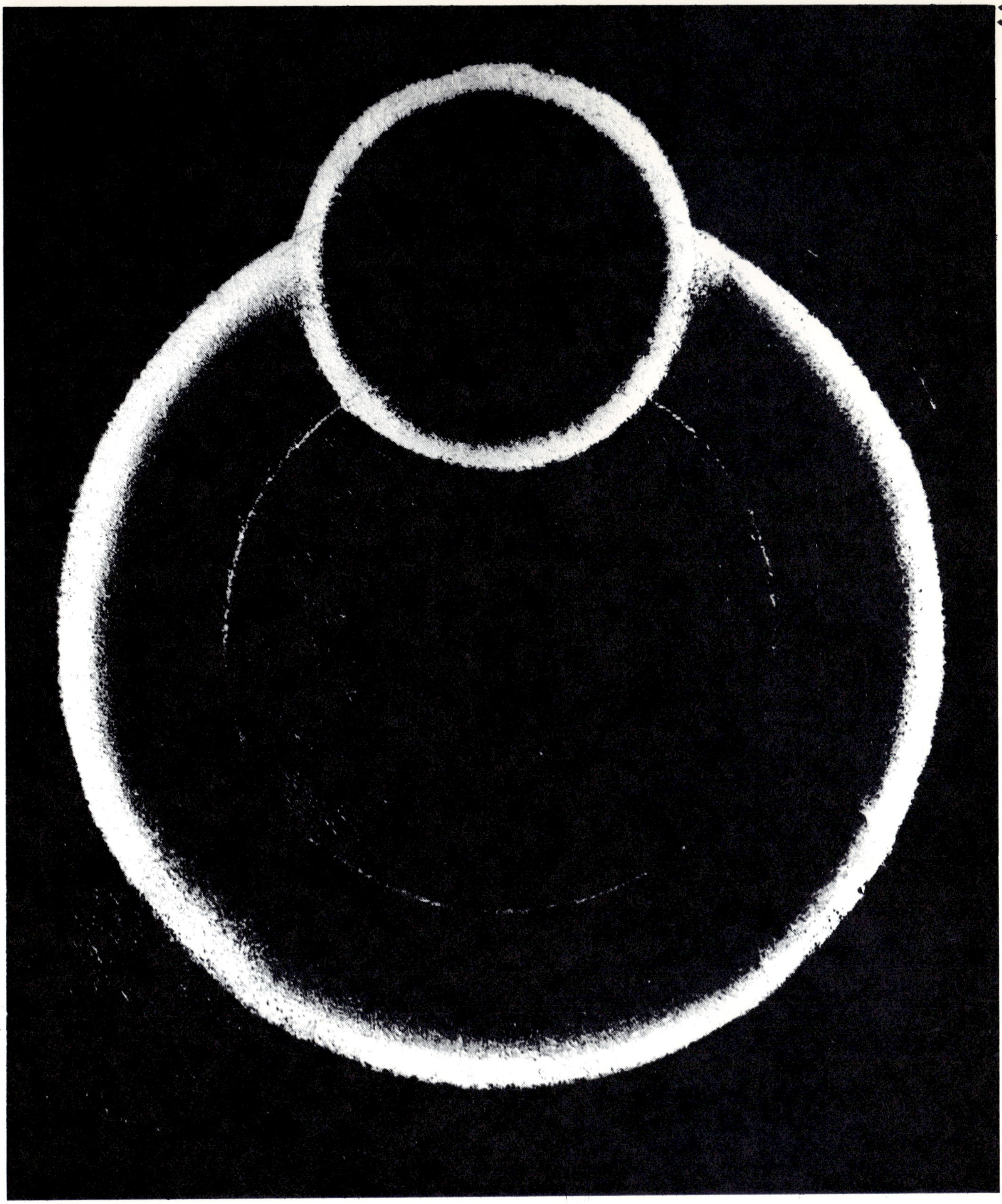

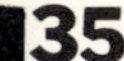

Untitled composition, oil on canvas, 1918

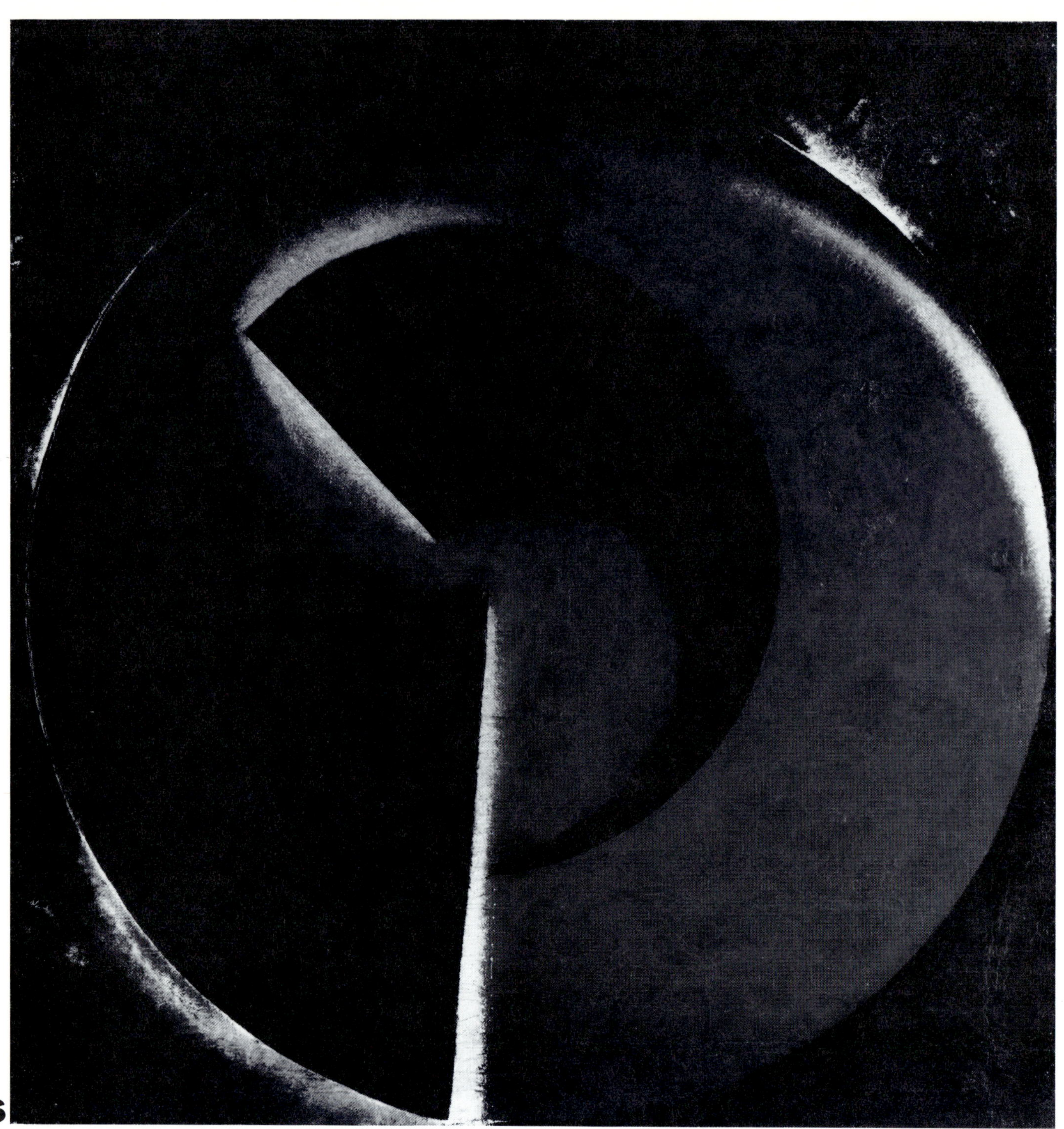

Non-objective painting: "Black on Black", oil on canvas, 1918.

Opposite page: Line construction, linocut, 1921

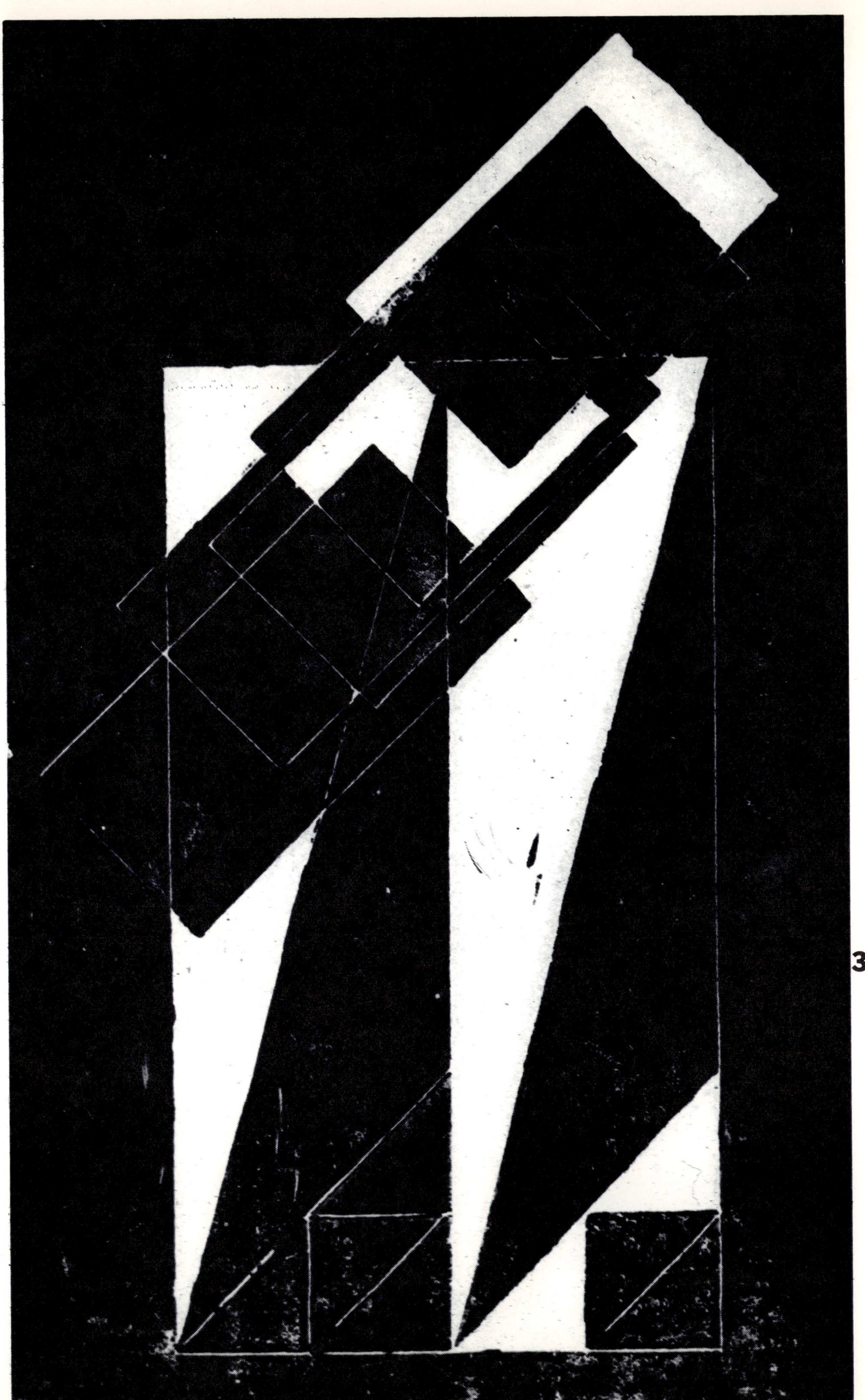

37

Opposite page: Untitled composition, oil on cardboard, 1919

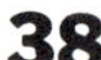

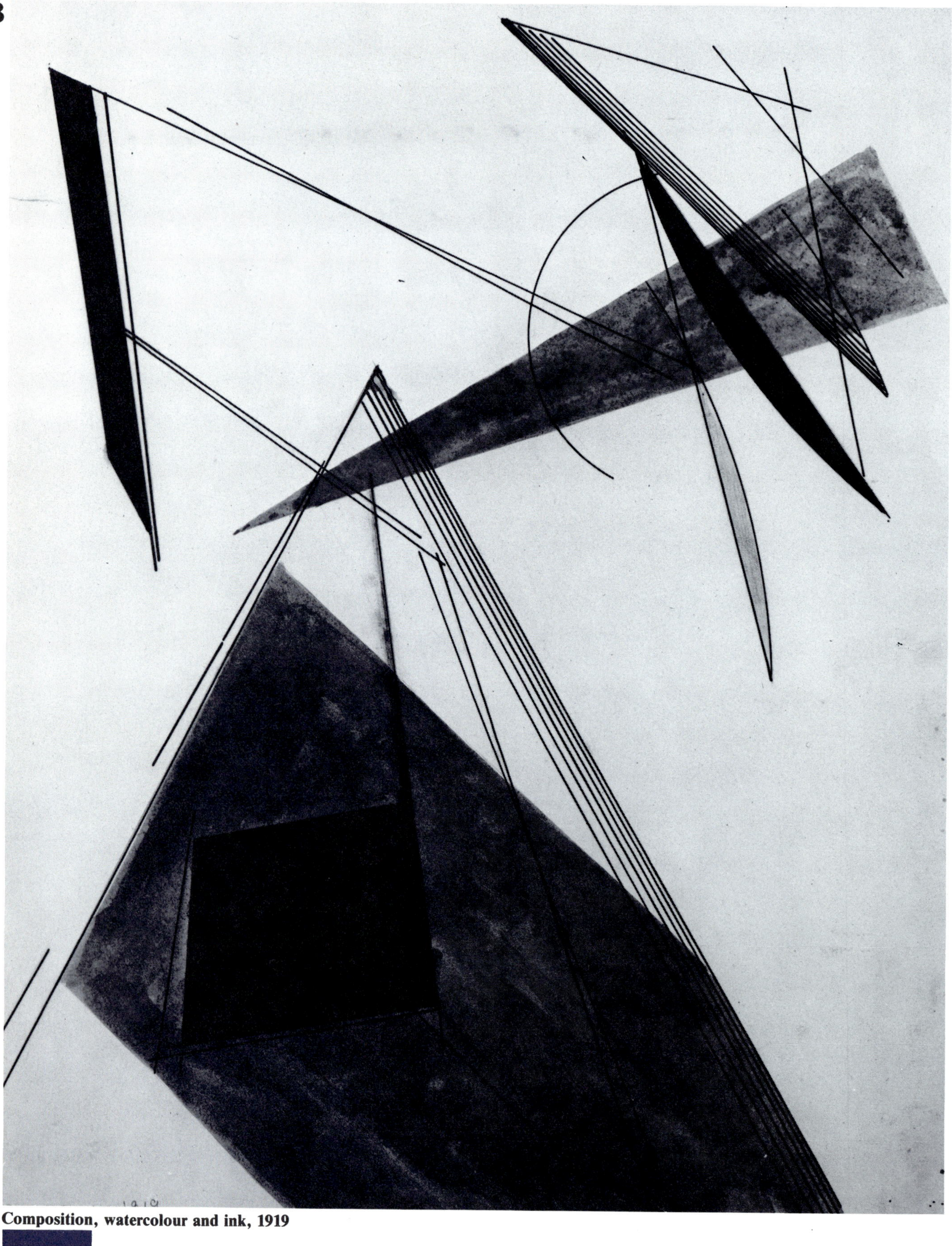

Composition, watercolour and ink, 1919

Page 40: "The Dissolving of the Surface", oil on canvas, 1920

Page 41: Rodchenko with "Hanging Constructions". Photograph by Mikhail Kaufman, 1921.

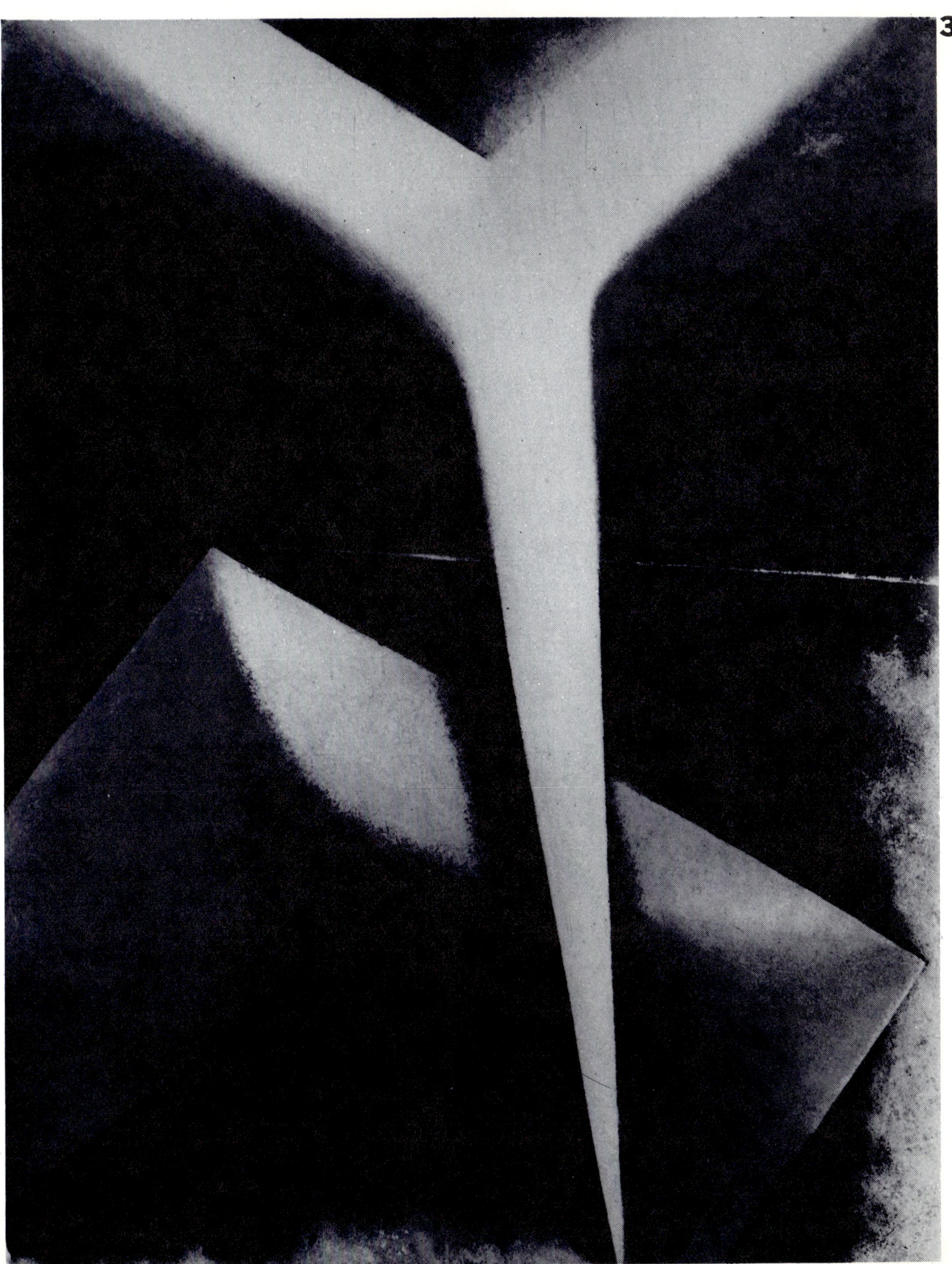

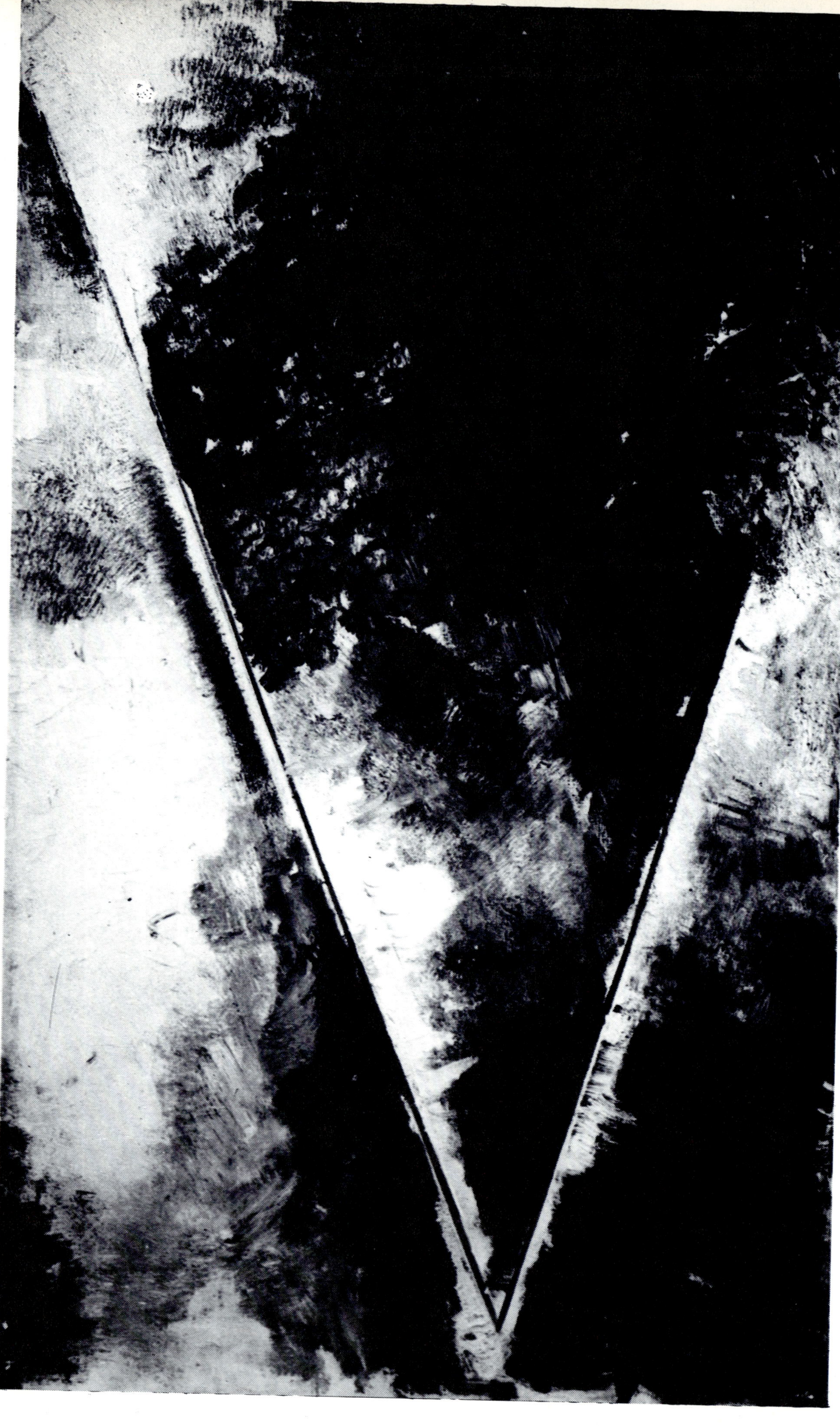

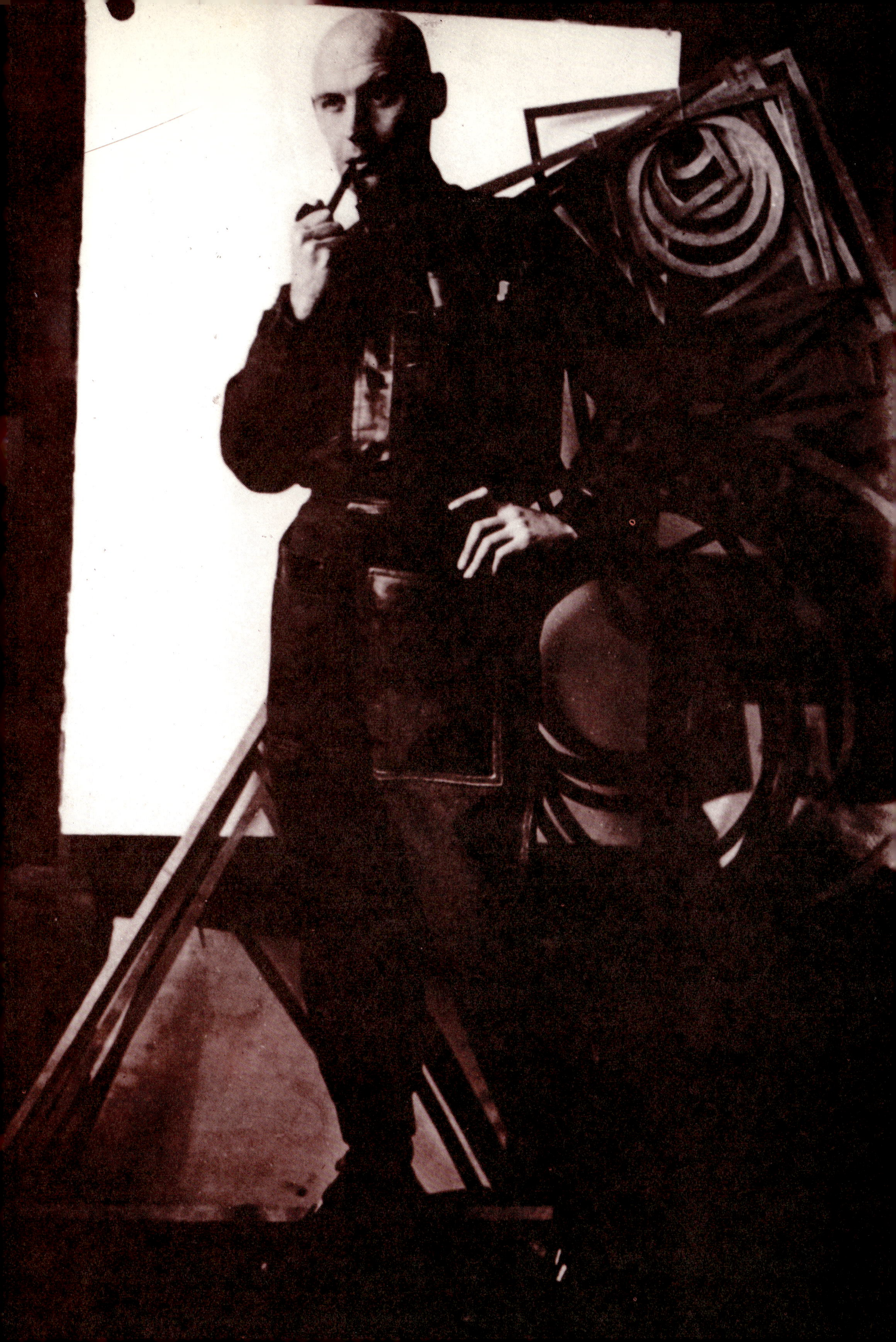

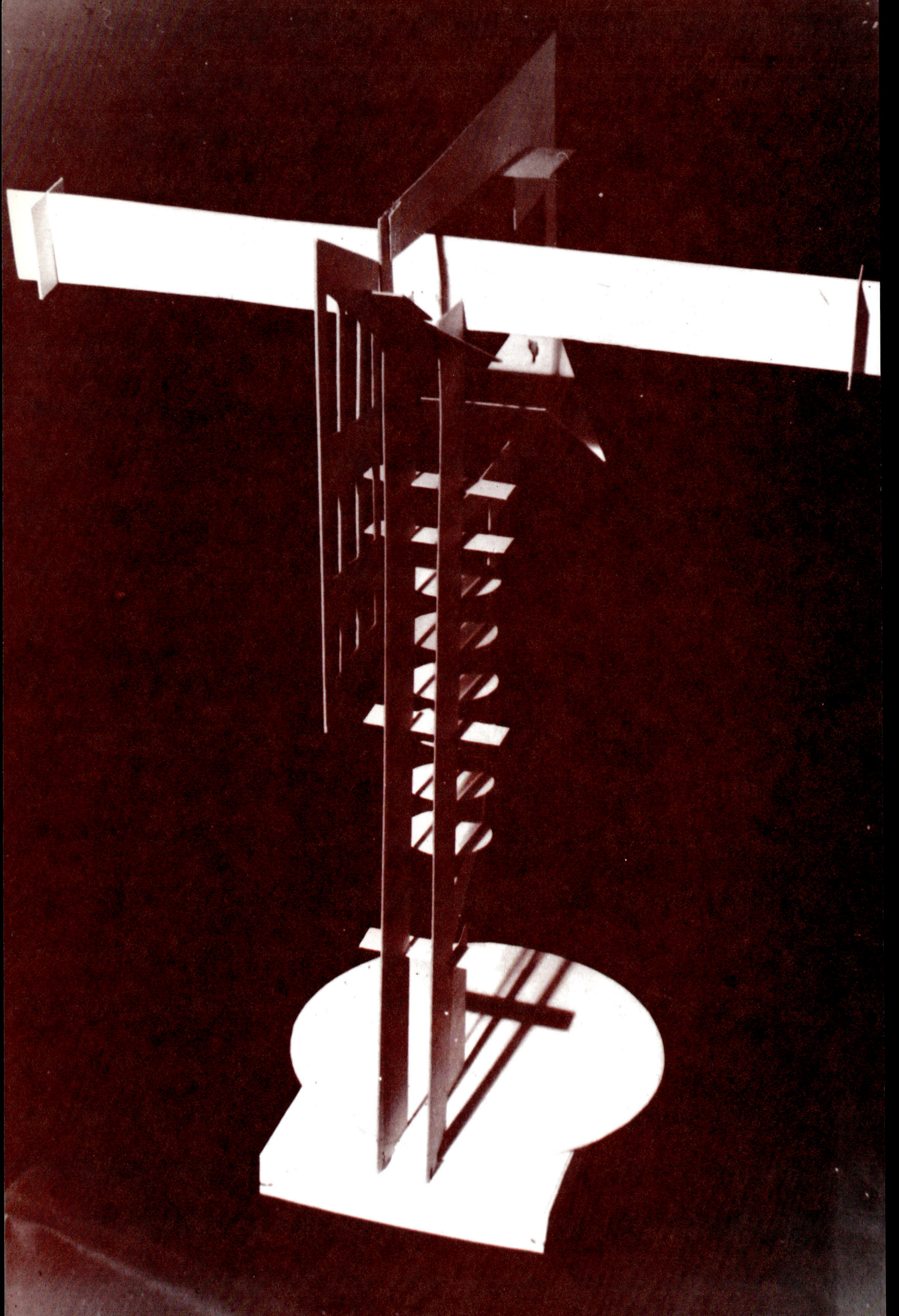

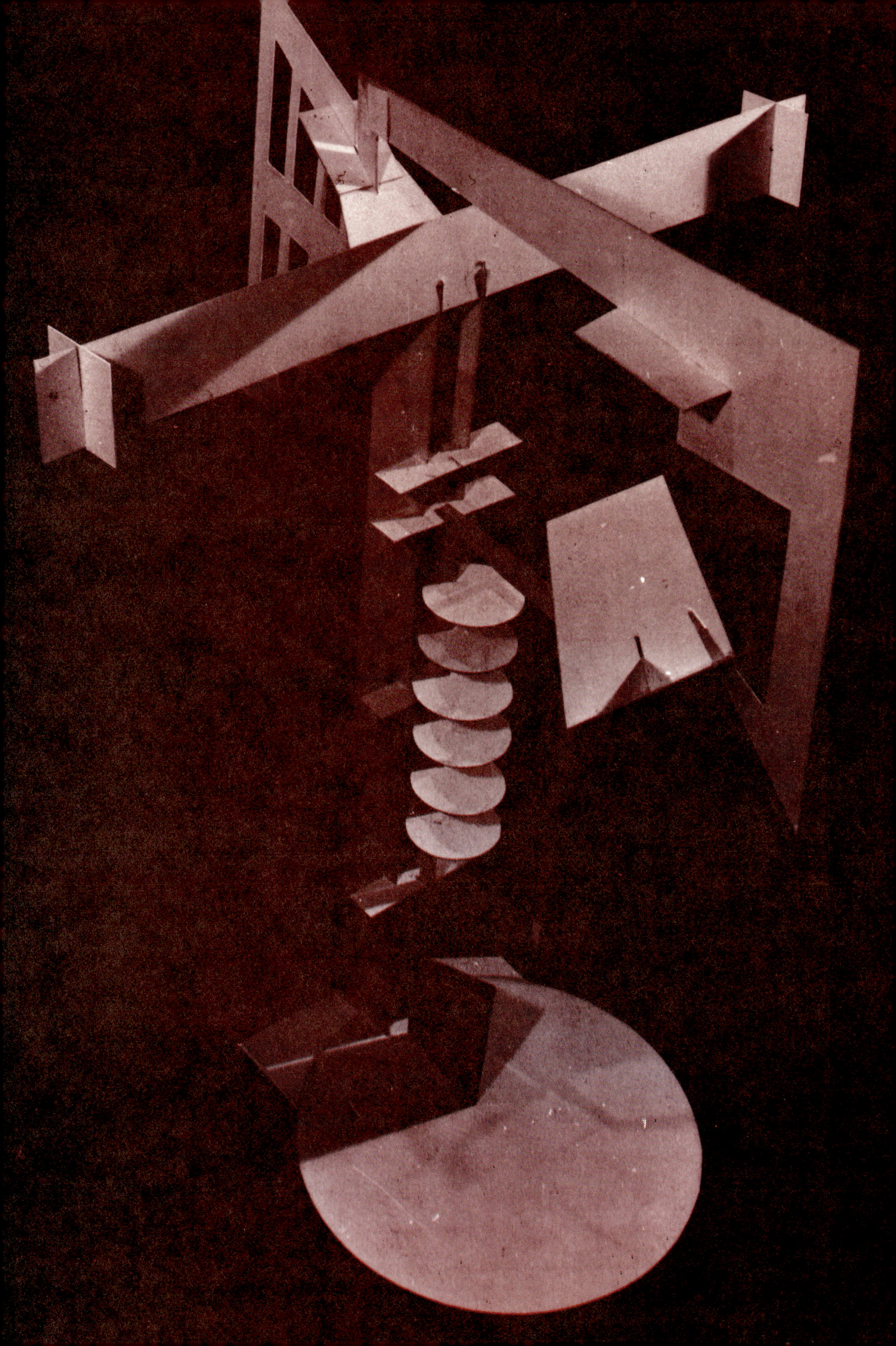

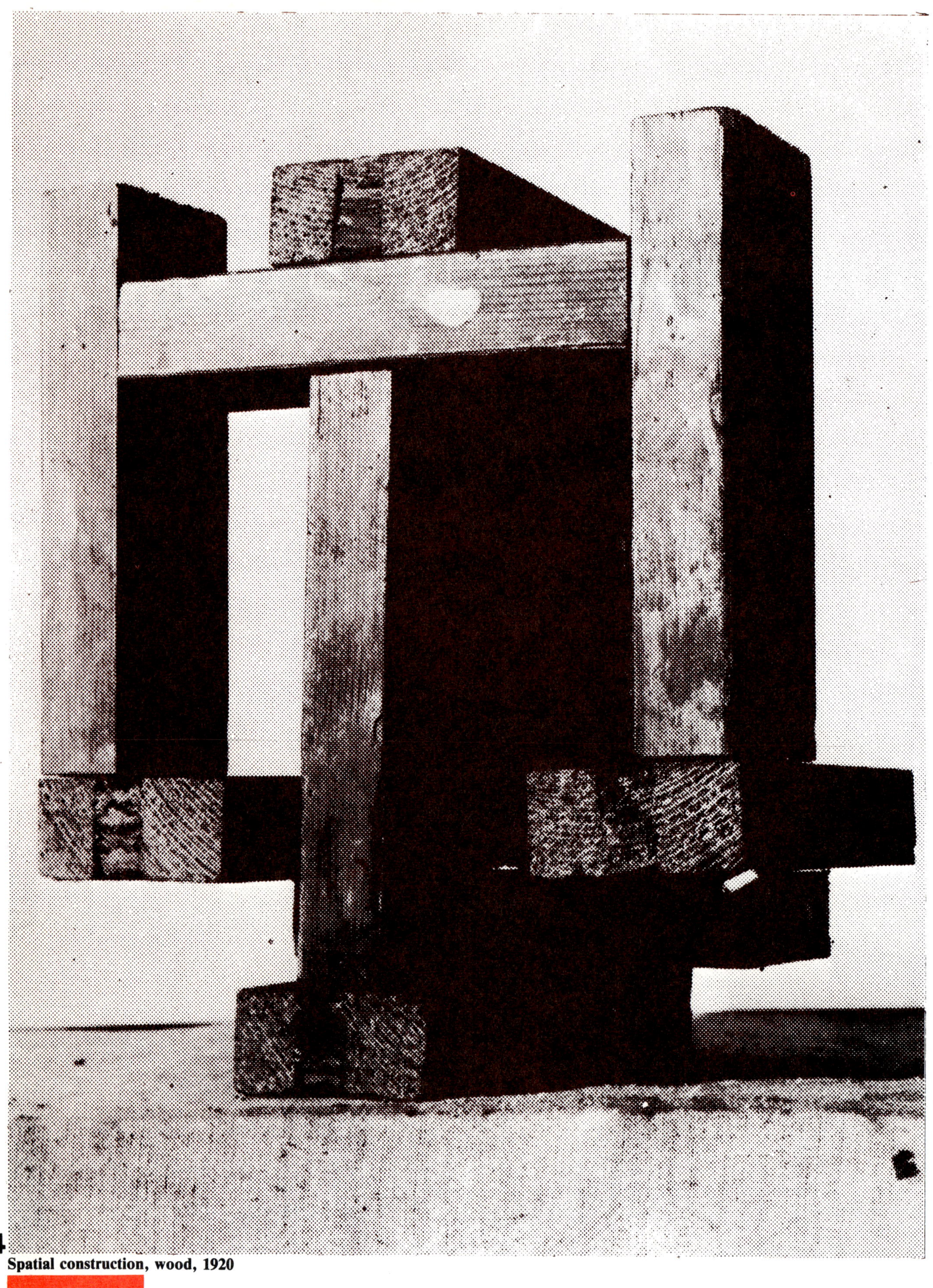

Spatial construction, wood, 1920

Pages 42/3: Two views of "Standing Construction (White Non-objective Sculpture)", 1918.

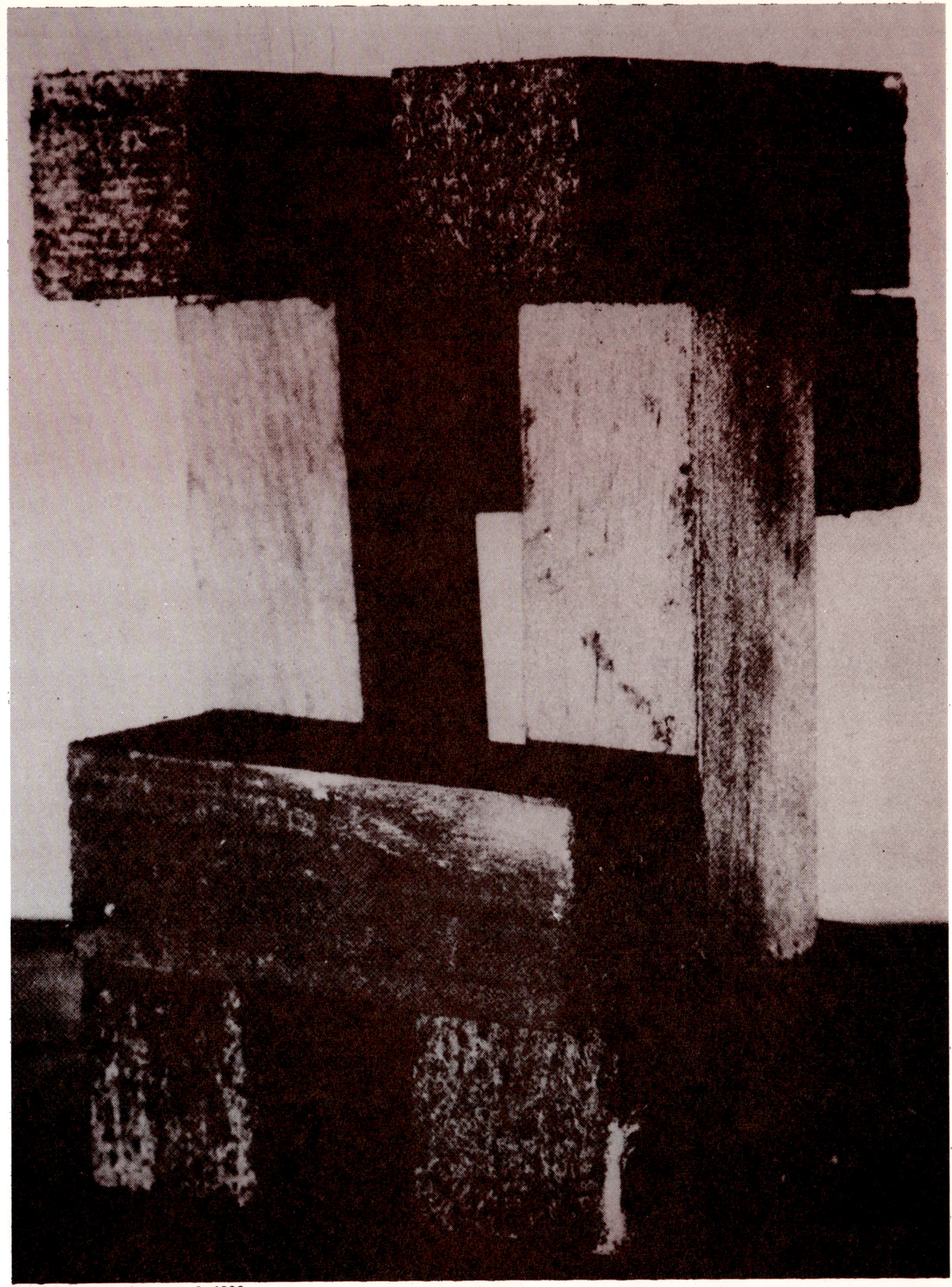

Spatial construction, wood, 1920

Below: Varvara Stepanova (second from right), with students at Vkhutemas, c. 1920

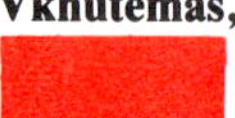

Bottom: Spatial constructions, (third series), wood, 1920-1

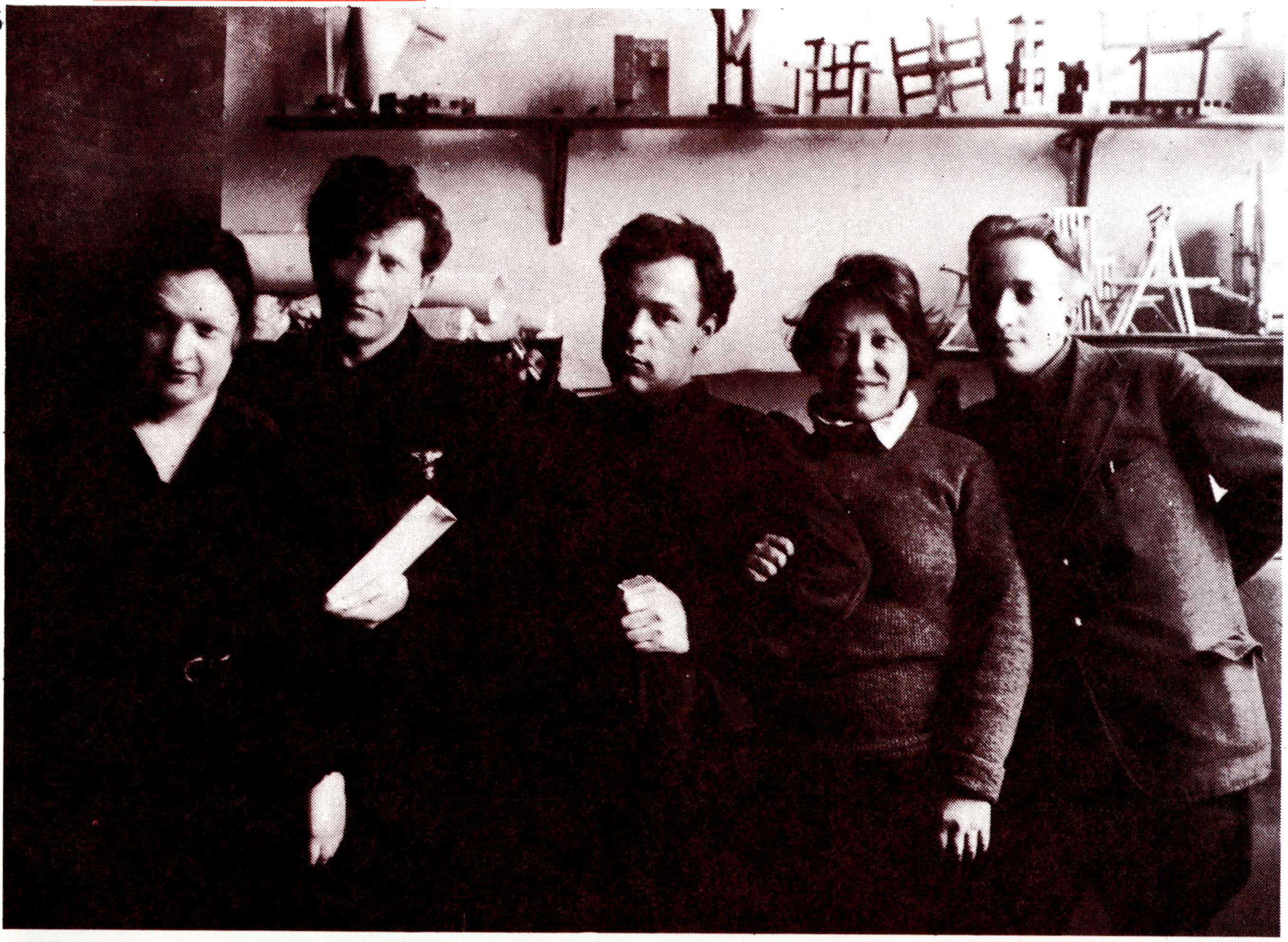

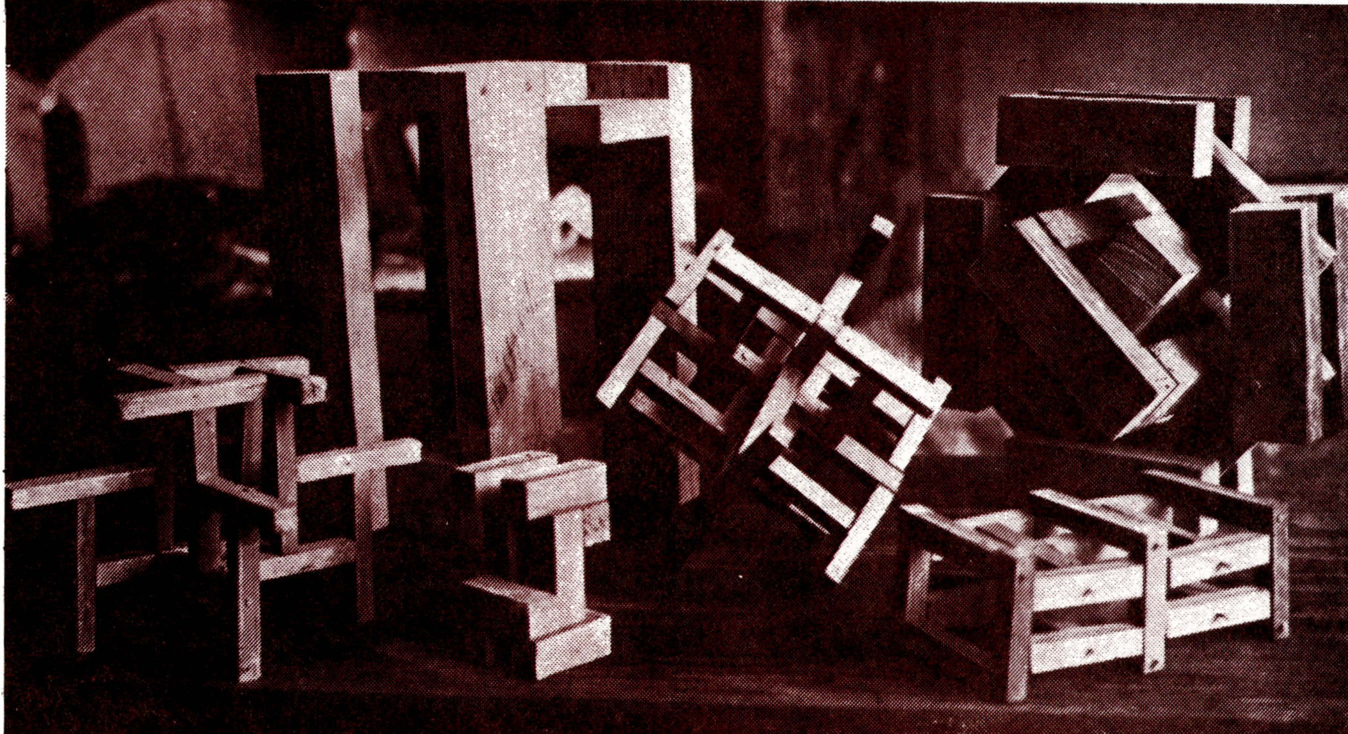

Spatial construction, wood, 1920-1

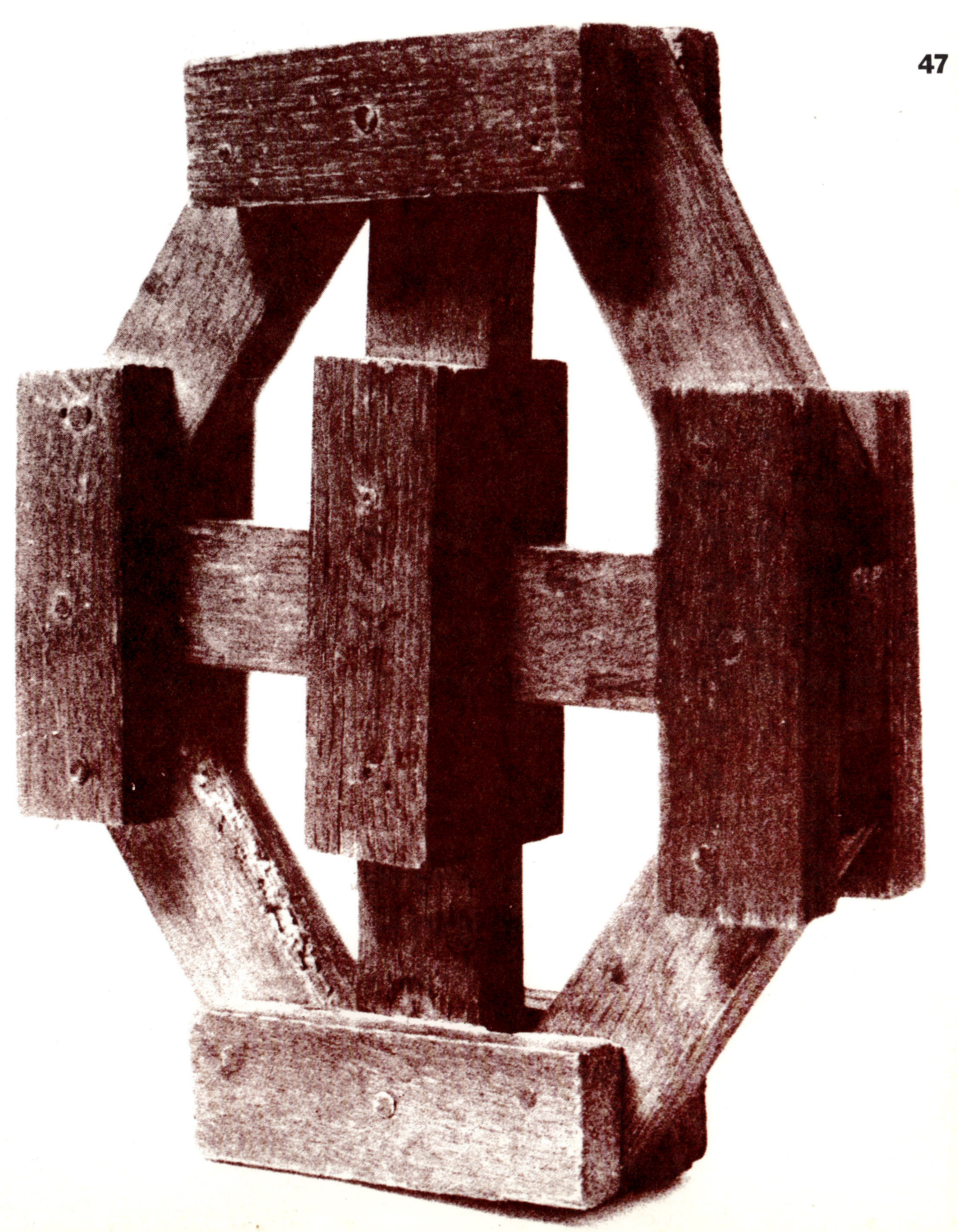

Four "Hanging Constructions", wood, 1920-1

48

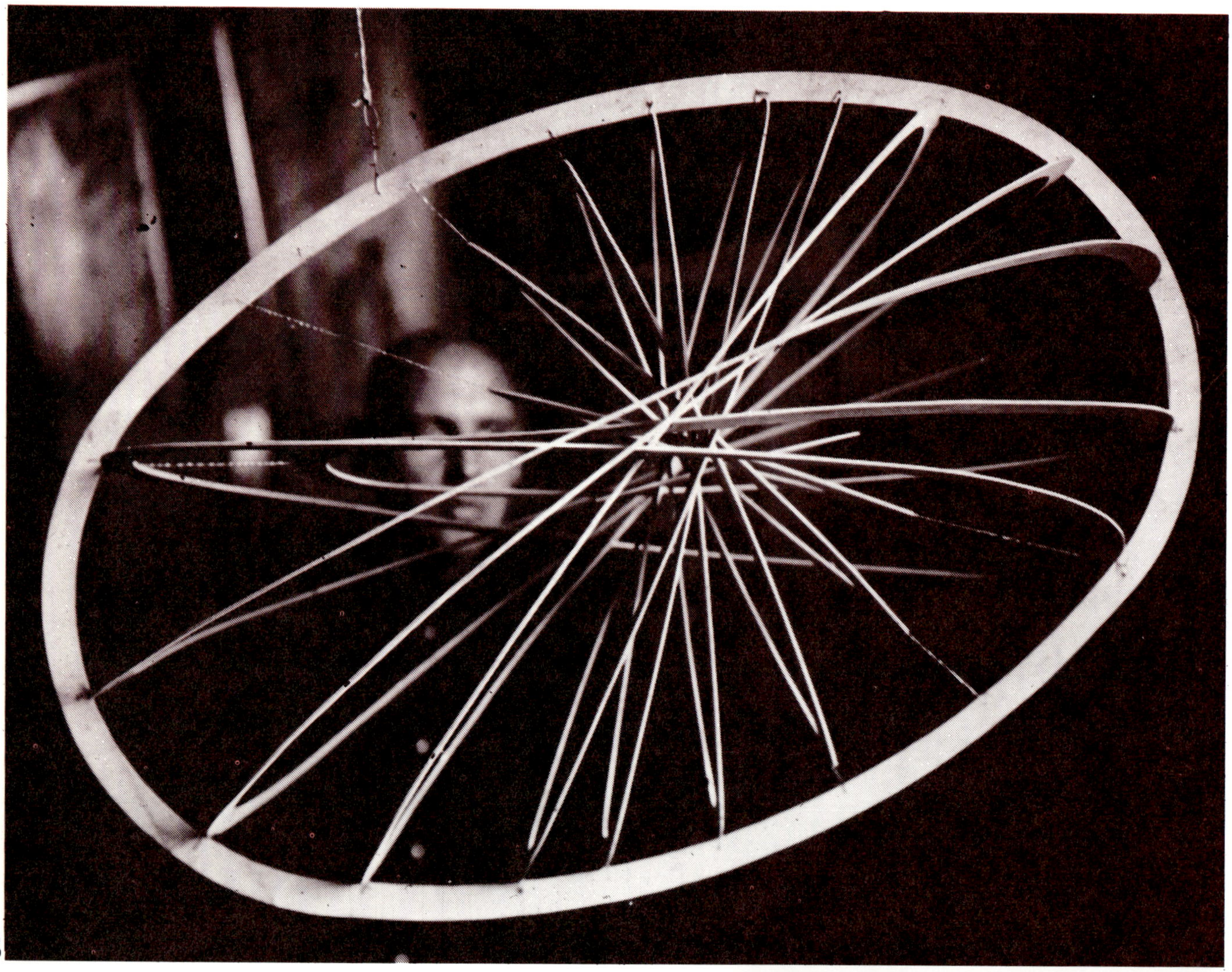

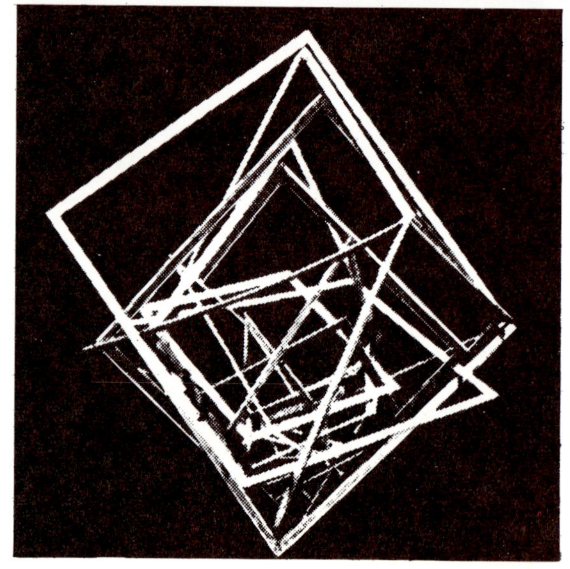

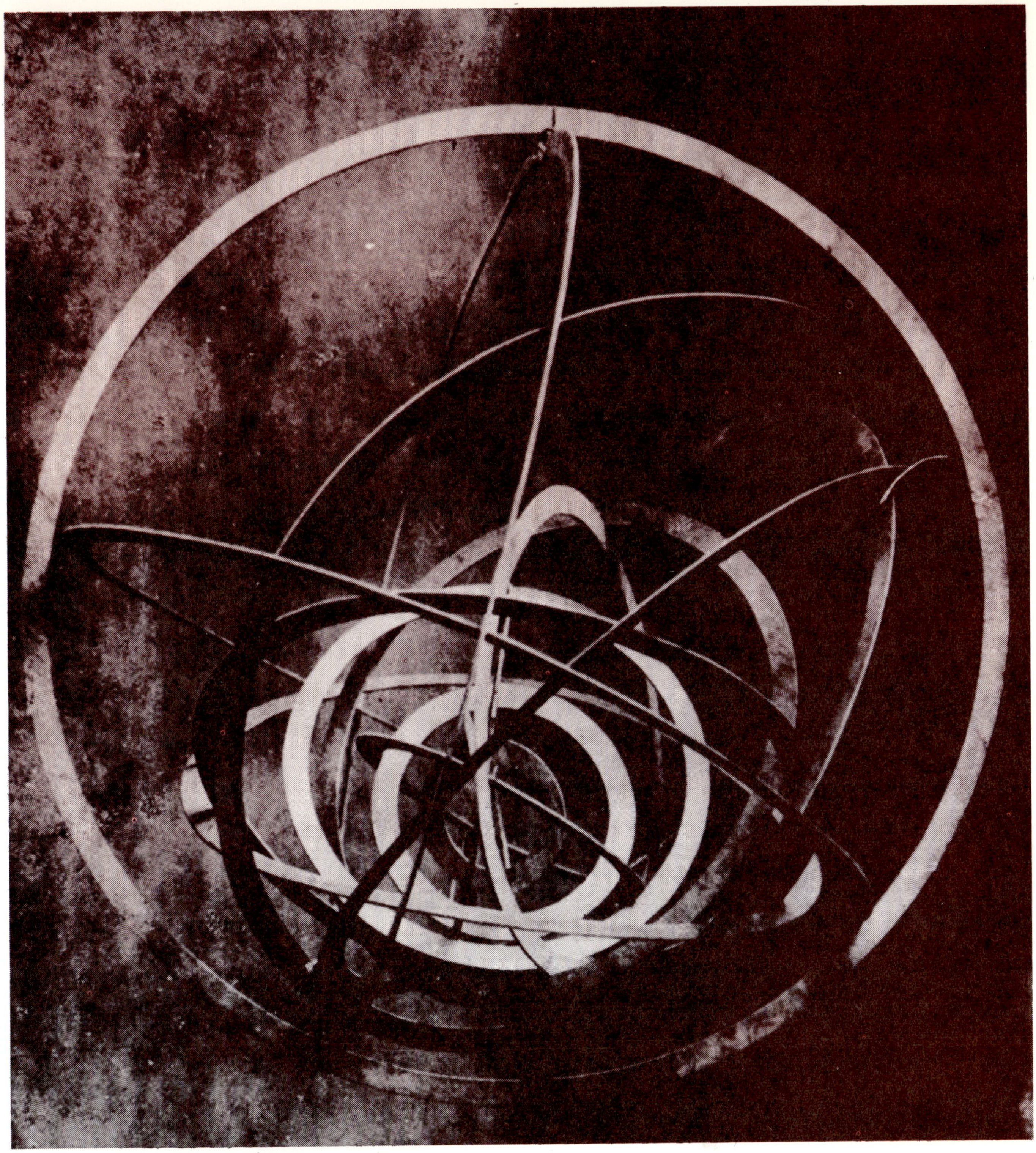

49

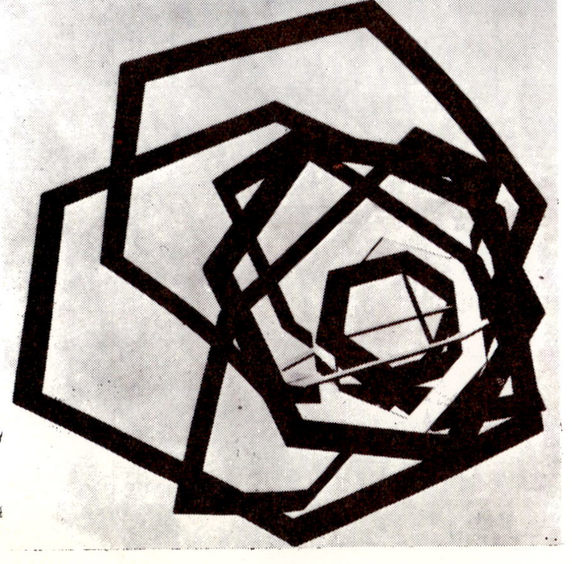

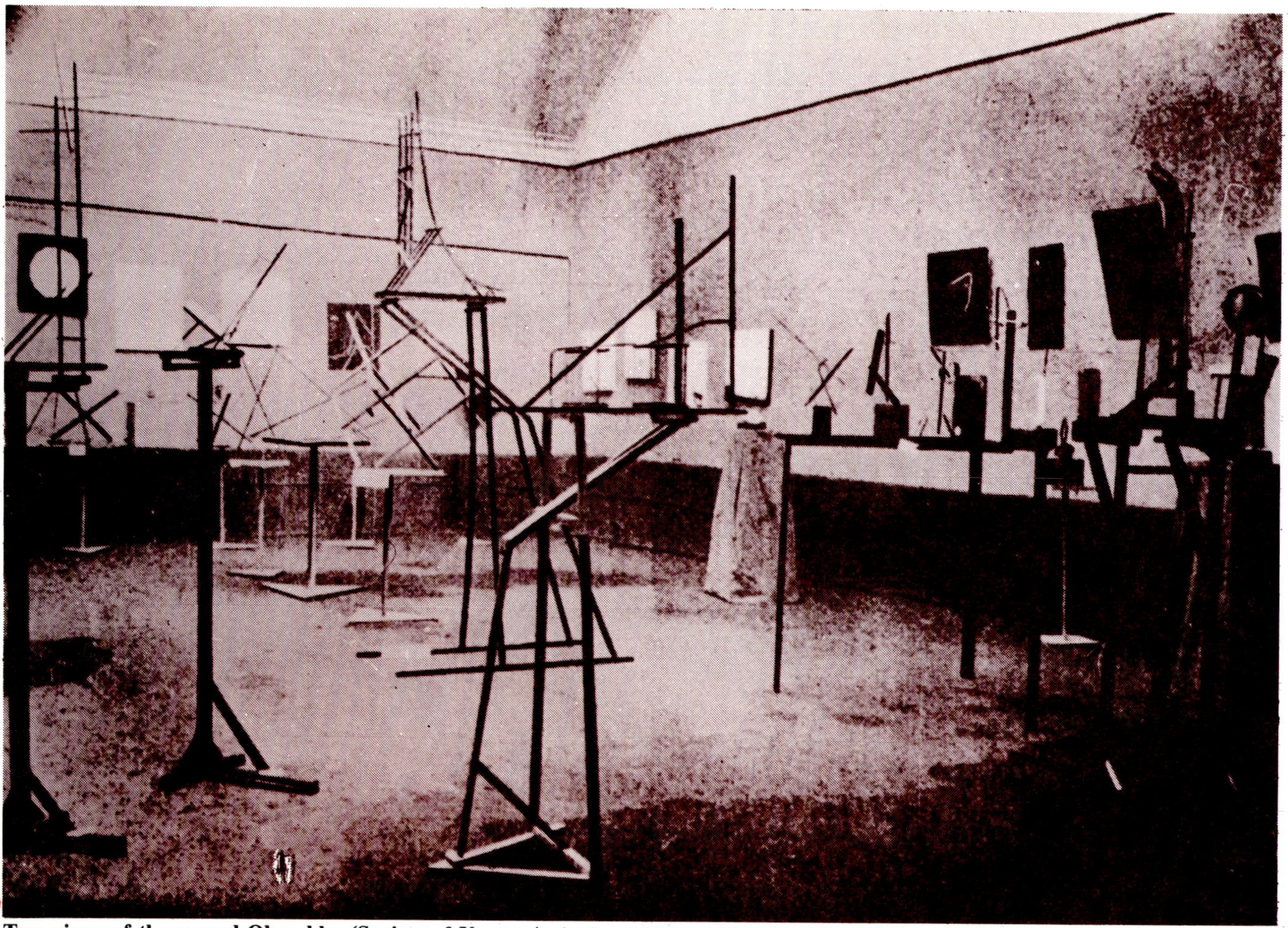

Two views of the second Obmokhu (Society of Young Artists) exhibition, Moscow, May 1921

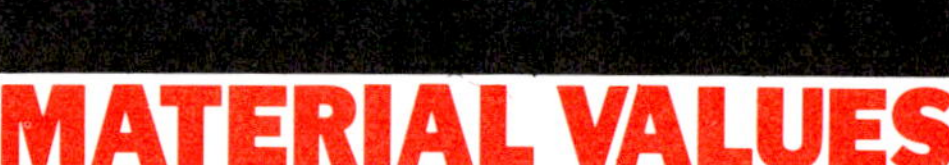

MATERIAL VALUES

Alexander Rodchenko and the end of abstract art by John Milner

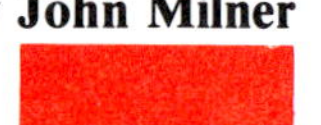

"As a basis for my work I put nothing", declared Rodchenko at the time of the exhibition "Non-Objective Creation and Suprematism" in Moscow in 1919. For a year he had been evolving a method of painting and of constructing objects which had led him not only decisively away from the Suprematism of Malevich and his followers but also clearly towards a new definition of creative activity which proved to be ultimately at odds with painting altogether.

In 1918 and 1919 Rodchenko had evolved a means of pictorial construction which systematically undermined those illusionistic pictorial conventions that had continued even into the abstraction of Kandinsky and the non-objective Suprematism of Malevich. By turning his attention to the succinct manipulation of material elements in his painting, Rodchenko was able to establish a system where that process of manipulation became the focus of activity; the focus of attention no longer remained with the forms themselves. These material elements tend to be of two kinds: the first comprises the specific material qualities of the pigments, grounds and so on employed, and for Rodchenko the importance of "handling" lay in the revealing of the materials employed and their process of application rather than in the suggestions of a personal style or of spatial recession. He employed many different kinds of paint, including metallic and reflective paints and varnishes, as well as gouache and oils, to emphasise these material qualities and necessarily on this level, the surface qualities of his paintings also were emphasised.

The second kind of element employed operated as an equivalent to imagery and at least in its origins, though not in its eventual outcome, owed a debt to Suprematism and to Malevich in particular. Rodchenko had derived from Malevich his use of geometrical form and his vigorous dedication to the examination not only of painterly but also of broader cultural questions. The black painting with which Rodchenko in 1919 replied to Malevich's "White on White" was a rejection of the latter's mysticism — but at the same time it was also a testament to the means Malevich had established. Having said this, it is crucial to consider Rodchenko's use of geometrical form separately from that of Malevich. For Rodchenko, the square, circle and straight line were employed for their material and impersonal characteristics; symmetry and repetition arise in his work as far as possible from the scale of the canvas and the dimensions of the elements on it. In other words, his personal involvement in terms of aesthetic predilection is minimal and his paintings are constructed rather than composed. The use of material

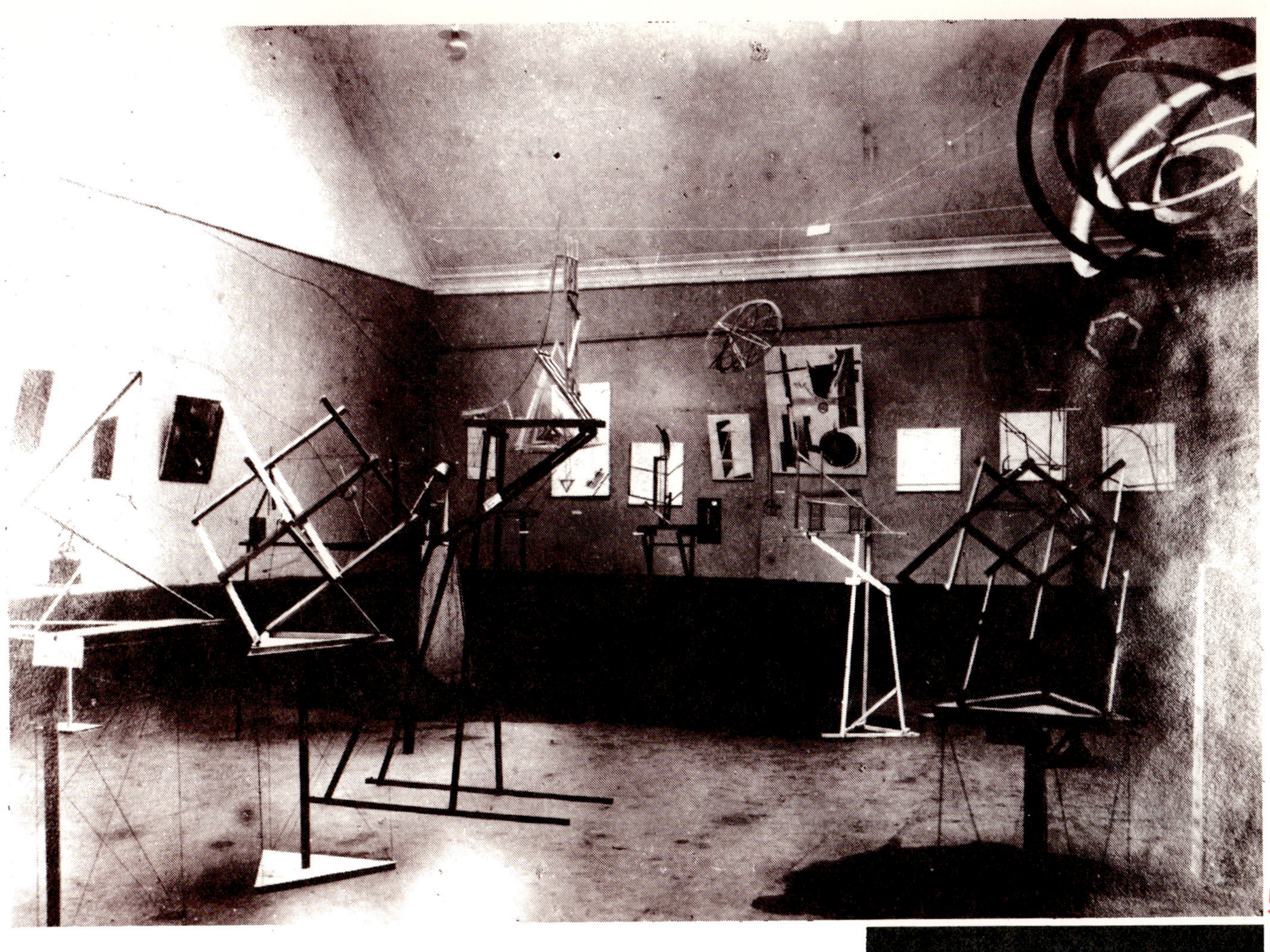

John Milner is an art historian and director of the Hatton Gallery, University of Newcastle upon Tyne. He was the organiser of the exhibitions "Russian Constructivism Revisited," Newcastle and Oxford, 1973 and of "Russian Graphic Art" Newcastle, 1978.

distinctions, (for example a gloss surface contrasted against a matt one) rather than tonal or colouristic distinctions, further reduced the possibilities of suggested picture-space with all its allusions to personal expression.

This material commitment on Rodchenko's part led to a rejection of stylistic considerations whilst retaining an important role for facture. It was impersonal in the elements employed (for geometrical figures are common intellectual property) and it fought against illusionistic picture space by employing the most direct means of undermining it: at first by reversing or contradicting spatially suggestive conventions and eventually by abandoning them altogether. His frequent use of mechanical means for making his circles and lines supported this extraordinary standpoint. These were later joined by the camera.

Rodchenko was engaged upon an investigation that in certain respects was clearly an anti-art activity, rejecting above all expressive abstraction.

By the dismantling of conventions his work progressed to define new means. Picture-space was amongst the first of these conventions that Rodchenko meticulously and with impressive economy made the focus of his analytical investigation. "The crushing of all 'isms' in painting was for me the beginning of my resurrection. With the funeral bells of colour painting, the last 'ism' was accompanied to its grave." The linear paintings of 1919 clearly reveal Rodchenko's investigation at work.

A note in Rodchenko's hand, dated September 7th, 1919, describes four such recent paintings. Accompanying the notes were drawings of the four paintings and details of their sizes. The four appear to comprise a series. He describes them as follows: (1) on a yellow ground (chrome) (40 x 68 cm, width before height); (2) on white lead (45 x 68 cm); (3) on ochre (72 x 84 cm) and (4) on green (46½ x 73 cm). Number three on Rodchenko's list appears to be the painting "Line Construction", 1919, now in the Museum of Modern Art in New York. For here Rodchenko employs colour as a ground for linear elements. Each line is even and flat without changes of application, texture, colour or width; they can be seen to move clearly across the surface of the painting. In this respect Rodchenko is dealing with pictorial construction of the most factual and material kind to date. As none of his individual elements is in itself at all illusionistic no single element relies upon picture space. On the other hand spatial effects of considerable elaboration do occur as the linear elements react together. The manner in which they do so is basically that employed in the linocuts of 1918-1919 in which the relatively closed forms of certain parts of the linocuts have been deleted to leave linear elements. The use of colour grounds in this series of paintings is also related to the lino cuts where the line incised into the lino becomes a lit-up and positive element in the print; in those paintings on a toned ground (number two is on white), the linear elements can be decisively to either side of it tonally. The ground thus becomes an active tone caught between those of the elements upon it. In order to resist an atmospheric perspective effect arising out of this (this can be seen, for example, in parts of the New York "Line Construction"), dark lines pass in front of light ones and elsewhere light in front of dark ones. This was not possible with the linocut technique.

Rodchenko's lines operate in three more ways. Firstly they congregate to establish edgeless transparent planes that are no more than the sum of related lines. The planar element in Rodchenko's painting continues therefore to have visual density, scale and spatial extension without recourse to firmly limited edges, firmly established surfaces or a firm commitment to colour, all of which Rodchenko had rejected earlier as they fostered a reading of an image upon a ground. As in his three-dimensional work of 1918 his material is ultimately the articulate manipulation of emptiness and space. Secondly, for all their even dedication to the material surface which they cross, whenever Rodchenko's lines are diagonal, as is usually the case, they imply perspective recession. This confounding of spatial systems, their mutual negation in a dynamic balance, can be seen earlier in Rodchenko's paintings. In the New York painting transparent planes intersect at angles implying complex spaces. The abrupt halting, for example, of the dark diagonals in the upper half of the work by a line comprising an almost vertical opposing diagonal implies that this line is the edge of a plane. Lower down the arrival of comparable diagonals is unimpeded so that the planar reading is contradicted. Indeed the crossing of both sets of dark lines over a suggested plane of white lines opens up complex spatial readings of an altogether different order. This opposition of spatial devices was characteristic of Rodchenko in 1918-1919.

The third sense in which Rodchenko's lines are active is in construction, for their spatial interaction implies spatial relations of planes however insubstantial and transparent. They not only form strictly two-dimensional constructions across a painted surface, but also articulate the shapes and surfaces of space within a balanced, negated and contradictory picture space. The economy of Rodchenko's means of achieving this complexity is stunning.

Surprisingly the elaboration of these means was for Rodchenko not at all incompatible, with the presentation of recognisable imagery. During 1919 and 1920 figurative imagery returned to his work in a variety of ways: as collages incorporating printed images and also in designs for buildings and costumes. But even in this work Rodchenko manipulates the pictorial elements which comprise these figures to avoid closed forms and his suggestion of contradictory and implied planes in them militates against the establishment of credible picture-space. The relation of means to image in these works is new and owes much to his linear investigations of pictorial construction.

1920 saw the further removal of Rodchenko's activities away from spatial illusionism toward the investigation of facture ("faktura" — the signs of the handling of a material). Further linear works, now incorporating the circle, often contain (as was the case in some works made in the previous year) smaller circles placed before larger ones to disrupt the implication of perspective recession which would otherwise arise. With means which are in themselves impersonal, Rodchenko creates and defies picture space. He employs means which not only move resolutely and evenly across the canvas surface but which also suggest contradictory and immaterial spaces. It is in these works that the discreetness of Rodchenko's achievement can most readily be appreciated. The sense of his 1919 statement that "as a basis for my work I put nothing" may be seen to contain an implication of positive achievement in opposition to its more obvious nihilism.

Increasingly his work becomes more diagrammatic, his reliance upon specific qualities of scale, or even of material becomes increasingly minimal. The revelation of the handling of ma-

Line composition, ink, 1918

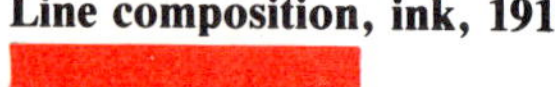

Below: Non-objective composition,

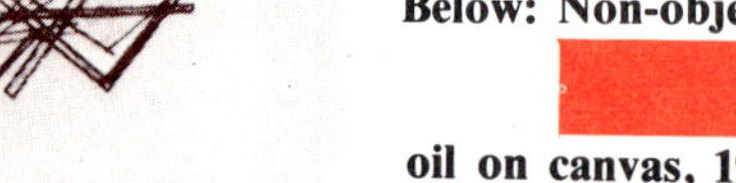

oil on canvas, 1919

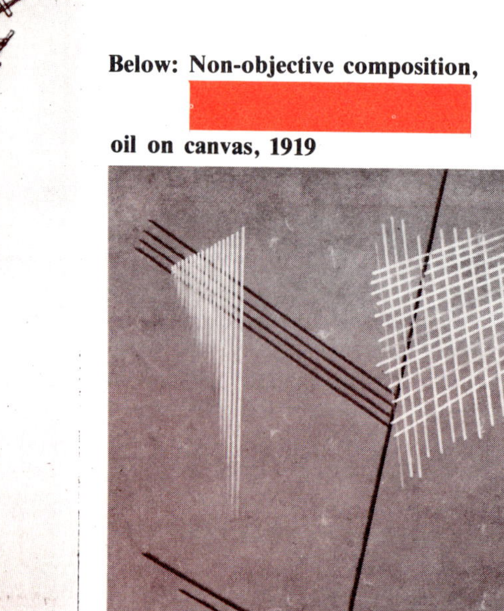

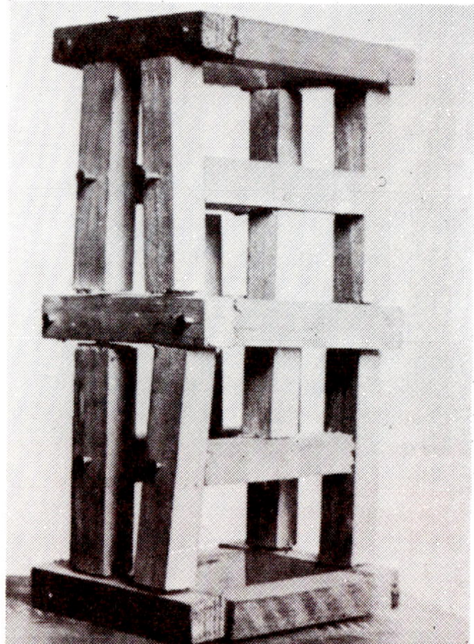

Spatial construction, wood, 1920

terials now becomes an important but incidental feature in his realisation of generalised conclusions in specific form. The wooden constructions, both free standing and suspended, evolved by Rodchenko in 1920 illustrate this clearly. As in his latest pictorial constructions employing ruler and compass, Rodchenko built up his work in wood from the repetition of units. These constructions are unlike the three dimensional works of two years earlier in that they do not attempt to reiterate in three dimensions the planar subtleties that Rodchenko had evolved in painting. They only relate closely to Rodchenko's current painting in the use of a repeated element to divide space and provide structure. Planes are suggested by the abrupt termination of elements at the level of a single, or rather six, single surfaces. A number of the wooden constructions would fit into a rectangular box, a little taller than a cube, with each of their elements contiguous with at least one side of the box. To a degree the wooden elements perform a role comparable with the plane — suggesting the lines of the linear paintings.

The use in these constructions of very rough wood recalls the strong "faktura" of other 1920 painting. The process of handling the wood, sawing it, in fact, is not concealed for the sake of finish. Despite the diagrammatic quality of certain of these wooden constructions (for example, their symmetry which is independent of particular materials), Rodchenko expresses clearly the quality of the material used and the method of its handling in these embodiments of immaterial principles of construction. Just as Tatlin's process of construction was distinct by its very nature from that of the engineer, so Rodchenko's was distinct from the traditional practices of the professional craftsman in wood.

Despite Rodchenko's concern with material values, particularly that of facture, in individual works, his geometrical elements were impersonal or supra-personal in that they comprised common intellectual property which may only be exemplified in but never exclusively attached to a particular material manifestation. In this sense, Rodchenko's process of construction became independent of particular forms and of particular materials, despite the solidity and precision of his work. The wooden constructions of 1920 for the first time carry these characteristics of construction beyond individual considerations, for whilst their material is emphatically wood, and whilst they are still very much the work of Rodchenko, they are above all embodiments of geometrical construction that would be undamaged by execution in other materials and by other hands. This remarkable achievement took Rodchenko out of the realm of non-objective painting and perhaps out of the realm of art altogether by undermining the personal link between the artist and his work. These constructions were no longer only visual — they did not rely upon aesthetic sensibility; they were not irreplaceable and were not therefore precious or valuable; they were easy to make and required little or no aesthetic education to do so. Yet, they were still constructions: cultural objects, which were communal rather than individual property. Particular realisations of the constructions would not affect their essential characteristics; these were constructions beyond the reach of non-objective art.

Elaborate symmetries and the inversion of elements led to the hanging pieces, Rodchenko's most complex, impersonal and ultimately scaleless works. Some of these were exhibited in the crucial second exhibition of the "Obmokhu" group in May 1921. The circle, the square, the triangle, the hexagon and the ellipse were manipulated into subtle and complex three-dimensional structures that arose directly from the original shape and concentric cuts within it. The nature and degree of Rodchenko's achievement as an anti-artist and the degree of his removal from abstraction is clear for he had produced impersonal work from impersonal elements, continuing an investigation without reference to style, expression, scale or material. These works together with the paintings exhibited at the exhibition "5 x 5 = 25" in Moscow in 1921 are the limit of his mapping of creative activity independent of externally imposed requirements. Having reached a crucial point in his dissection of cultural activity, Rodchenko relinquished what little remained of the personal in his work as he undertook the exploration, instead, of creative work within a communal context towards politically committed ends. Both "Obmokhu" and "5 x 5 = 25" were communal ventures in themselves. Rodchenko contributed to both, offering works that represented lucidly the axial point of his development and the

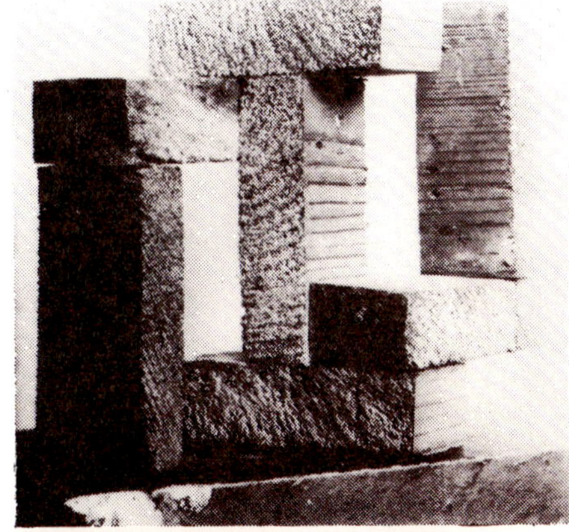

Spatial construction, wood, 1920

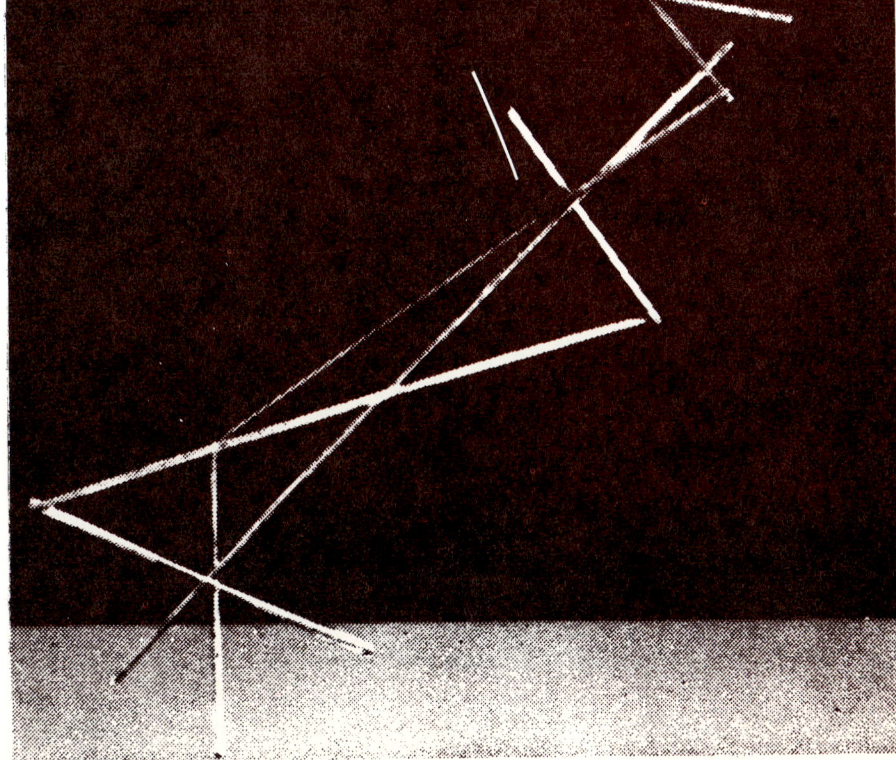

Right: "Vibrating Structure", metal, 1921

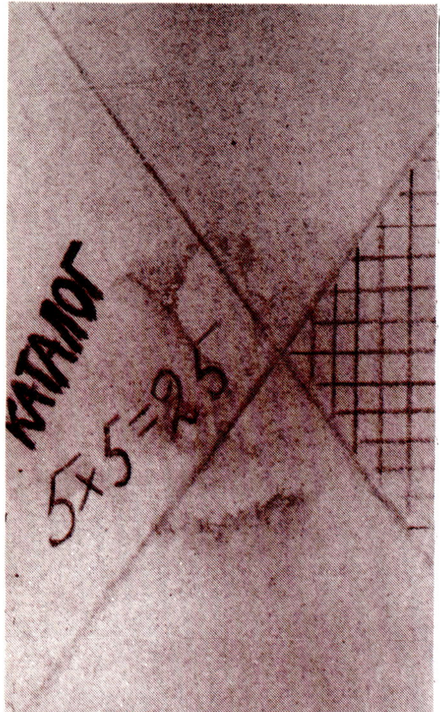

Catalogue cover for "5 x 5 = 25", 1921

conclusions that emerged from his investigations.

Small original drawings were given away in the catalogue of "5 x 5 = 25", and in Rodchenko's case the preciousness of the art-object was further attacked in his sequence of works entitled and comprising, together, the "Last Painting".

Rodchenko's contributions to "5 x 5 = 25" were characteristically austere. Drawings for the catalogue comprise a few lines, sometimes one, drawn in crayon on squared paper. For all their simplicity, these linear drawings shared qualities with the wooden unit constructions made by Rodchenko in 1920. They comprised units single or repeated in an arrangement that was reversible and symmetrical in a number of ways.

The paintings which Rodchenko exhibited in this exhibition were equally elemental constructions. He wrote in the catalogue, "At the present exhibition for the first time in art the three primary colours are declared". His exhibits included three monochrome paintings, "Pure Red Colour", "Pure Yellow Colour", "Pure Blue Colour". They corresponded to the three dimensions of colour. As his catalogue drawings had described elements of two-dimensional construction and as his wooden unit works of 1920 had described elements of three-dimensional construction, so here Rodchenko is returning to the two-dimensional canvas surface and describing in three works together, the elemental dimensions of construction in colour. The separation, employed by Rodchenko over a number of years, of colour from plane in picture-space, was maintained. "Faktura" was maintained, however illusionistic picture space was finally relinquished as the canvas became a coloured surface permitting no apparent recession. That the surface was one of three, emphasised the abandonment of the "special" picture-space of each canvas: they were now evidently three aspects of a single construction in the prime dimensions of colour. The canvas itself became a mere unit, an element, an object that was merely part of the construction. Painting, for Rodchenko, no longer proferred special pictorial qualities for construction: it had become one set of materials amongst many.

For Rodchenko, 1920 saw his creative energies shift their sphere of activity. The question of whether he had been an artist or an anti-artist became finally resolved through practical involvement in public and communal work. His contribution to the history of Constructivism was vital yet self-effacing, as it continued to be in the Productivist period after 1921, where his relation to the role of designer was every bit as complex as had been his previous relation to the role of painter or sculptor. In communal work on furniture, posters, films, exhibitions, books and many other activities Rodchenko's discreet and impersonal manipulation of elements grew no closer to aesthetic criteria; it was seen much more as work than art, and in these works no rapprochement was sought or found with the aesthetic qualities fought and undermined in his days as a painter. In this respect Rodchenko shared a platform with his more explicitly ideological contemporaries, in particular Ossip Brik who in 1921 was an active organiser of Inkhuk and a key figure in its investigation of the theory of creative activity. In a statement on November 24th, 1921, Ossip Brik announced the renunciation of art as a distinctive activity separate from broader socially oriented creative activity. Rodchenko and twenty-four others followed Brik's lead. The step by step evolution of Rodchenko's study of construction led him in November 1921, to stop painting altogether and to view his own creative work as an active contributory element in the creative work of the large social body. This relation inherent in the "Biziaks" Kiosk and other architectural projects, in his own nonpersonal works and in his recent abandonment of painterly concerns in the work for "5 x 5 = 25", here became explicit. Construction had led him out of painting. It was construction with all of its implications that he continued to investigate with tenacity. Brik's announcement of November 24th, 1921, marked the coming together of theoreticians and the practitioners of construction. The social dimension which in 1920 had been inherent in works by Rodchenko and others, now became a primary consideration. For the twenty-five who followed Brik's lead, the pursuit of art was typified by an outlived and self-sufficient devotion to easel-painting; the activities of painters were considered "merely aimless". Instead, the twenty-five proposed "the absoluteness of production art and of constructivism as its sole form of expression". Brik in 1921 had already elucidated his theories in "Art into Production", a collection of texts published by the "production-art council of Izo Narkompros". "We know", he wrote, "that so-called pure art is a craft like any other. We do not understand why a man who makes pictures is spiritually superior to a man who manufactures fabrics". And just as Brik wished to identify artistic creativity with work, so he wished, too, for the converse of this: "We want every worker who gives a definite form and colour to an object to understand why precisely this colour and this form are necessary. We want the worker to cease to be a mechanical executor of some plan that is alien to him. He must consciously and actively participate in the process of creating things. Then there will be no need for a special group of artist-decorators. Artistry will blend into the very creation of things".

For Rodchenko as a constructivist, creative work was incompatible with aesthetic predilection. If this was anti-art, the tenacity and lucidity of Rodchenko's investigation was as original as it was impersonal. It was an achievement to be recognised, as it was an invitation to self-effacement, communal work and an intimate involvement of the creative person amongst the public growth of creative activity.

Opposite page: The view from Rodchenko's studio, Kirov Street, Moscow, 1927. The Vkhutemas building is to the left

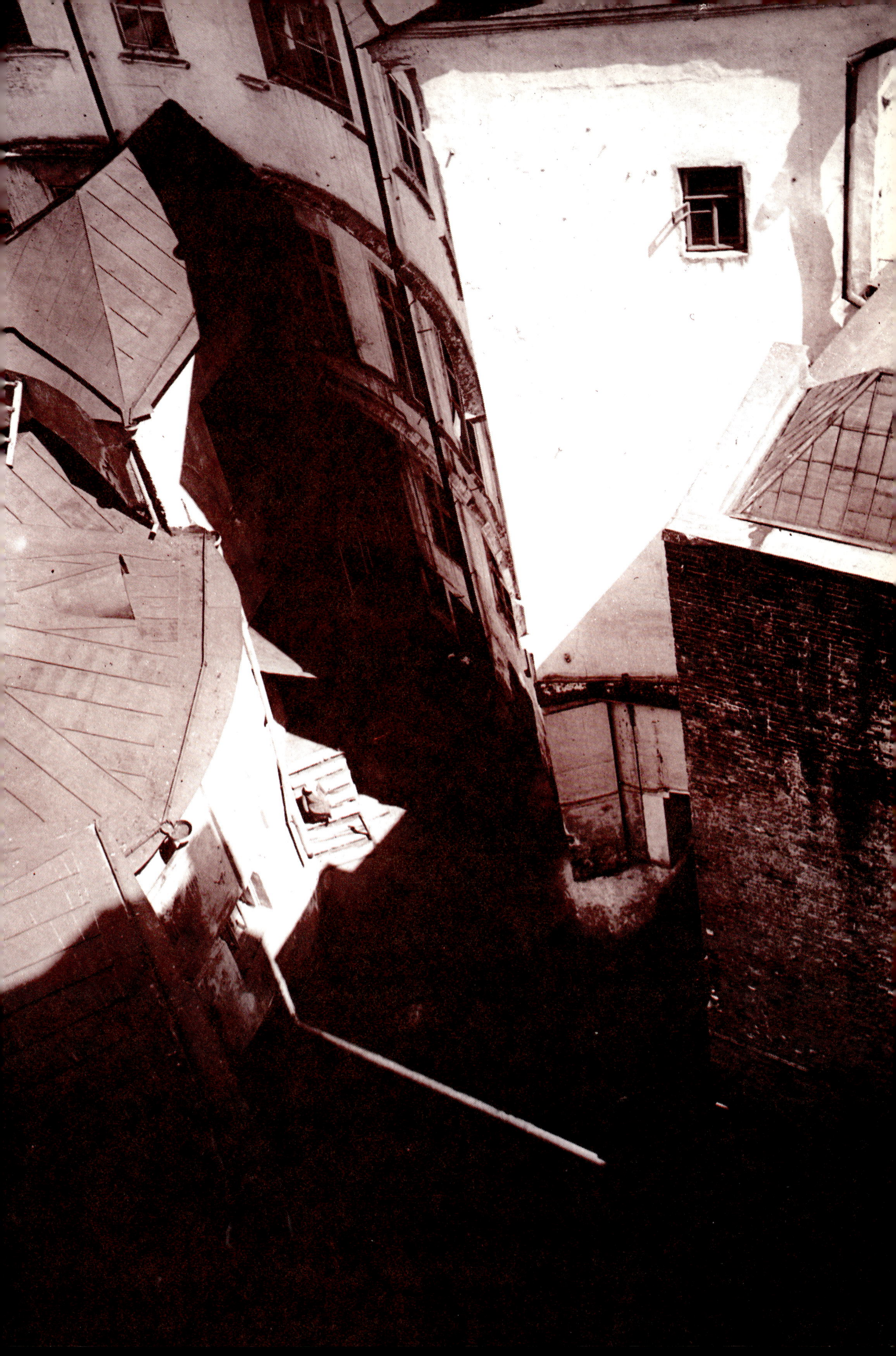

STYLISTIC CHANGES

Painting without a referent by Andrei B. Nakov

56 "Luckily I'm not like you, which gives me the strength to venture further and further into the barren desert. For the transfiguration is to be found there... My philosophy is to destroy the old towns and villages every fifty years, to banish nature from the realm of art, to suppress love and sincerity in art, but under no circumstances to drain the living origins of man (war)."
K. Malevich, letter to A. Benois, 1916

There is a strange passage in Rodchenko's autobiography concerning this first meeting with Malevich. It took place in Moscow during the winter of 1916 at the time of the exhibition "The Store" ("Magazin") where Rodchenko showed his non-objective works of art for the first time.

"Malevich came up to me and said:— You are the only painter here, but do you know what you are doing?
— I don't know.
— Do you know that everything they're doing (the other exhibitors) has already been seen and done? It's all out of date. Now there is something new in the air, something closer to ourselves, something more typically Russian. That's what I'm working on myself and I can see it in your work already, intuitively, I can feel it's there!"

It is no coincidence that these words of Malevich were engraved in Rodchenko's memory and that he recalled them twenty five years later in his autobiography. They reflect, with the pertinence that only sudden revelations can contain, the true essence of his approach to art.

This interpretive hypothesis must not be understood in purely critical terms, but rather as an approach to the true essence of the artist's formal attitudes, the internal structure of his plastic system, the first functional characteristic of which lies in the amazing dynamism of his stylistic changes. (Between 1914 (the year we can take as the starting point of his independent creation), and 1923 (when at the age of thirty-three he had unquestionably achieved a maturity and stability in developing the set of formal characteristics which defined "the Rodchenko style") several radical stylistic changes had taken place. These changes were so radical that at each the artist seems to adopt an attitude diametrically opposed to the one preceding.

The skilful arabesques of "art nouveau" (1913) and the affectation of highly varnished Chinese curios (1914) are succeeded by a short period (winter 1914-15) of hazy Cubism "à la Marie Laurencin" (theatrical characters, costume designs for "The Princess of Padua" by Oscar Wilde). This very same style is replaced at the end of 1915 by the calculated coldness of the first non-objective works, in which mechanical pirouettes are drawn with the help of precision instruments — the slide-rule and the compass. Once he had achieved the dexterity of craftsmanship in 1914 — the delicate finesse of his Chinese curios bears witness to this — he repudiated this very skill ("the hand-instrument is neither sufficient nor precise" he said) for the sake of "new instruments capable of working the surface plane in a simpler, more suitable and more adequate way". But this purely formal tendency is not the result of a need for a (philosophical) transcendance of the old logic of object-representation.

If we refer to Viktor Shklovsky's "objective" theory, a theory developed at the same time (in about 1916) which eliminated any symbolic connotation from interpretation of art, then Rodchenko's work, unlike that of Tatlin, Malevich or the other non-objective artists, is the best — if not the only — example of materially objective formalism; "formalism" in this context being understood in the new sense given to it by the linguistic theories of the time.

The year 1917 stands out because of the same variety of research, for next to wholly non-objective works, we find works which explore the problem of the intersection and transparency of planes as well as figurative compositions in which problems of mass and weight seem to preoccupy the artist.
The overtly futurist style of the period — Tatlin's influence is especially perceptible in this aspect of Rodchenko's work — is discarded a few months later to allow for a more pictorial manipulation of planes. This sudden change with its declamatory insistence on the figural aspect of non-objective plastic representation contrasts once again with the anecdotal, narrative aspect of those compositions of 1917 which were overloaded with formal elements.

Rodchenko's paintings made in 1918 constitute perhaps the most original phase of his entire pictorial work. As we can learn from the catalogue of "The X State Exhibition: Non-Objective Creation and Suprematism" (January 1919), this results from strictly material and visual researches:

Works from the first half of 1918.
"A rigorous immobile construction of coloured surface planes.
A simple construction of colour.
Texture.
Movement of colour in relation to form (for the first time colour moves away from form).
A construction of colour on ovals.
The colour which is withdrawn from the surface plane is reconstructed on the ovals but is no longer subordinate to them.
Colour sliding on to the ovals.
A variety of colour and texture on the same surface plane.

Works from the second half of 1918.
A construction of picto-writing in colour.
The colour which renews itself freely becomes its own objective.
Luminescence of colour.
Light-colours.
Texture of colours.
Abstraction of colour.
The withdrawal of luminosity (without an object, colour or light)."

The explanation given by the painter of his system — the title of the text is "Rodchenko's system" — may seem a little chaotic and almost contradictory. If this is so, it perhaps results from the formal and stylistic confusion and from an elementary lack of command of syntax (which inevitably upsets the logical sequence of the discourse); yet these do assert the painter's purely objective tendency, his wish to avoid the symbolic superstructure which can be grafted on to non-objective creation from the very moment of its conception.

"Literature and philosophy are for specialists in those subjects, I am the inventor of new discoveries in painting. Christopher Columbus was neither a writer nor a philosopher, he was merely the discoverer of new countries". Following this, a quotation by Otto Weininger, used by Rodchenko in the same

Andrei B. Nakov is an art historian who has studied and published widely on the topic of 20th century Russian art. He is resident in Paris and was organiser of the exhibition "Liberated Colour and Form", Edinburgh and Sheffield, 1978.

catalogue at first sight seems somewhat superficial, but further explains his a-theoretical and totally anti-idealistic frame of mind: "The murderer strives to prove, by the act of murder, that nothing exists". This is much more than a frustrated attempt at provincial sophism and we should note, in the reference to this maxim by Weininger, the announcement, as early as January 1919, of Rodchenko's ultimate positive experience: the idea of the "last paintings"; these were not to appear until September 1921. When seen in this formal-materialist light, these ideas seem no less radical, but their audacity is somewhat diminished by the materially experimental justification that the reference to Weininger unequivocally implies. It is more than a suicidal gesture—as it is described in N. Tarabukin's commentary. "From the Easel to the Machine" — and we must see in it the audacity of encompassing the unknown. By means of a frontal attack on the essence of representation in painting, Rodchenko wanted to reveal its limitations by the reduction of the semantic connotation to a demonstration of minimal materials: one single colour (without contrast or opposition, thus in a state of absolute neutrality which excludes any polarisation or discourse) and a completely neutral format (square or almost square forms). Does not this "murder of painting", which took place in 1921, certify, as Weininger foresaw, the absolute vitality of existential activity against which the murderer stumbles blindly and impotently, unable to act? In 1919, Rodchenko comes close to a kind of semantic "tabula rasa" which follows Malevich's "Black Square" (1915), the first "zero degree" in painting. This approach provides him yet again with the antidote to the rich and formal non-objective language he had developed in various pictorial works in 1919.

It is not surprising that all the interpreters of non-objective painting took Rodchenko's "black circles" to be a truly pictorial (thus purely stylistic) response to Malevich's white Suprematism; this results from the strictly formal attitude adopted by a large group of the followers of non-objective art at the time. In many respects this view is incorrect, especially with regard to the cultural meaning of forms, their philosophical iconology. During the winter of 1918-1919 the philosophical symbolism of Malevich's white Suprematism had moved further and further away from the ideology of form as such, which is ultimately derived from the formalist and materialist aesthetic of "Art for Art's sake", an ideal by which Rodchenko was undoubtedly influenced during his artistic training. At this point we can see the philosophical differentiation between the symbolist basis of Malevich's aesthetic ideal and Rodchenko's pure formalism, the origins of which can be found in the flamboyant decorative elements of "art nouveau" — the formalist aesthetic ideal "par excellence".

This tendency, which was diametrically opposed to the philosophical bases of white Suprematism, is made explicit in the text by Rodchenko on "Line", written in May 1921: "Non-objective painting has dedicated itself exclusively to its specific tasks... it has cultivated colour for its own sake... the final phase of this undertaking has been achieved with the attainment of a monochrome intensity within the limits of one single colour, a unique intensity (undiminished and unintensified)".

As early as February 1919 the painter plunged into a new stylistic dispute, that of "linearism". This new process seems to place itself in opposition to the preceding phase, to seek "the total victory (of the line) which reduced the last vestiges of painting: that is to say colour, tone, texture and surface plane to — nothingness. The line traced a large red cross on the concept of painting." As a consequence of this phase of semantic suppression, Rodchenko finished in September 1921 by radically questioning the very essence of representation in painting in the work shown in the exhibition "5 x 5 = 25", held in Moscow that autumn.

Once again purely formal comparison, one that doesn't take the philosophical symbolism of forms (Malevich) into account, falsifies the analysis. At first sight it seems to be Rodchenko who most radically abandoned pictorial practice (in his case to take up photography), whereas Malevich continued to teach a system of Suprematist forms at "Unovis", in Vitebsk . Nevertheless the transcendence of a certain pictorial practice led Malevich towards a new kind of plastic conceptualisation, whereas Rodchenko remained a visceral painter who merely changed the tools he worked with.

A new logic of practice is revealed in the internal dynamics of Rodchenko's work. The extent to which the blinding brilliance of these intuitive changes, based on the most elementary logic of "formal counterpoint", could bear the seeds of new expressive procedures is evident in one of the artist's least known works: a long composition on paper dated "winter 1942-43". In order to free himself from the post-cubist stylisation of decorative forms, which had developed in his paintings around the years 1939-41, Rodchenko had resorted to a pictorial process which consisted of its very antithesis. Thus he produced an automatic and gestural painting that was an amazing anticipation of Pollock's "drip painting" and Hartung's fury of "electric" lines.

Rodchenko's work provides a model of artistic development based on the radical alternation of successive phases; this seems over the past half century to have become one of the current bases for a supra-stylistic attitude, which works as a much more general level than that of traditional unitary form, of form in the sense of "a model to be improved". Thus "style", which in the classical tradition expresses and consolidates the meaning of plastic creation, is now replaced by a relationship between different series of works and it is their juxtaposition in time which enables us to perceive the painter's fundamental intention.

The recent evolution of American art from 1960 onwards shows the vitality of this new stylistic structure and if we look back a little further into the past we note that Marcel Duchamp suggested a similar creative attitude in which style transcends a highly individualistic approach to become the end result of a series of inventions. It is only in the analysis of their logical sequence that we are able to fully comprehend the real intention of the artist's approach and to understand the true essence of his message.

Opposite page: Cover, featuring Lilya Brik, of Mayakovsky's poem, "Pro Eto" (About This), 1923.

Pages 60/71: Twelve photomontages by Rodchenko illustrating the text.

Pages 68 to 71 were not included in the original publication. Page 69 has never previously been published.

"Pro Eto" describes the poet's affair with his lover, Lilya Brik.

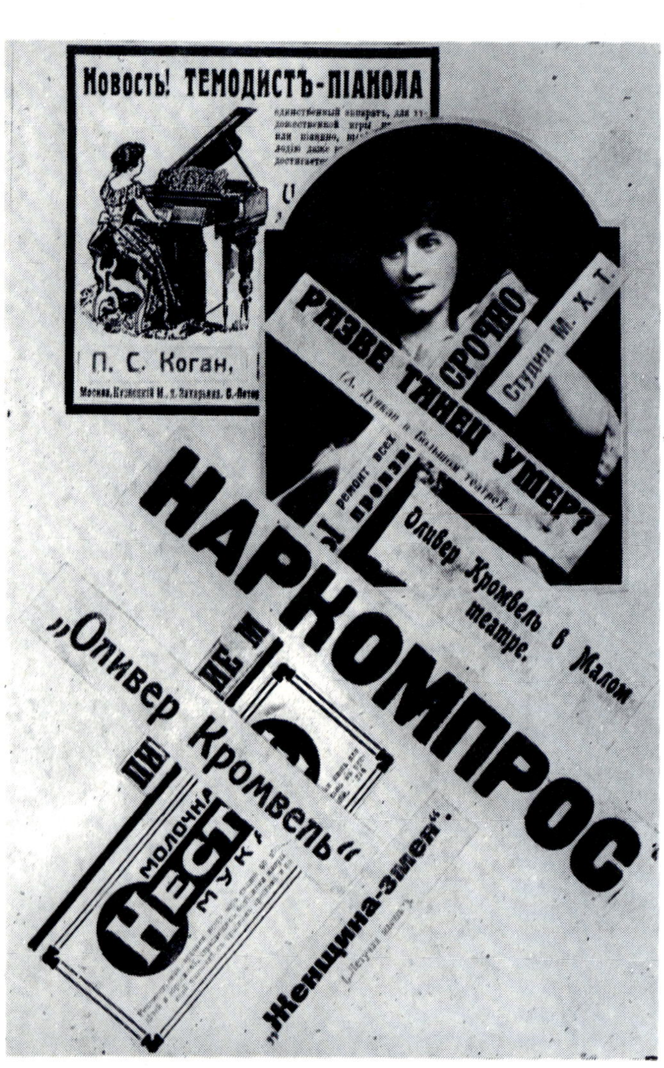

"Narkompros/Oliver Cromwell", collage, 1922.

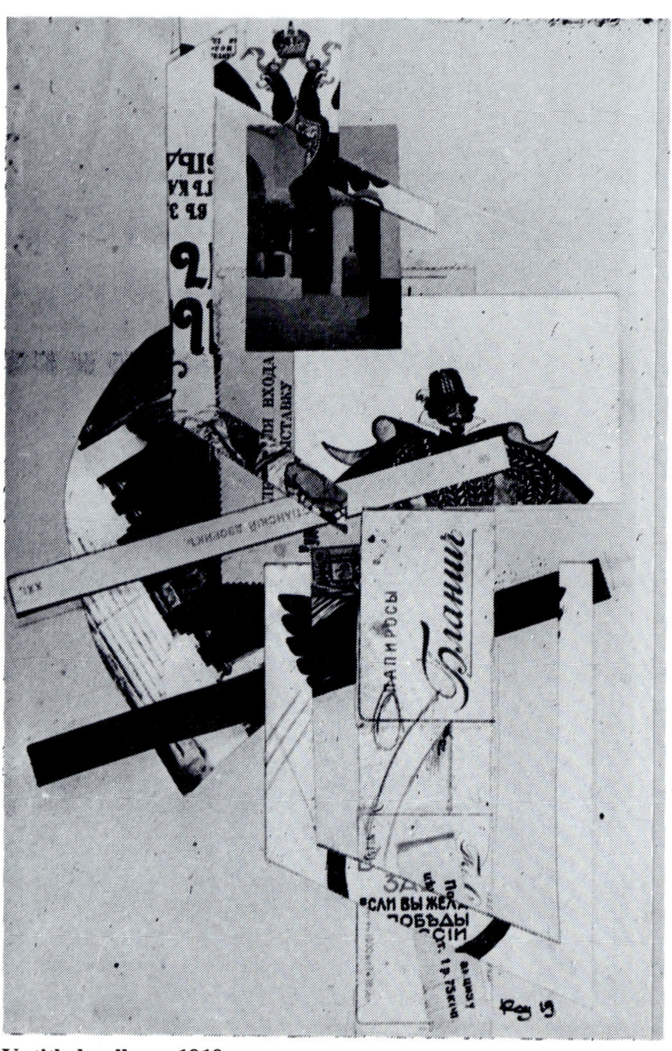

Untitled collage, 1919

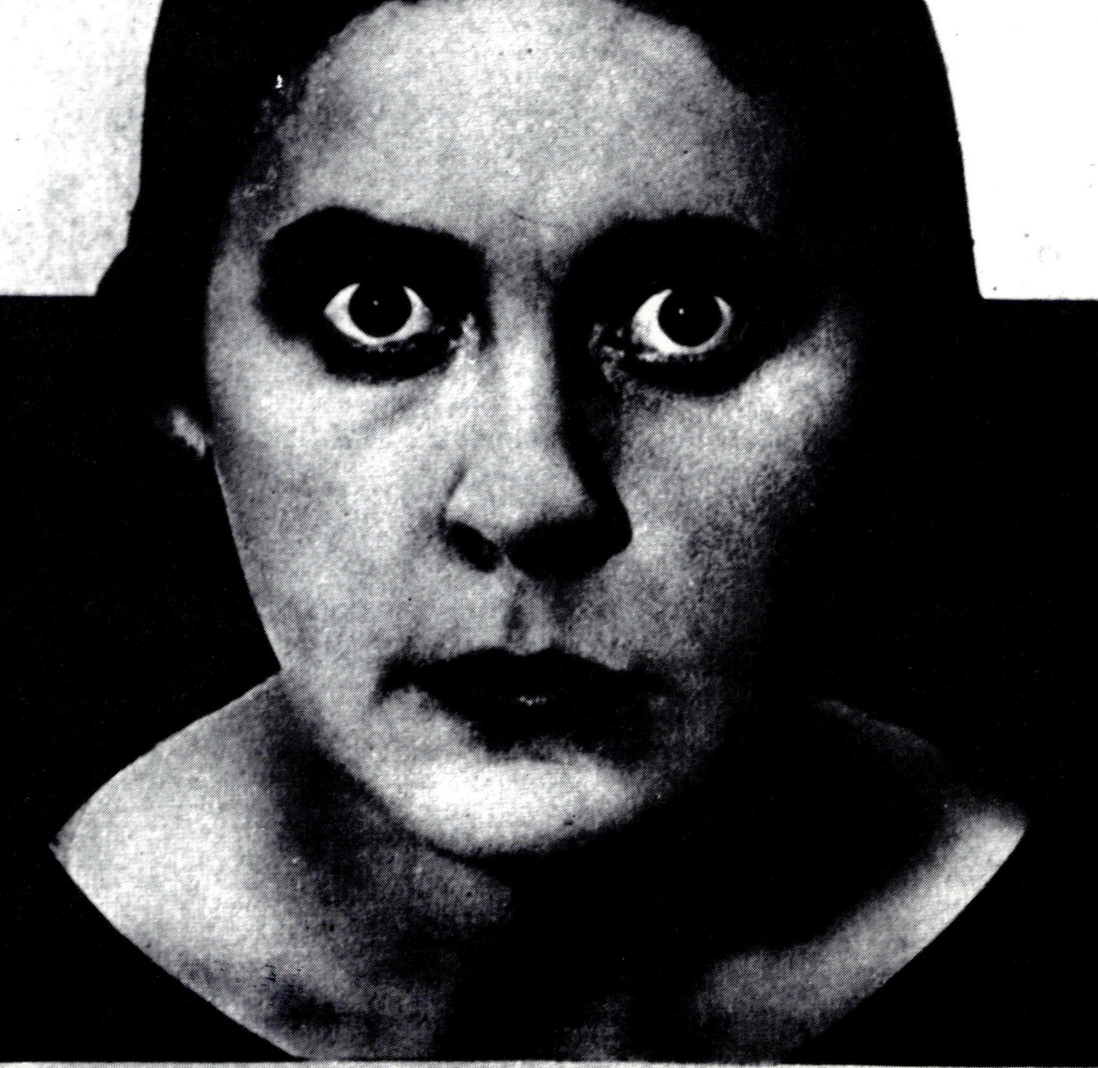
ПРО ЭТО
МАЯКОВСКИЙ

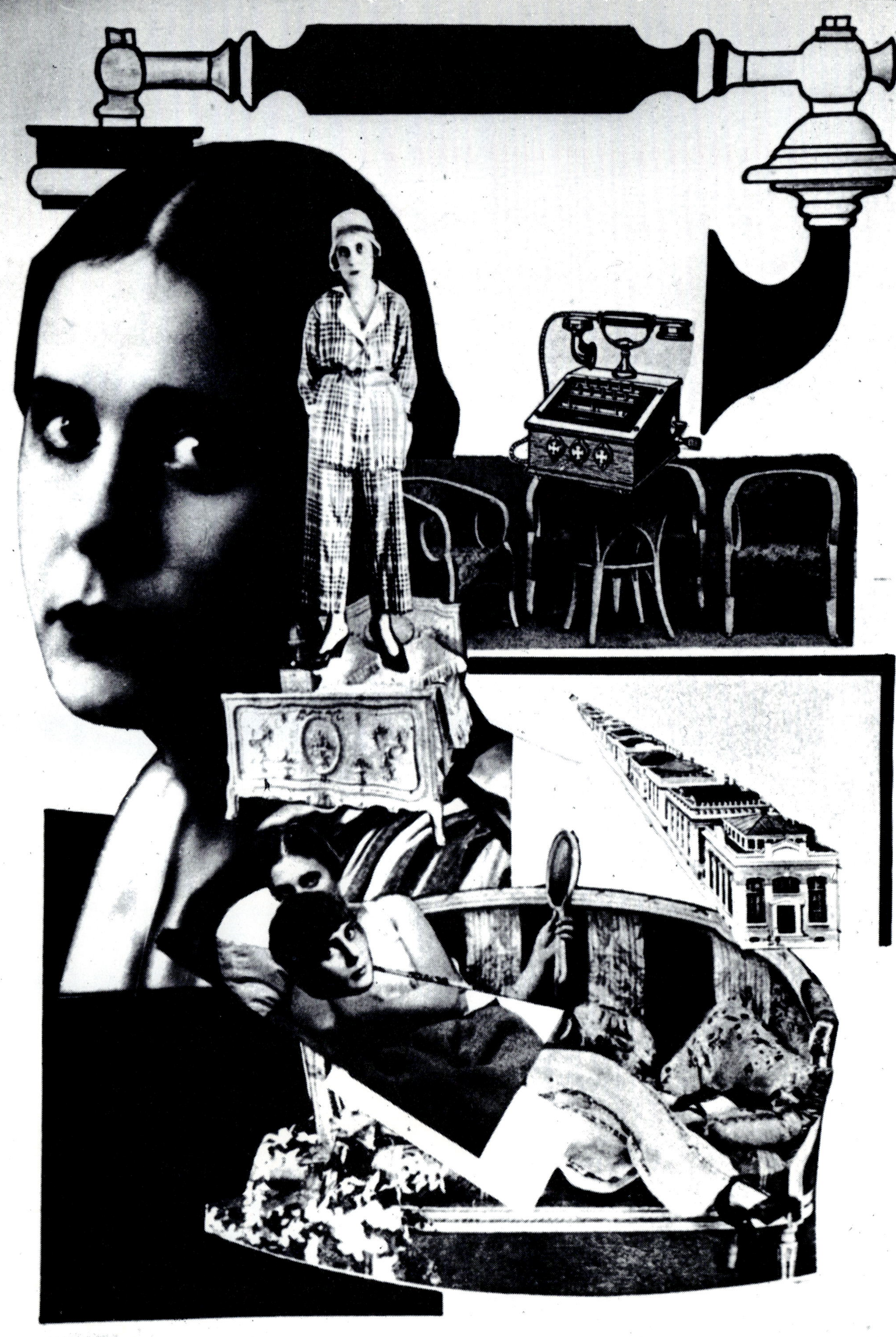

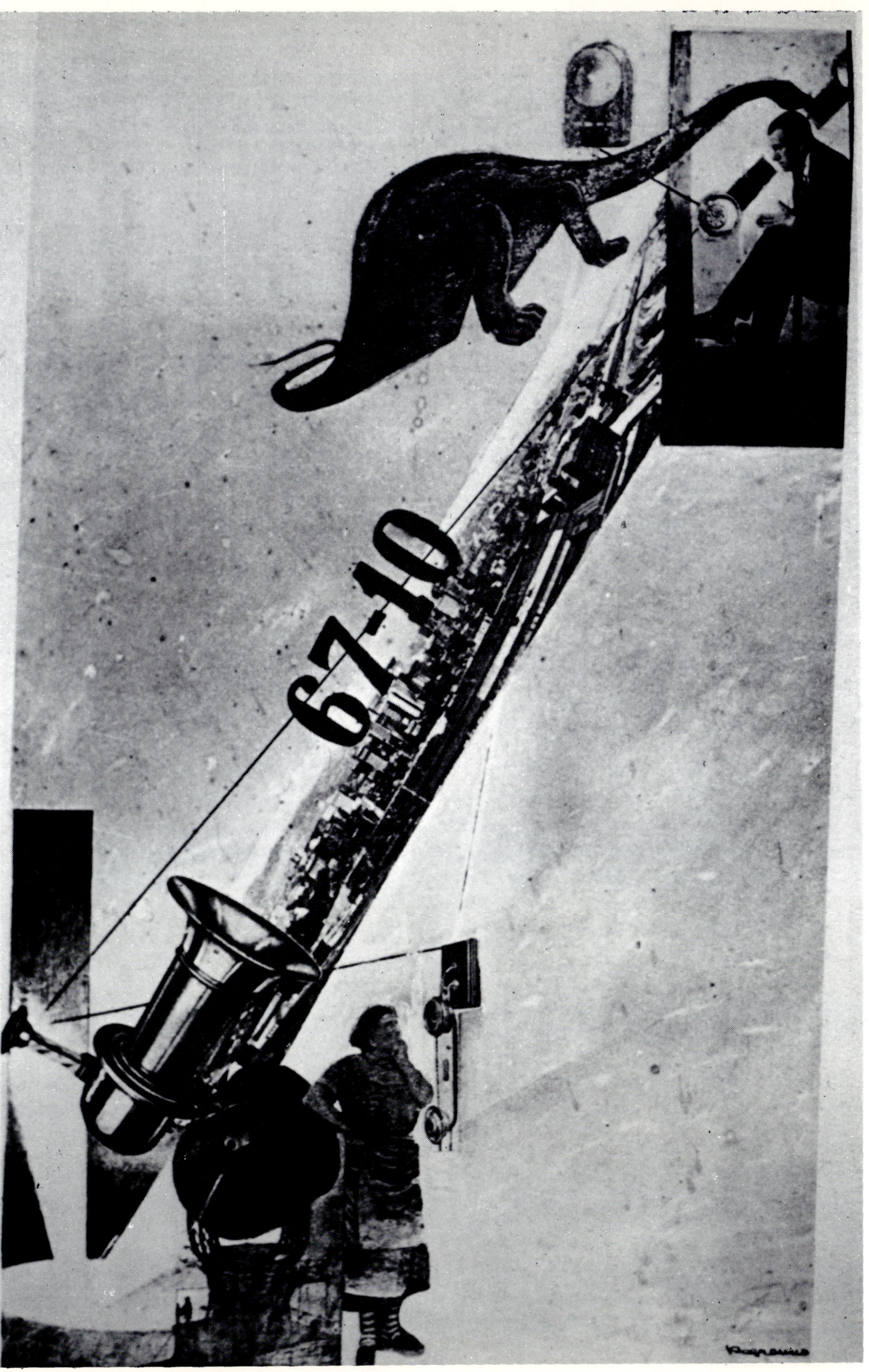
67-10

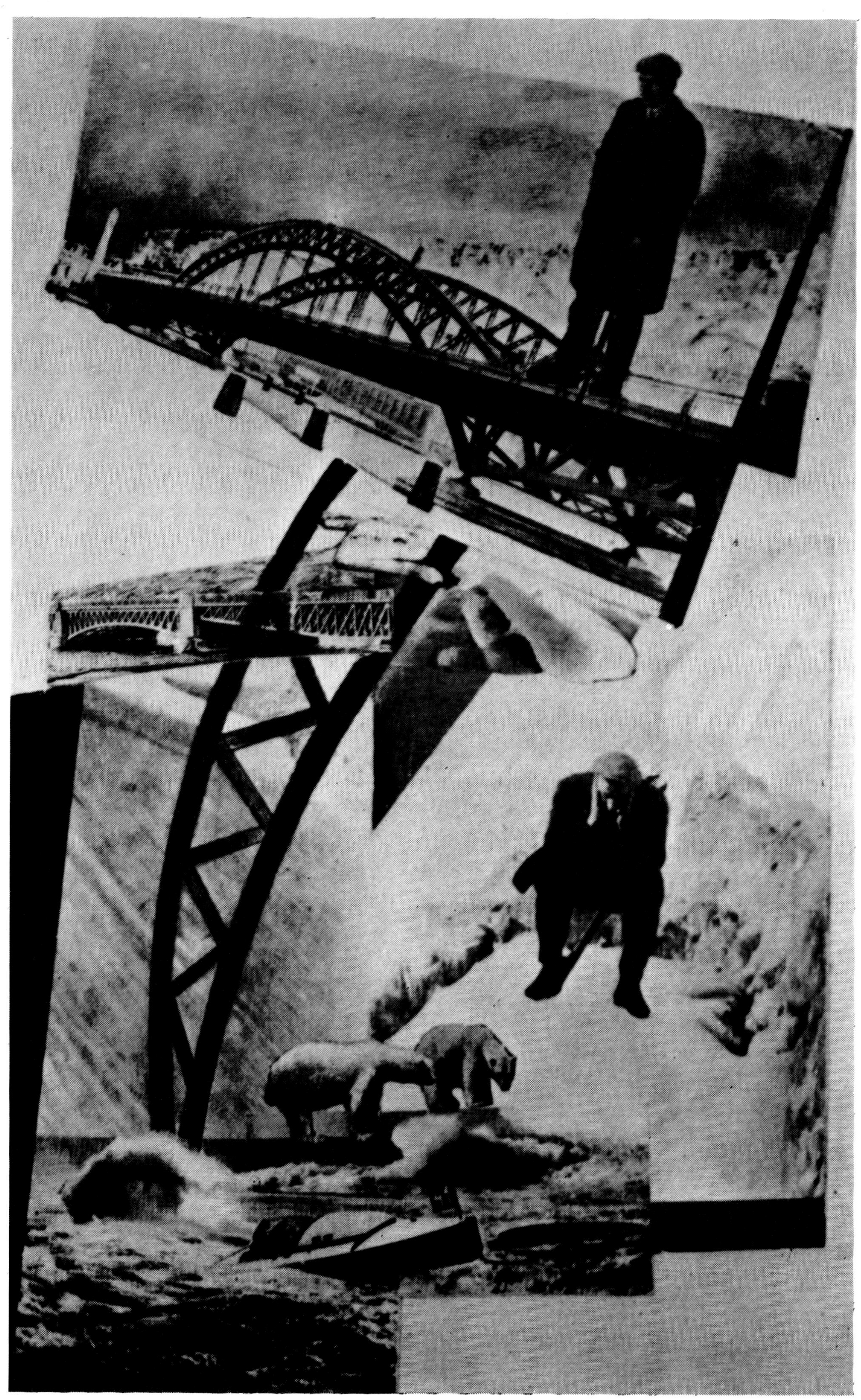

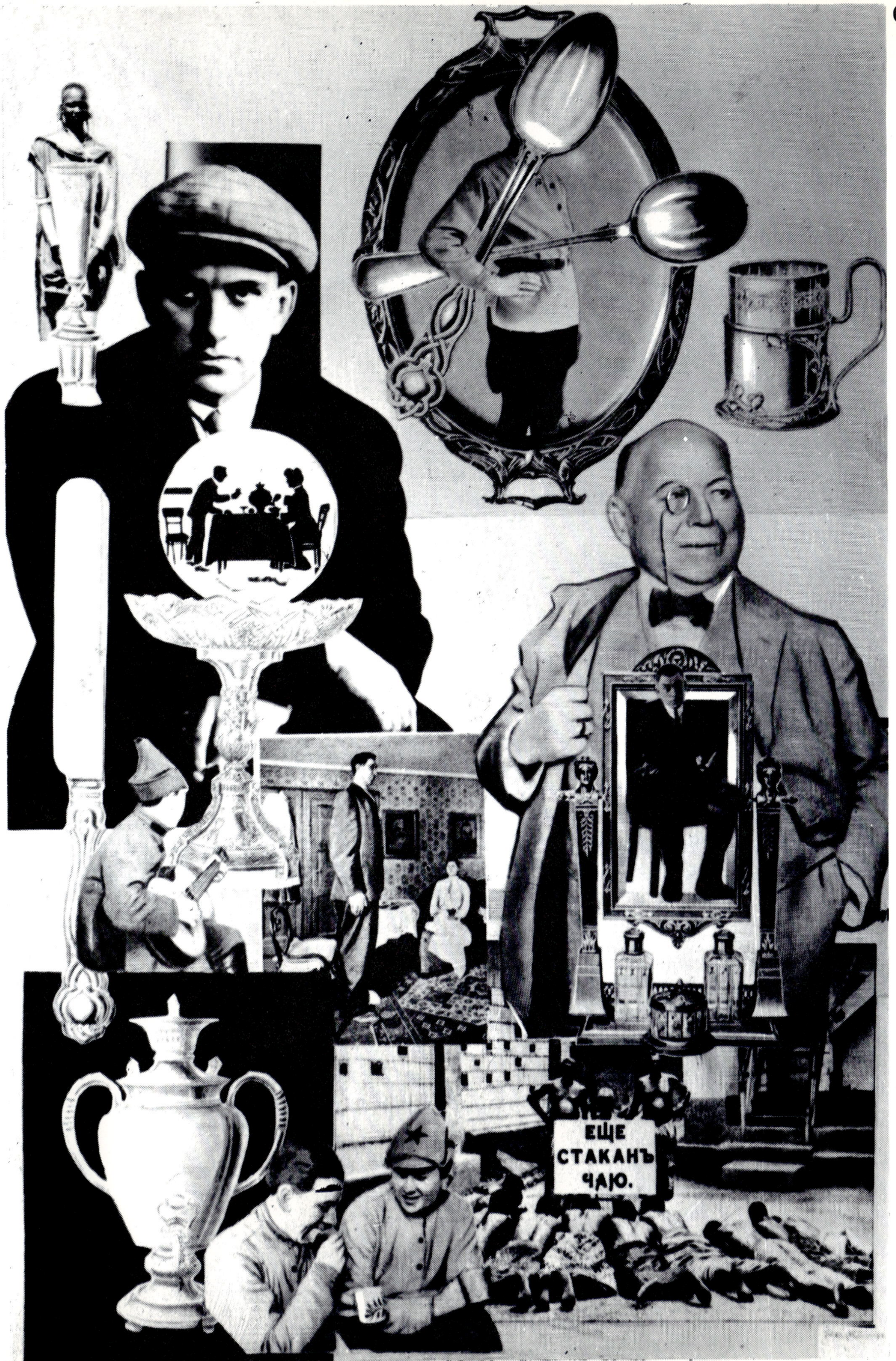
ЕЩЕ
СТАКАНЪ
ЧАЮ.

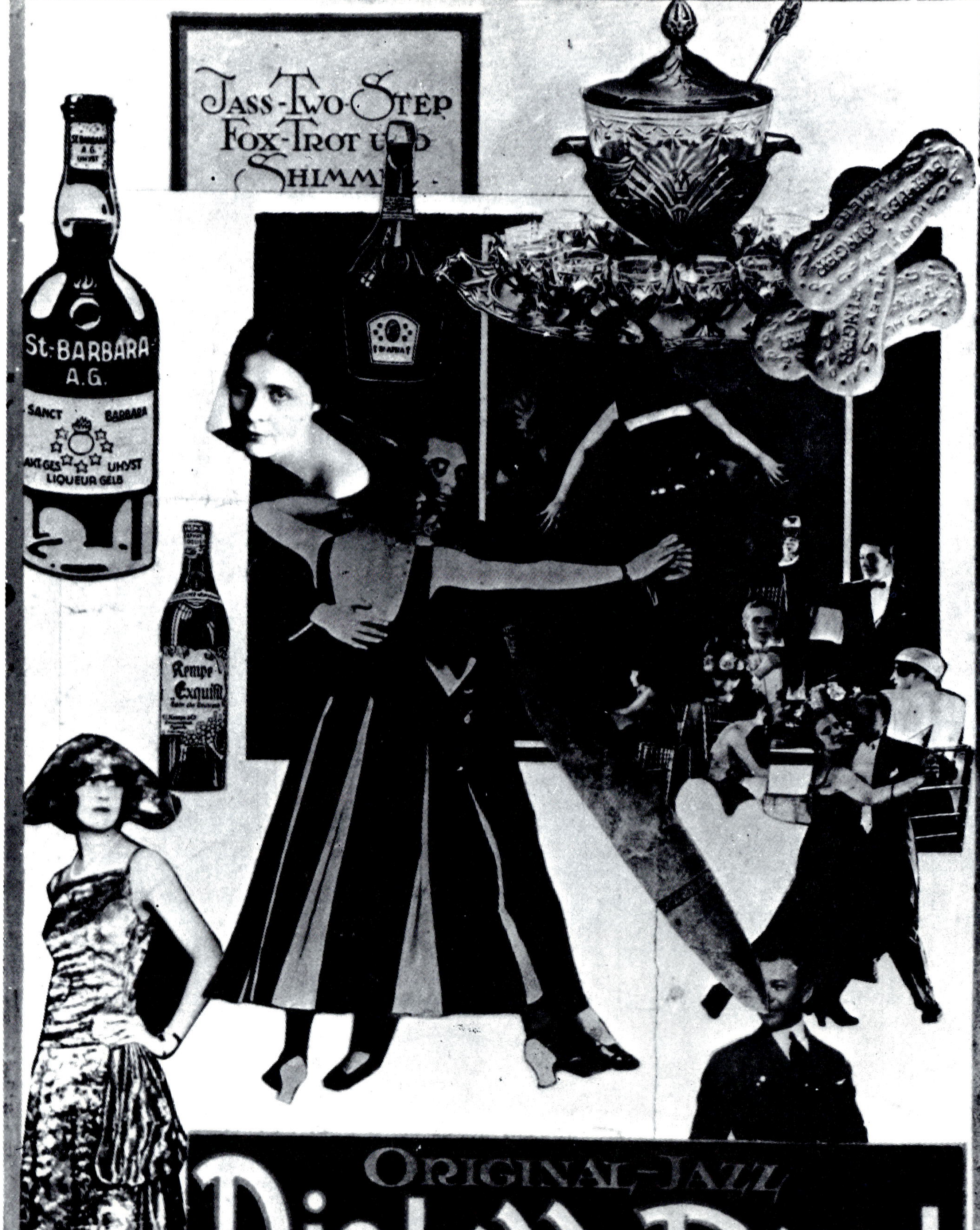
JASS-TWO-STEP
FOX-TROT U
SHIMM
St-BARBARA
A.G.
SANCT BARBARA
AKT.GES. UHYST
LIQUEUR GELB
ORIGINAL-JAZZ
Die Jazz-Band

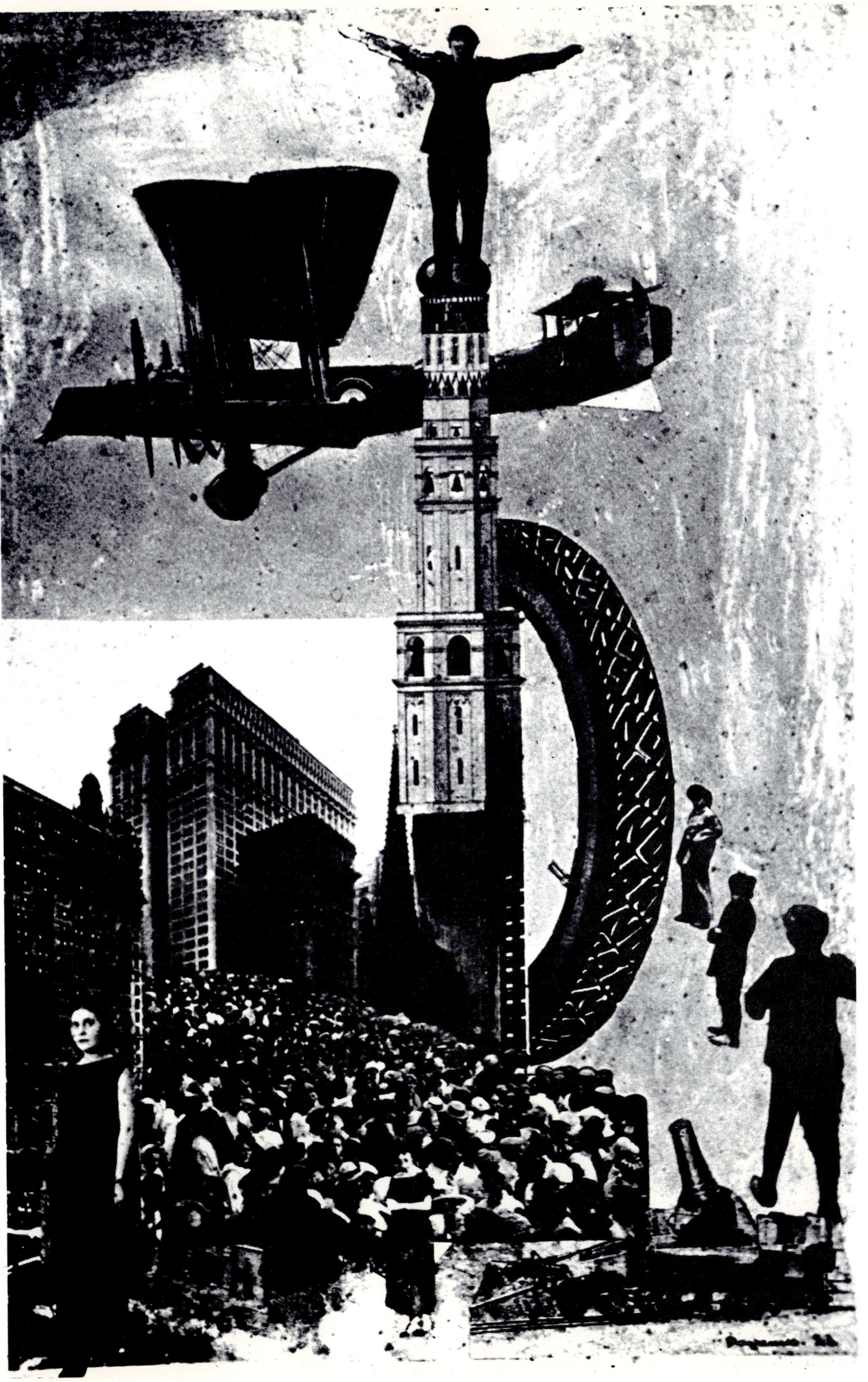

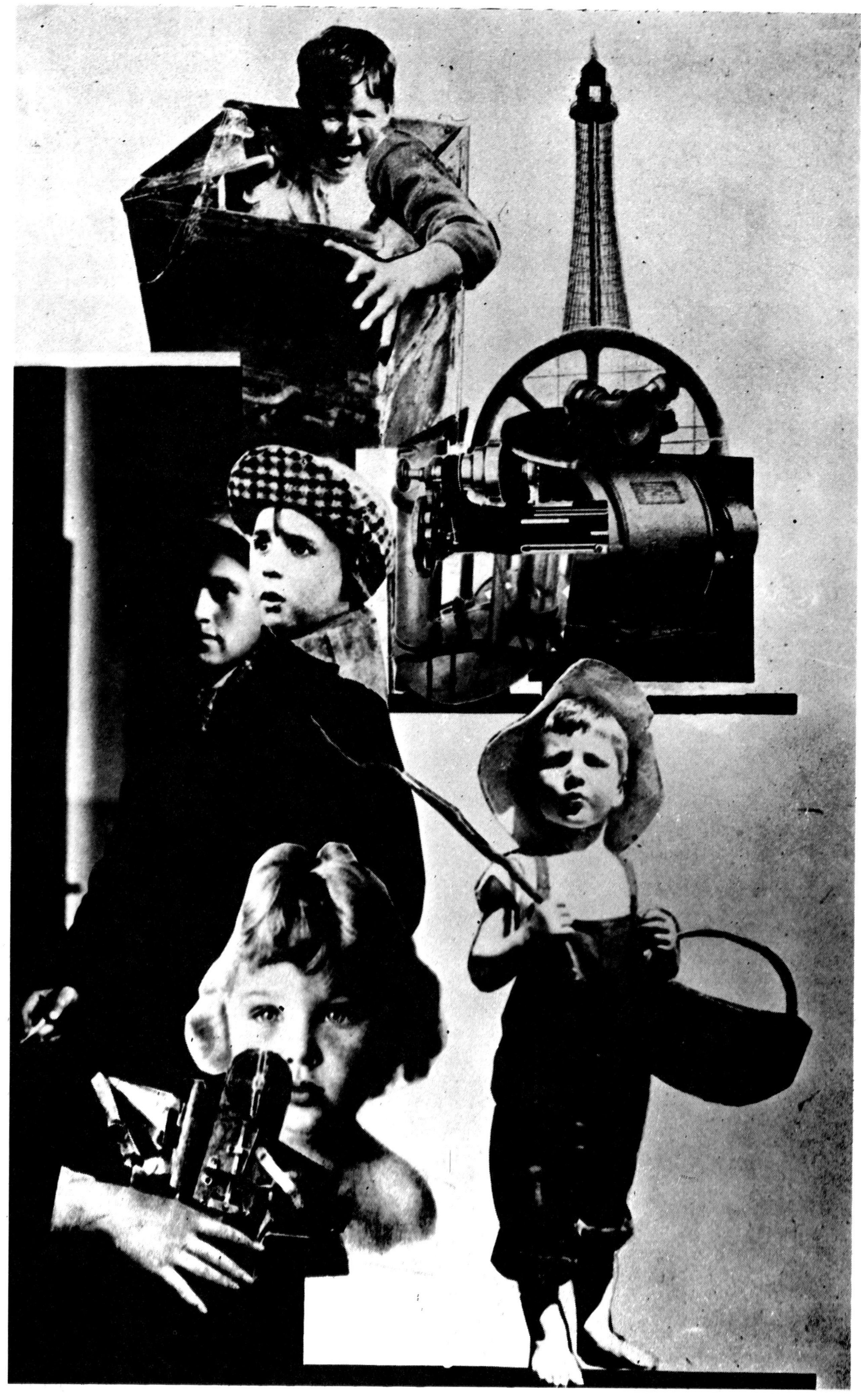

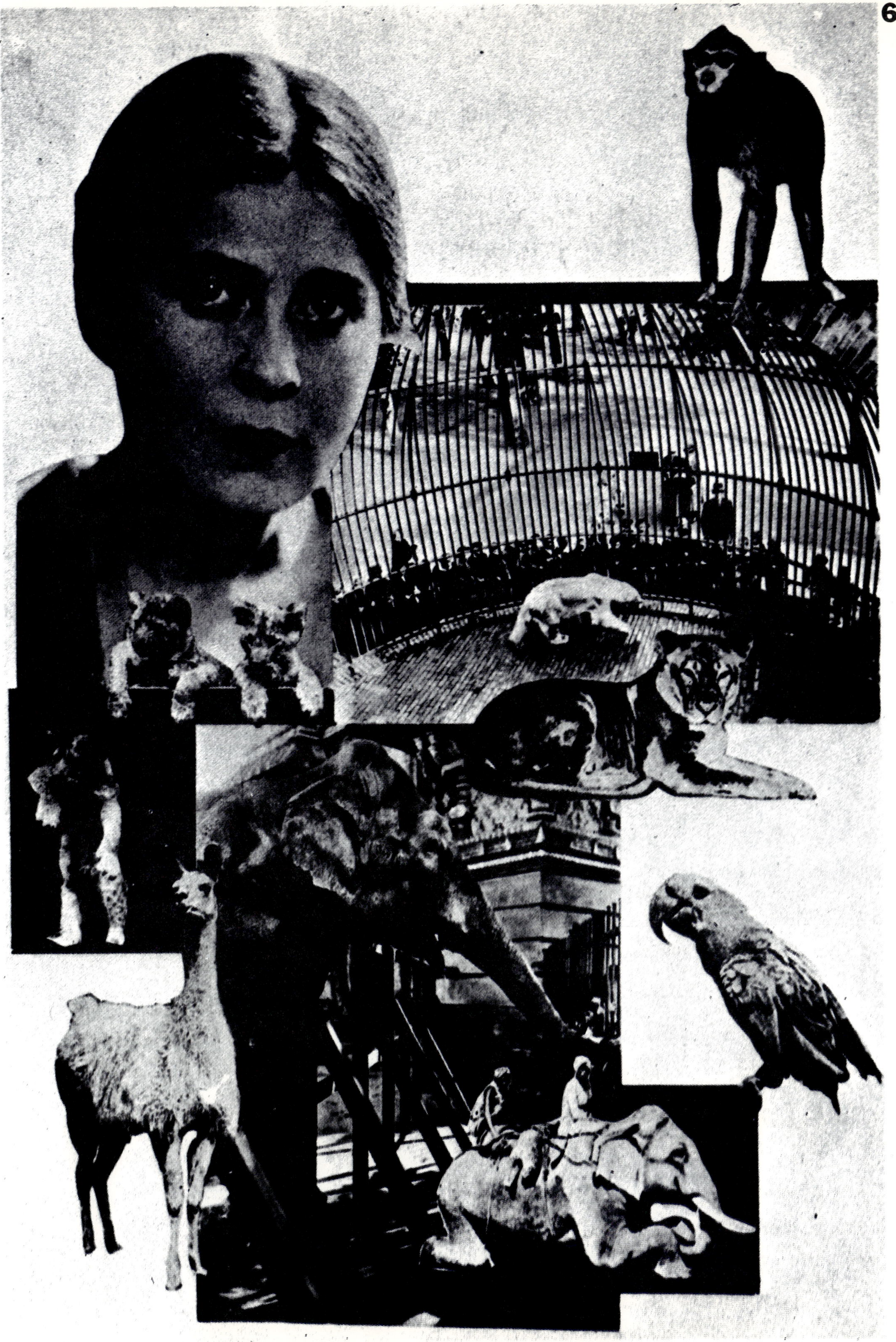

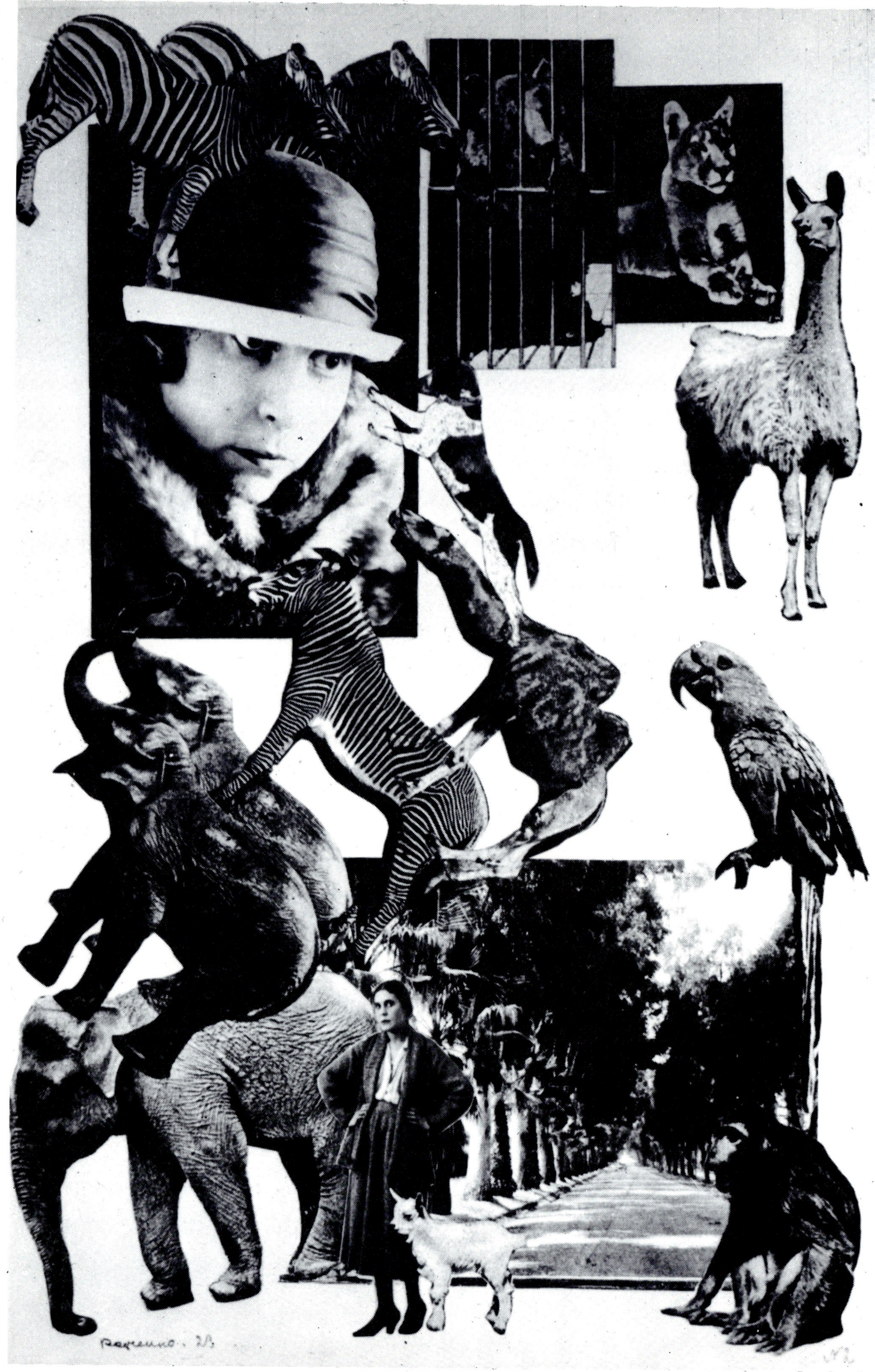

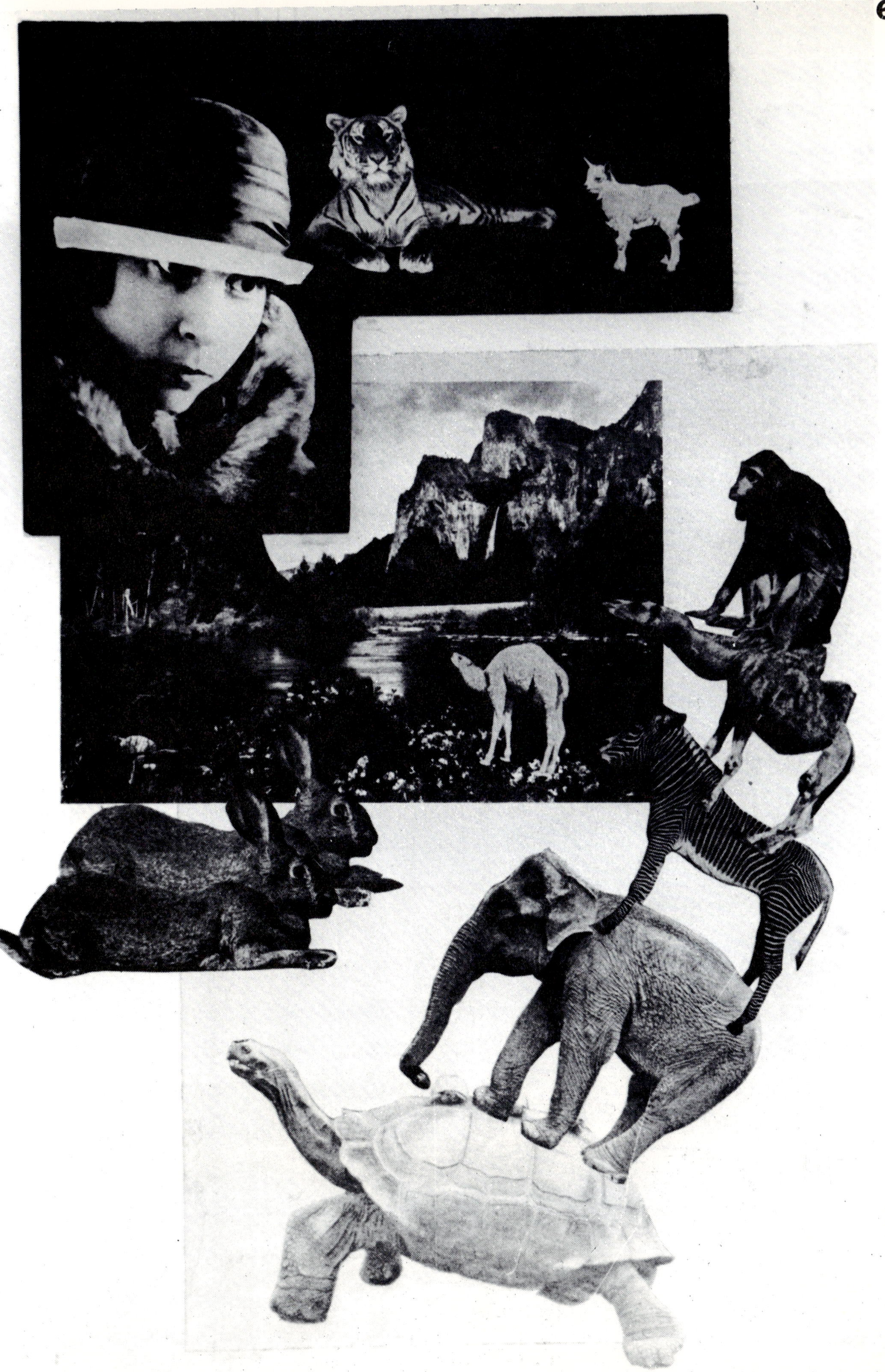

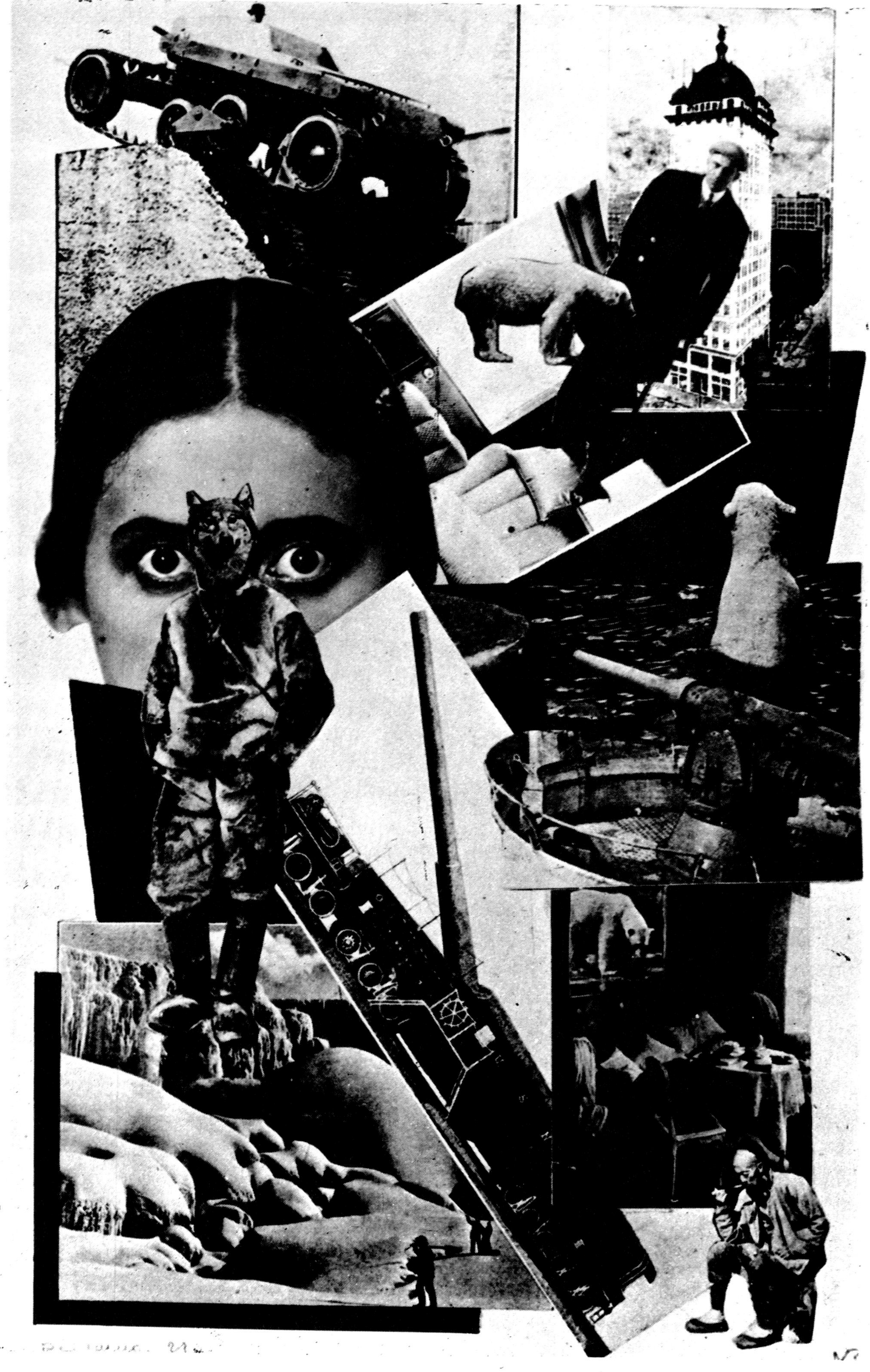

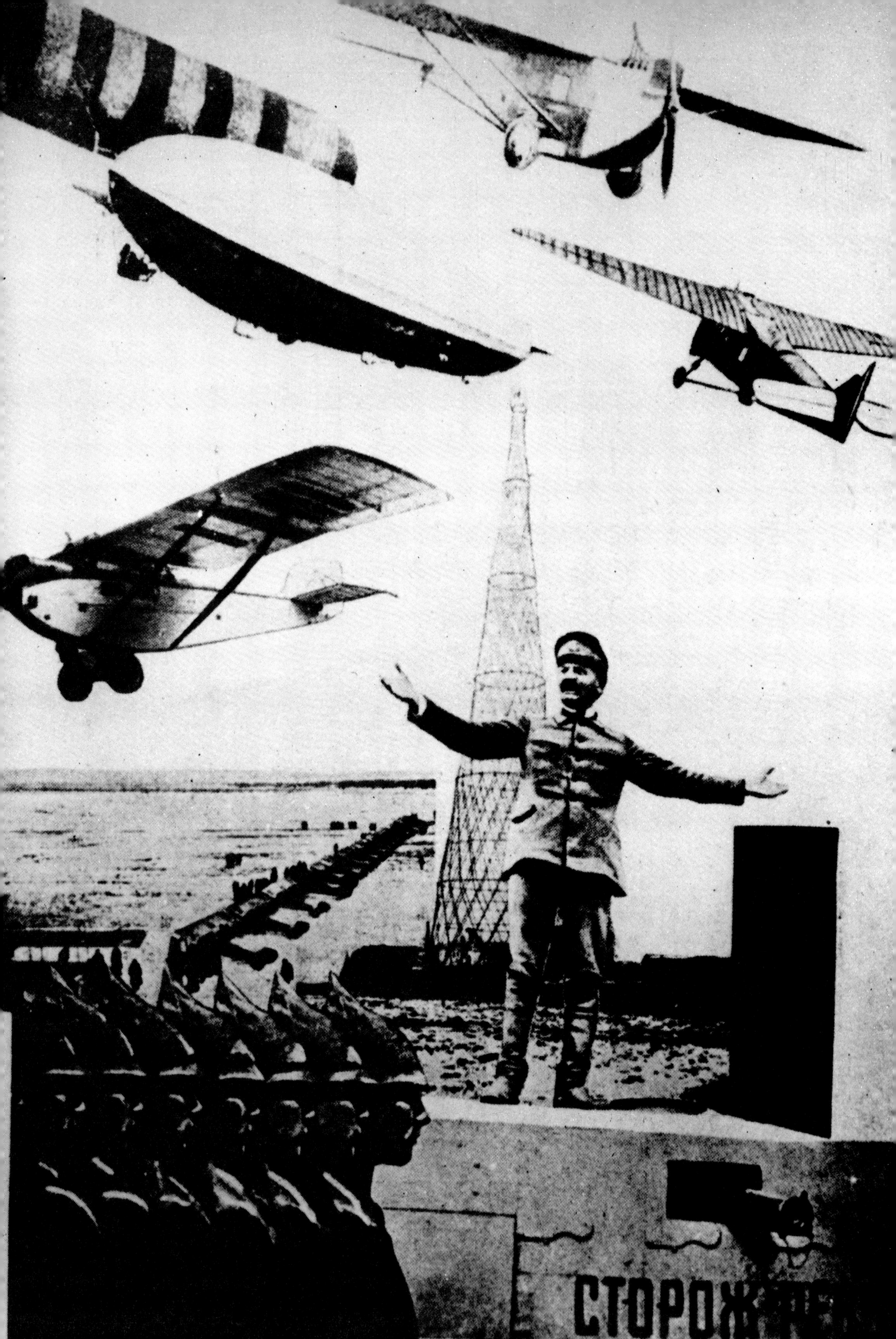
СТОРОЖ

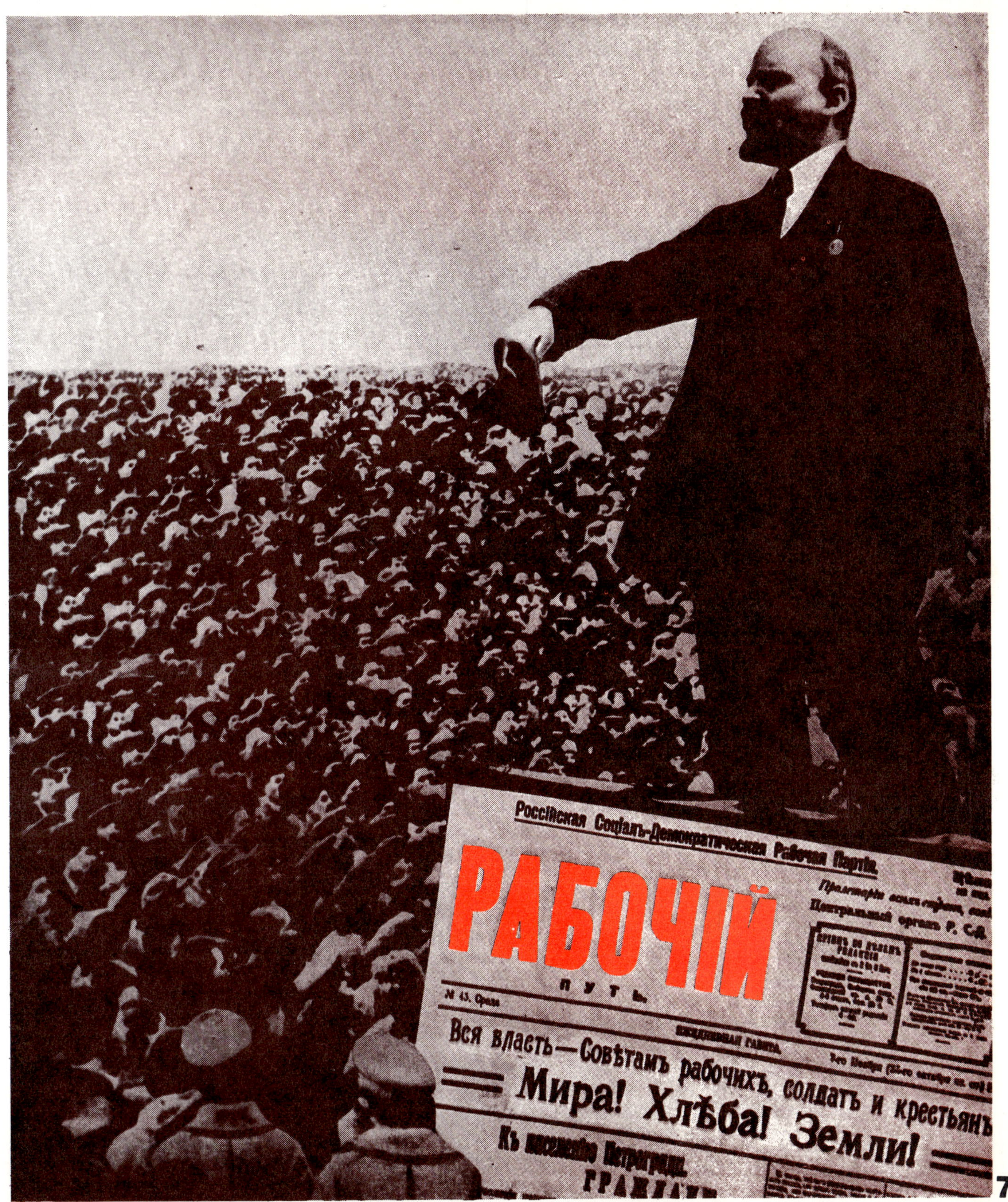

"Peace! Bread! Land!" photomontage of V.I. Lenin from the photo-album "First Cavalry", 1937

Opposite page: Photomontage 1923

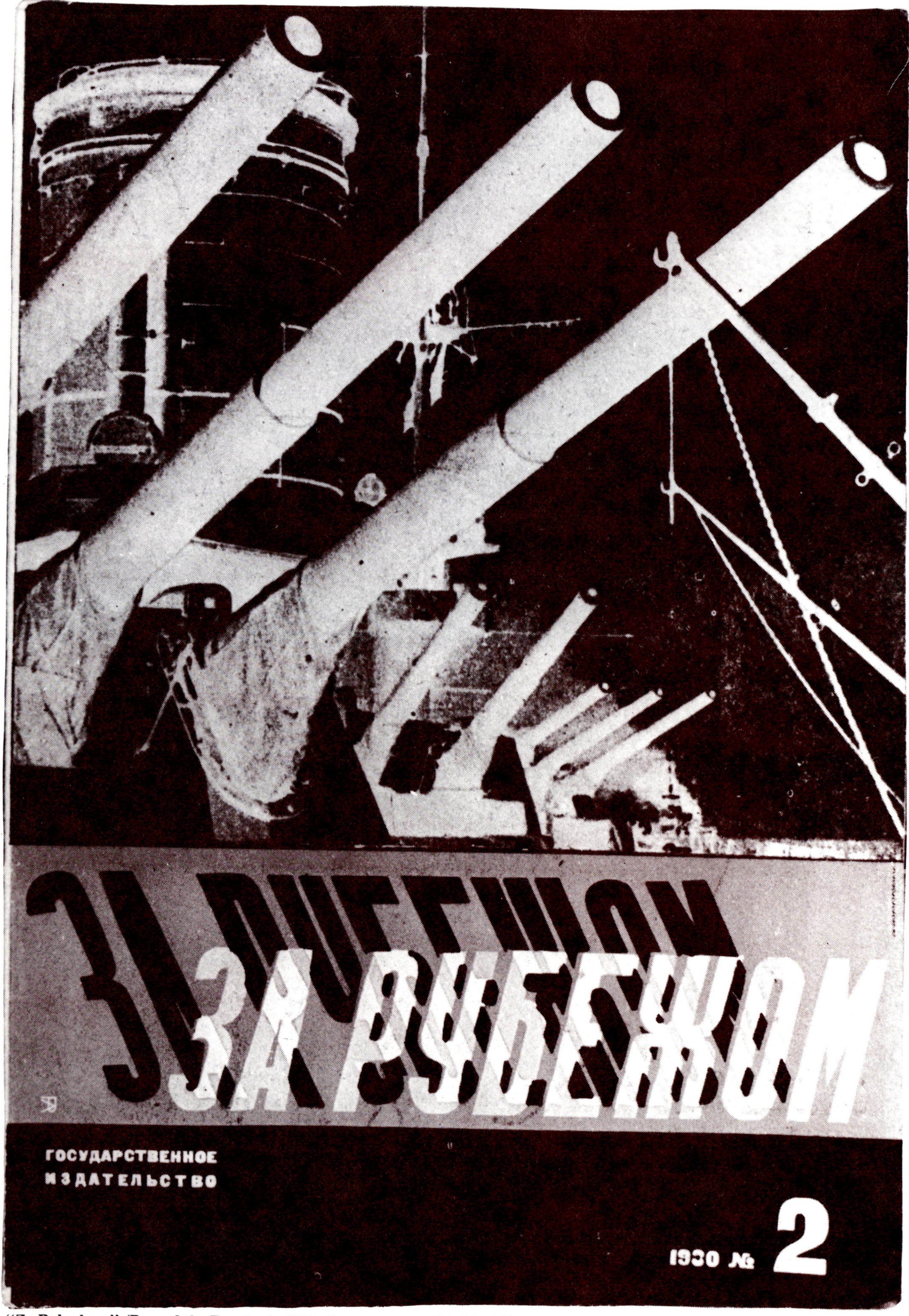

"Za Rubezhom" (Beyond the Frontiers), 1930. Opposite page: "Political Football", photomontage from "Za Rubezhom", 1930

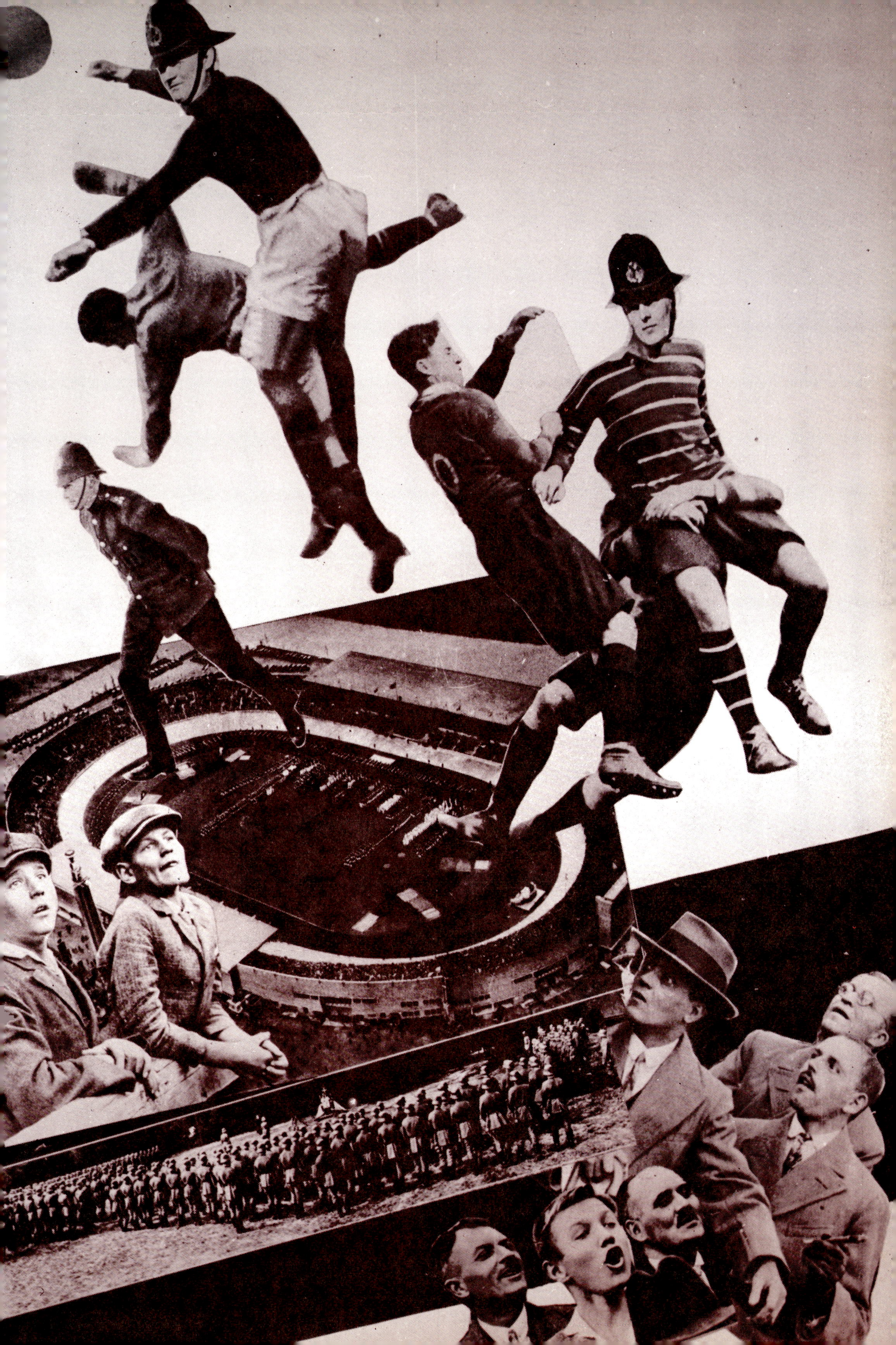

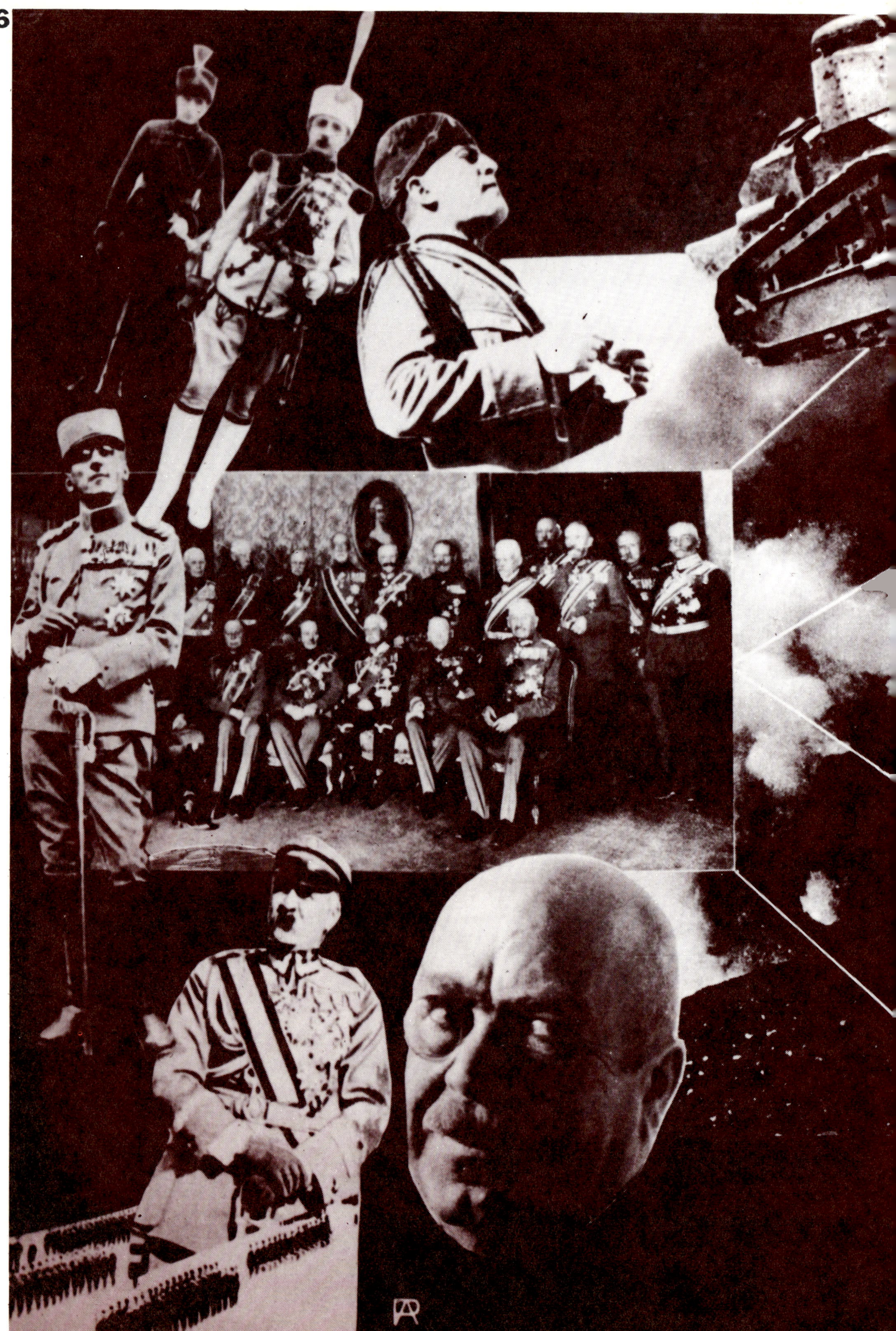

Anti-fascist photomontage from "Za Rubezhom", 1930

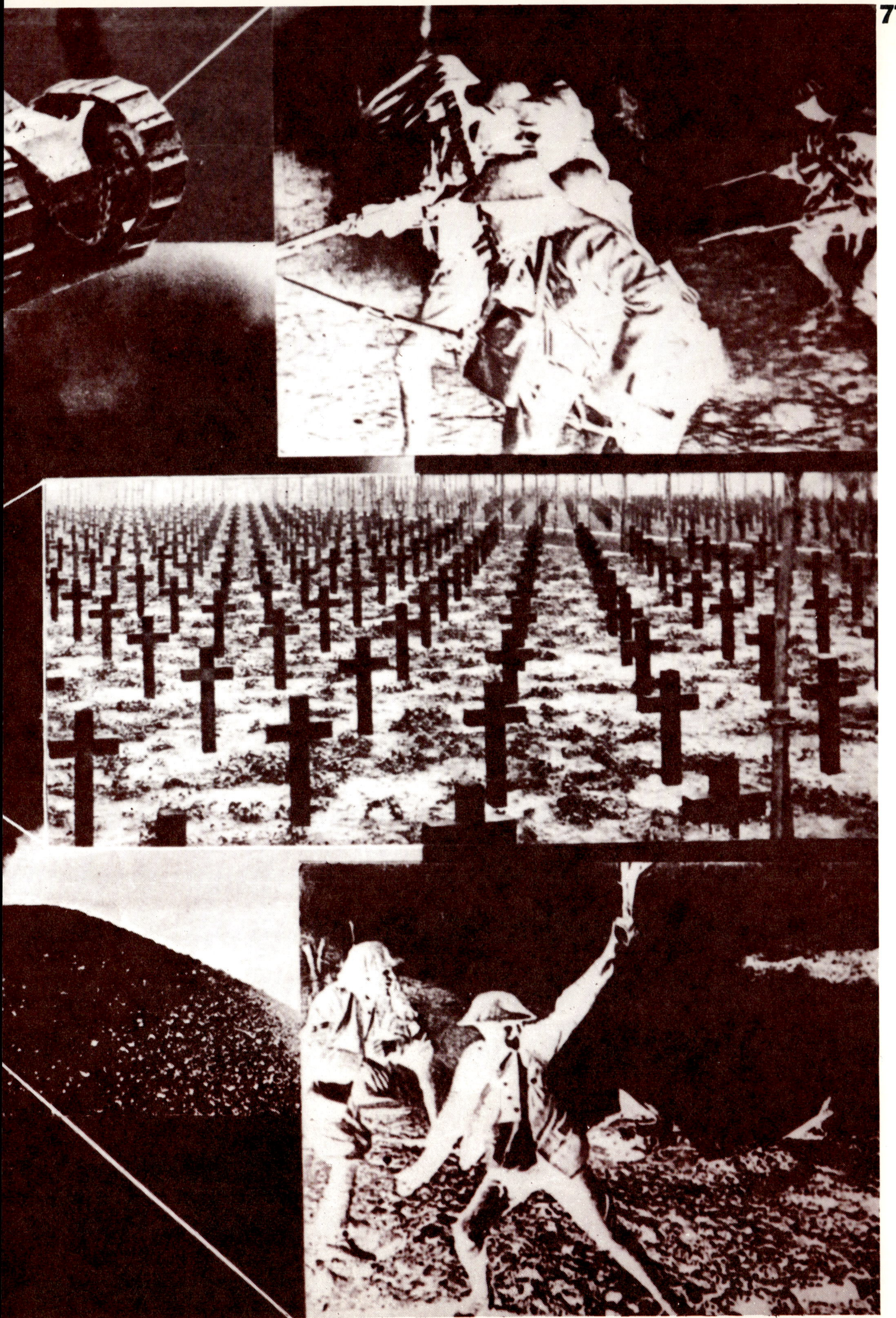

PRODUCTIVIST LIFE

Alexander Rodchenko as a graphic artist by Szymon Bojko

Alexander Rodchenko was born at a time when the acceleration of both social consciousness and cultural change in art were transforming Russian society. At the beginning of the twentieth century there was massive class conflict and aesthetic revolution. By heralding a new sensitivity for the man of the industrial era, the arts were disposing of provincialism and of a limited and patriarchal world outlook. The movement for this revival of art started around 1904 with the Modernism of artists belonging to the World of Art movement (the Russian variety of Art Nouveau) and did not stop at half measures. The generation which had lost heart with academic realism and with ideas of a didactic mission for the artist had reconsidered the axioms, judgements and ideas which had become immured in the artistic theory and practice of previous generations.

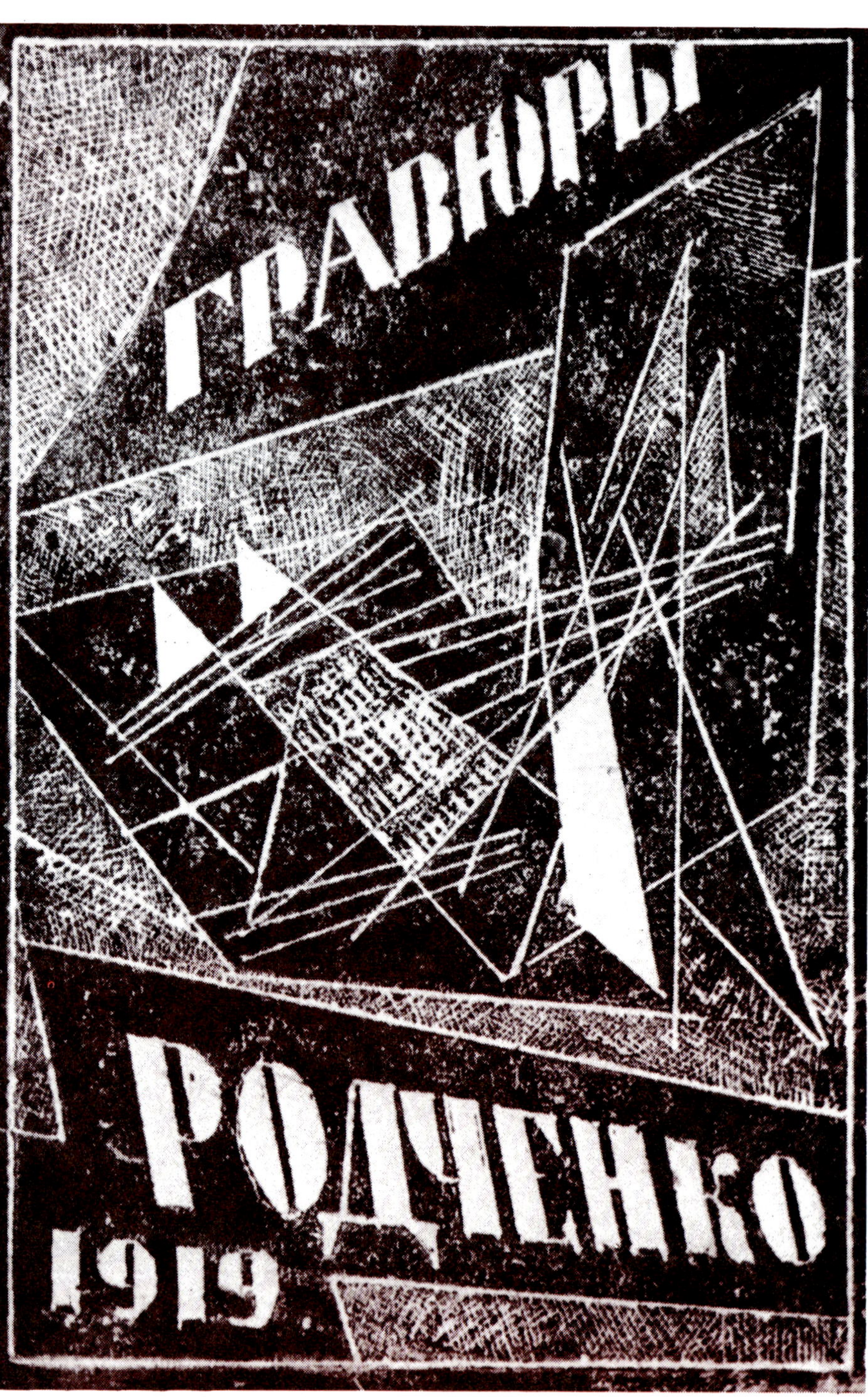

Cover for a portfolio of linocuts, 1919

The early work of Rodchenko reflects over a very short period, the mosaic of such changes. He arrived in Moscow in the first years of the First World War. He came there after art studies in Kazan, a university town where he was brought up and educated. News from the outside world reached such provinces with difficulty if at all. Neither his father — a stage-property maker at the local theatre, nor his mother — a washerwoman, could have assisted their son in the shaping of his consciousness and his aspirations. Yet his adaptation to new conditions took place rapidly. Continuing his art studies at the Stroganov Art Institute in Moscow, he took part in many events of historic importance. Now he came to know the artistic formations nearest to himself from personal experience and not from reading. Well-differentiated groups and movements still existed side by side: Colourism, the Cézannists, the followers of the Ecole de Paris, and of German Expressionism, and the Fauvists; there were exhibitions by artists grouped in the "Knave of Diamonds", the "Donkey's Tail", and in the more radical "Union of Youth". The modernism of the World of Art was also not yet extinct but by this time there appeared Cubism and

Syzmon Bojko is a critic and art historian resident in Warsaw. He has extensively researched graphic art of the twenties in the Soviet Union and has written a number of catalogues and books on the subject.

Futurism in their specific Russian varient of Cubofuturism. The march of innovations and discoveries became more and more intense, and in the period 1913-16 it became more like a landslide. Unending refutations and counter-tendencies became a widespread phenomenon; as Malevich announced the new order of Suprematism, he was opposed by Tatlin's Constructivist vision of the world. Rodchenko was faced with a choice as to which path he should follow. His convictions and aesthetic sympathies gravitated towards the avant-garde originating from Futurism, and it was with this avant garde that he identified himself. But in this development he was not free from some diversion; other ways were not at first alien to him, not even excluding the "Modernist" style. An analysis of his drawings and graphic work proves that he took advantage of various valuable experiences. The pen-drawings and gouaches of the period 1910-13, which have recently appeared in Karginov's book, as well as many other examples of his work known from the family archive, point to their relationship with the formal manner of Art Nouveau, represented in Russian Modernism by such painters as Borisov-Musatov, Somov, or Benois.

Nor can we exclude the probability that he also adapted Aubrey Beardsley's stylistic legacy in counterpointing the elements of line and infill, the thin line and the plane, black and white to make use of their expressive and linear contours. We could suppose that this was the origin of Rodchenko's estimation of linear values and his sensitivity to the constructional value of line in modern art, which he expressed in his statement on the "Line" of 1921.

His incidental interest in Modernism very quickly gave way to Cubism in its developed, synthetic phase, and then, as if in a sequence, it was placed at the meeting-point of Futurism and Suprematism, in order to stay to the end true to Constructivist ideals.

Passing through successive stages of mastering the current language of art, he investigated various aspects of form with increasing technical efficiency. Cubism marked the turning-point. Having shown the possibilities of freeing oneself from the outward appearance of things, Cubism opened a perspective for a new way of comprehending space and mass. Futurism was connected with the category of movement, reached by purely graphic means with the elimination of illusion and of literary undertones. Suprematism ensured maximum conciseness through the rejection of the last remnants of figuration and the working out of a system of non-objective form as the basis for new planar, spatial and colour relations. Suprematism, considered by some Soviet art historians as a departure from Cubism, contained an important metaphysical motivation which Rodchenko did not share. Although he was opposed to Malevich in respect of the motivation behind Productivist art, he found in his painterly theory some points of support which were important for himself.

Already in 1915 Rodchenko manifested the need to express his attitude to the world through complex geometrical structures. These were small-size Indian-ink drawings made with instruments used for technical drawing: ruler, compass, ruling pen. The technical objectivity of the drawings, at times they seem like engineering drawings, pressaged later designs. At first, the axis of the structure was provided by a circle, arcs, which passed into groups and spirals of rhythmic and sometimes decorative expressive forms. In the next phase, the alphabet of lines became more rigorous (he also made the following aesthetic recommendations to his students at the Basic Design Studio of the Vkhutemas): the vertical, the horizontal, the diagonal — this was, he said, the material with which one could put the image of the world in order. Cubist and geometrical principles served Rodchenko as the basis for a series of innovatory graphic designs and cycles of drawings. They included an album of dresses (never made) for A. Gan's play "We" (1919-20), where the human silhouette, marked out by a dismembered mass, was transformed into an ideogram — a graphic sign devoid of any psychological element. A similar tendency for using a schematic graphic design appears in a series of drawings on sport, called "Champions" of 1919, which was striking in its late-Cubist deformation of the human body and grotesque treatment of the subject. The simplicity and logic of modular, rhythmic and repeated geometrical motifs, was applied in designing patterns for the textile industry, as well as in designs for stage settings (as in "Inga", 1929; "The Bedbug", 1929, and for film decor as in "The Journalist", 1927).

The characteristic of Rodchenko's work mentioned earlier, which was expressed in the union of art and public life, evolved with an intellectual movement developing at the time which entered twentieth century cultural history as Constructivism. Looking at it in retrospect, with reference to Russia, Constructivism was not just one of several current trends in art but a developed artistic outlook encompassing in its intellectual scope the whole spiritual, cognitive and material activity of man. It tended to create an ideal model for "Constructivist life", rationalised and guided by an economy of thought and action. The victory of the Revolution in Russia, despite the whole heritage of ignorance and economic underdevelopment, seemed to open the perspective for a real embodiment of such a distant aim. Declaring themselves for the Revolution, and contributing to the consolidation of its achievements, the Constructivists expected to be able to introduce their own programme for a new outlook. This was the programme of the Left Front of Art and its leading figure, Mayakovsky. In the "LEF" periodical, and later, after an interval, in "Novyi LEF", it was proposed, not infrequently in a declamatory way, to interpret the quality of life and Socialist culture in a Constructivist way. The past was finished, and the chief targets for criticism were the selfish middle-class standards which were threatening the new life. A typical representative of everything outdated which, being conservative, stood in the way of most developed forms of life. It was no mere phantom. It existed, took on a revolutionary pose, adapted itself by the law of mimicry, and was still a force to be reckoned with. Yet, in spite of its revolutionary fervour, after several years, as a result of developments unfavourable for the avant-garde of the "LEF", Constructivist ideas were ruled out.

At a soirée held to commemorate Rodchenko in 1957 in Moscow at the Journalists' Club, this drama was characterised by the notable writer S. Kirsanov in the following way:

"...Rodchenko, Mayakovsky and others...tended to create new art, taking a break with the past as their point of departure. Their hate of the past was not just negative but was an indispensable step leading to the new... The past, which meant the previous social formation, spread to everything which was lavish, starting from ornaments on the 'plafonds' in landowners' houses, and ending on pink lampshades in middle-class rooms. These intruded insolently into the flats of the new community.... An ascetism of simplicity, straight lines, and a rejection of embellishments... A departure from ascetic habits, and the drawing of a curtain of oblivion over them, has led to mass-spreading of middle-class art.... And yet, we were forming a highly-motivated art of simplicity and more suitable to forms of new life.... than the one which is supposed to be the art of the new community.... Therefore, in looking at covers and posters designed by Rodchenko I see in them the leavening for that which failed to develop. It is sad that middle-class art has put an end to these beginnings...."

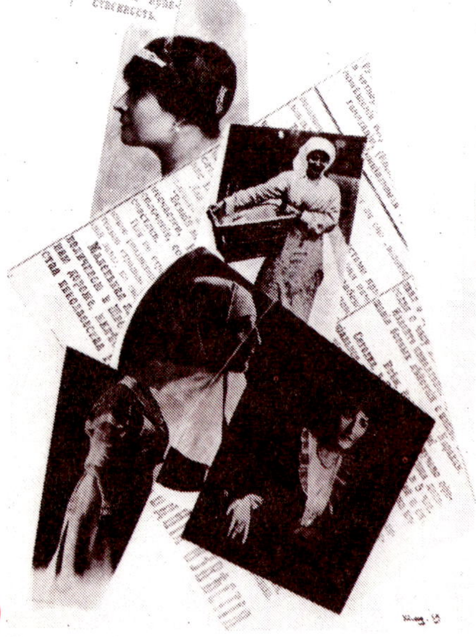

Collage, 1919

It is fitting to develop the observations just quoted on asceticism and simplicity as positive determinants of Rodchenko's art which were consistent with its anti-middle-class edge. Here I shall limit myself to just one part of it, namely to that of the graphics of the mass media, including typography. In this field, the spirit of innovation and experiment was developed intensively; it did not yield to pioneering works made in Western Europe, and often took precedence over them. What became a harbinger, heralding a break with the aesthetics of exclusive and richly ornamented print, highly elevated by the Modernism of the World of Art movement, were the volumes of Futurist poetry by Khlebnikov and Kruchenykh, published in 1912-13. In order to oppose "elegance", these volumes featured the values of "poverty": using low-grade paper, semi-craft production with stone lithography, and with parts added by hand. There was no traditional illustration; its place was taken by freely laid out pages, with reference to Futuristic poetic stylistics. They were folklore-inspired to a larger degree than in any other European country. Relaxation of the canon of illustrated books seen, for example, in the interpenetration of words and pictures, had outlined further developments. They made an impact on the theory and practice of Russian Constructivists. El Lissitzky deliberated on a "visual book" the construction of which was based on type, whilst the kinetics of succeeding pages were developed as if according to the rules of film; for Rodchenko, graphic design belonged to the mass media and was subject to general rules of visual communication, which meant that communication must be a coded sign, unambiguous and objectivised, free from ornamental superstructure. Soon there began to appear books which still today are examples of a search for a new formula for book illustration. The most important were: "The Story of Two Squares" and "For Reading Aloud" by Lissitzky, Rodchenko's photomontages to Mayakovksy's poem "Pro Eto" (About This), books for children designed by the sisters Galina and Olga Chichagova, as well as photomontages by Klutsis and Senkin for a popular publication on Lenin.

While Lissitzky laid stress on the dynamics of functional typography, and the 'cinematographicity' of the book, Rodchenko was more interested in its tectonics, texture and construction. The consciousness of a dialectical connection of these categories, and their joint action, assisted the artist from the start in painting, in spatial construction, in design, and in graphics for the mass media. 1919 had marked the beginning of the first collages, which were an introduction to the complicated problems of the texture of flat forms: compositions resulting from the assembling of bits of coloured papers, fragments of packaging, wallpapers, entrance tickets, cuttings from publicity material and advertisements. These were devised from Cubist collages by Picasso and Braque, as well as from collages by the Italian Futurists Severini and Carrà, and by Russian artists: Malevich, Puni, and Rozanova. The series of "topical" typo-collages of 1922 did not produce anything new, either, even though they were of some interest on account of the satirical content coded in them. But it was not until the experience gained during work on Mayakovsky's poem "Pro Eto" (1923) that Rodchenko was able to start on a mature composition, which was not just an illustration but a particular visual commentary. This resulted from a personal acquaintance with the life and lover of a friend, and also from feeling the climate of a period, as well as its material and moral realities. Moreover, by now the artist felt easier with material of a mechanical origin and introduced photography, which faced the anonymity of print with a form of counterpoint — the value of a document.

All this time Rodchenko used the work of a professional photographer, named Sterenburg, but it was a sign of his interest in the new medium. He took up photography a year later and this made a great impact on the whole of the further development of his work. In his reminiscences, written down later, we read: "In connection with work on photomontage, I became occupied with photography myself. This was a case of necessity, since I always needed to enlarge, reduce or reproduce. I bought two cameras 134 x 18, with a triple extension of the bellows and a Dagor lens, a camera for reproduction, and a pocket-size Kodak." He also noted earlier on: "I was the first to make photomontages in the Soviet Union; at first for the "Kinofot" periodical, and later for posters for films by Vertov and Eisenstein... It was exactly for that reason that Mayakovsky wished that I should make photomontages for his poem." (From an unpublished typescript.) It is of lesser importance that Klutsis claimed priority (see, for example, "Dynamic City", 1919), while Lissitzky practiced this medium simultaneously with Rodchenko. The essential point is that photomontage, stemming out of formal investigations of European art (Cubism, Futurism, Dadaism), found a wide response among the common people. It was the language of the street, belonging to the same family of material as the film documentary, propaganda poster, decorations for celebrations of revolutionary anniversaries, and street spectacles. Prevalent in various forms, in the course of time it was transformed into a popular form of art, like a cheap print of previous centuries.

The beginning of photomontage coincided with the birth in the Soviet cinema of an original film language using exclusively visual means, the main idea of which was montage. By using montage, film gave an intensified vision by revealing the invisible connexions between phenomena and objects. Rodchenko's photomontages fulfilled a function similar to that of Vertov's chronicle "Kino-Pravda" and also had a similar structure: simultaneous action, superimposition of two or more frames, the showing of detail in close-up, the rhythmical use of multiplied elements, the featuring of perspective foreshortenings....

Rodchenko had produced only a few posters which used photomontage in the strict sense. The most interesting of these are three versions for Vertov's "Kino-Pravda", containing all of the above characteristics.

Most graphic posters belonged to the artistic partnership of Mayakovsky and Rodchenko, being set up and active in the NEP period, in order to satisfy advertising commissions. The need for visual advertising appeared as a result of the coexistence on the national scene of the nationalised and private sectors. The real sense of NEP advertising was not so much commercial, since there was still a scarcity of goods, but for propaganda purposes. The aim was to stress the dominating role of the nationalised commerce and services. In this way Mayakovsky understood advertising and he wrote propaganda poems and slogans for it. He showed unusual inventiveness in devising slogans and rhymed texts for posters, packaging, leaflets, signboards, kiosks, and wall advertising. All Moscow was dominated by products of the partnership, who signed themselves as "advertising constructors". These advertisements hit pedestrians' eyes with a strong geometric drawing, large areas of pure colour, clear lettering, and an amusing text.

The design of lettering and typographical layout opened a separate chapter in the practice of Russian Constructivism. In this area, subject to technological determinants, there was a confrontation between the rules of Constructivist architectonics and the requirements of perception — between legibility and economy. According to Constructivist theory, there is an interdependence between the visual composition of the text and its semantic notation. Since this composition is governed by laws of typographical mechanics, it must reflect the course and rhythm of its contents. Following these assumptions, Lissitzky, Gan, and later Telingater, their junior, analysed the text and broke it into parts of varying rhythms. Rodchenko did not go as far in typographical radicalism. He rather consolidated the text, taking care to keep his lettering in strict order. His lettering, with its varieties and shades, is characterised by a horizontal rhythm. Heavy sanserif letters with sharp edges, most often condensed and with small spaces, static and with a coarse appearance, supplement the graphics with that ascetic simplicity mentioned earlier by Kirsanov. Hand-drawn lettering designed by Rodchenko became the basis for extra bold sanserif type in his country. Popularised in the press, on book covers, and in innumerable headings, it now appears as an historic document of that time. In the minds of several generations, this form of lettering was identified with the style of the new art of the Revolution. The coarseness of forms, their bulkiness, and lack of decoration, corresponded to the purism of life itself and to the atmosphere of renunciation for a better future.

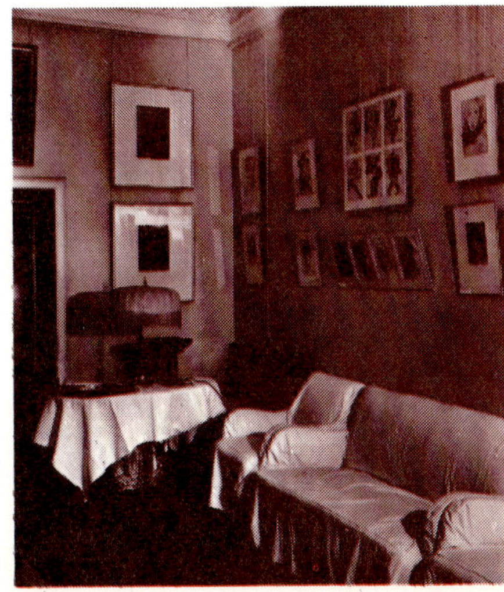

First posthumous exhibition of Rodchenko's work, House of Journalists, Moscow, 1957

Alexander Rodchenko as a book designer by Gail Harrison

Gail Harrison is an art historian, who lives in New York. She is at present researching the work of Vladimir Tatlin, and early Soviet book design.

GRAPHIC COMMITMENT

In 1921, Alexander Mikhailovich Rodchenko ended one career in art and began another. Declaring that "the downfall of all the isms of painting marked the beginning of my ascent," he abandoned sculpture and easel painting and turned instead to domestic design, typography and photography. Along with Vladimir Tatlin (1885-1953) and others at Inkhuk (an acronym for the Russian "Institute of Artistic Culture") in 1921, Rodchenko perfected the "productivist" aspects of Constructivism; i.e., the creation of mass-produced utilitarian objects for everyday use, the simplified forms of which embodied an ideal of machine-made precision. Throughout the 1920s, Rodchenko devoted his efforts increasingly to printed modes of communication: to books, posters, and film-titles. His book designs are particularly noteworthy not only as examples of the synthetic approach to art promulgated by the Constructivist avant-garde, but also as vibrant manifestations of the dynamic optimism inspired by the young Soviet Union. Experimental "modern" literature and book design in Russia date from as early as 1910, but post-Revolutionary activity in the arts encouraged the greatest proliferation in number and variety of avant-garde books and periodicals. Selected book designs by Rodchenko are discussed below both as outstanding examples of the collaborative efforts of artists and writers in the two decades following the Revolution and as illustrations of his individual approach to typography and photomontage.

As did many Russian and western European artists during the teens and twenties, Rodchenko used collage in order to extend painting beyond its two dimensional confines. By introducing textured elements onto the canvas, collage also provided the opportunity to incorporate everyday objects, or fragments of them, into artworks.

Photomontage dates from the late teens, when it was developed simultaneously in Russia and Germany. It involved the manipulation of one or several photographs in a variety of ways, such as the combination of two or more photographic images into a single print, the combination of multiple exposures on a single negative, or the combination of several negatives; it could also include prints obtained by directing light through cut-outs or by objects laid onto photo-sensitive paper. However, an even broader definition of photomontage as any combination of photographs with text, colour or drawing apparently guided Rodchenko's own designs. In the words of the German Dadaist Hannah Höch (1889-1978), whose photomontages displayed a strong affinity to Rodchenko's own work in that medium, "Our whole purpose was to integrate objects from the world of machines and industry in the world of art."

Rodchenko's involvement in book design was both political and artistic. His work as chief designer for the journals LEF (Levyi front iskusstv; "Left Front of the Arts"), from 1923 to 1925, and its successor "Novyi LEF" ("New LEF"), from 1927 to 1928, demonstrates his sustained commitment to the leftist principles established for art and life during the Revolutionary years of the 1920s. The second number of "LEF" carried an exhortation entitled "Comrades, Organisers of Life!" Printed in Russian, German, and English, this declaration called on artists to "exercise your artistic strength to engirdle cities until you are able to take part in the whole global construction! Give the world new colours and outline!... Break down the barriers of beauty for beauty's sake..." In response to the claim that "only October has given us new, tremendous ideas that demand new artistic organisation," Rodchenko produced covers, title pages, illustrations, and layouts for "LEF" and "Novyi LEF", charged with enthusiasm for innovative art forms as a manifestation of the new social and artistic organisation of Soviet life. His designs employed a wide range of Constructivist typography, technological and industrial imagery, photomontage, and illustrations of new artistic methods and products.

In 1923, "LEF's" editor-in-chief, Vladimir Mayakovsky (1893-1930), wrote in his autobiography: "...one of the greatest achivements of "LEF" [is] the de-aestheticisation of the productional arts, Constructivism. A poetic supplement: agit-art and economic agitation..." Rodchenko's Constructivist typography and design for "LEF" was decidedly "unaesthetic" in its boldly coloured, geometrical precision, which related it directly to "productional" art. Just as "LEF" itself was to play an "agit-role" in the development of the Soviet arts, its logo epitomised the Constructivist forms that the (visual) arts were about to take. This synthesis of style and intent in Rodchenko's work conforms to the dicta established by El Lissitzky (1890-1941) in his manifesto "The Topography of Typography," published the same year as "LEF's" inception:

1. The words on the printed sheet are learnt by sight not by hearing.
2. Ideas are communicated through conventional words, the idea should be

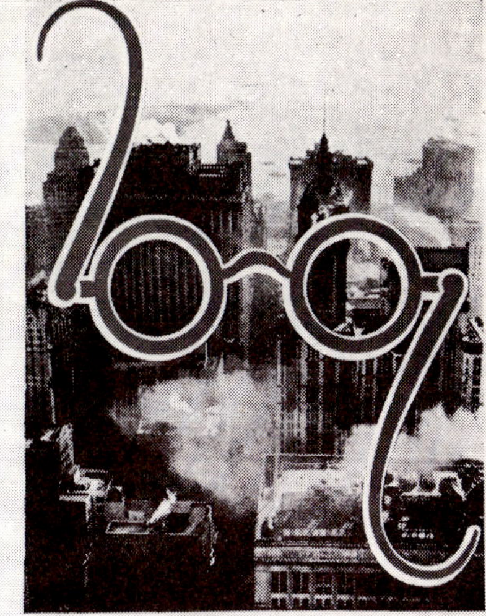

Cover of "Biznes", 1929

given form through the letters.
3. Economy of expression — optics instead of phonetics.
4. The designing of the book — space through the material of the type, according to the laws of typographical mechanics must correspond to the... content."

For Rodchenko, as for Lissitzky, the actual lettering "en page" had to function not only on a substantive level but emotionally and visually as well.

For example, large-scale lettering dominates the cover of "LEF", occupying one-third of its surface and commanding visual attention through its massive proportions and bold two-colour composition.

Rodchenko had begun to experiment extensively with photography during the early "LEF" years, and photomontages dominate the covers of "Novyi LEF"; architectural fragments, portraits, figures, ships, and emblematic forms fill the allotted space, with the title lettering sometimes relegated to a single corner. Here, Rodchenko has separated typography from illustration, exercising a clear preference for the pictorial image over the printed one, and his decorative placement of the title "Novyi LEF" seems far removed from the brashly "heraldic" role of the earlier "LEF" logo. Rodchenko's later covers display greater contrasts of colour either in two-colour typography or in monochrome letters against a coloured background, and the shape of the letters L E F was altered. For "Novyi LEF" Rodchenko abandoned the precisely geometrical, angular type of "LEF's" "L E F" in favour of an almost fanciful style of lettering, characterised by its plasticity and bulbous, curvilinear forms. This change seems to have been motivated by Rodchenko's desire to ensure that the aesthetic integrity of the typography would not be subordinated to the increasingly dominant photographic illustration on the covers of "Novyi LEF".

The poet Vladimir Mayakovsky and Rodchenko both shared LEF's activist, productivist approach to art and life, and the numerous designs that Rodchenko created for his friend's books during the 1920s attest to their common affinities. Rodchenko's photomontages for Mayakovsky's personal exegesis, "Pro Eto" ("About This"), in 1923 express the two great passions of the poet's life: his lover Lilya Brik, and his desire for a revolutionary society.

This series of photomontages, eight of which (excluding the cover) were included in the published version of the poem, are intimately tied to the narrative and style of Mayakovsky's text.

LEF's standard definition of creative work as an agent in the transformation of society was reinforced by Mayakovsky's memorial poem "Sergeiu Eseninu" ("To Sergei Esenin"), published in 1926, one year after Esenin (b. 1895) committed suicide in a Leningrad hotel after writing a valedictory poem in his own blood. The final lines of Esenin's poem conclude that:

In life dying is nothing new
But neither is living, of course, new.

Saddened and angered by Esenin's negativism, Mayakovsky responded poetically with his own exhortation to creative labour:

In life it is not difficult to die.
To make life is far more difficult...

Why increase the suicide rate?
Better to increase the flow of ink!

Rodchenko's cover for this poem depicts a railroad bridge seen head-on with a black disc superimposed on its tracks, over which the book's title is inscribed in red. The disc ambiguously suggests the mouth of a tunnel and the engine of an oncoming locomotive, inviting the reader towards its dynamic force and rhythm. Close examination reveals that there are stalks of wheat inscribed within the disc, an allusion to the co-existence of the Soviet economy's agricultural base with its growing industrial capability. This alternative version of the Soviet hammer-and-sickle no doubt summarises Mayakovsky's recent whistle-stop lecture tour through the Russian countryside to speak on poetry to provincial audiences. The illustration on the rear cover reinforces this analogy. A worm's-eye-view photograph of a tall building (in fact the eight storey block in which Rodchenko's studio was situated) forms the background to another montaged disc which illustrates a peasant hut. For both Mayakovsky and Rodchenko, these juxtapositions of urban and rural imagery represented pleas for a united effort to build the Soviet Union, an appeal made all the more urgent by contrast with Esenin's suicide. Although shaken by Esenin's death, Mayakovsky's response was, characteristically, not to mourn but to seek action. He declared that workers would need the concerted energy of the entire human race in order to carry out their revolution; suicide was unthinkable.

Among the many impediments to the creative construction advocated by LEF was taxation introduced under the New Economic Policy, or NEP, of 1921-1928. Mayakovsky voiced his scornful opinion of the new taxes in his poem "Razgovor s Fininspektorom o poezii ("A Conversation with a Tax Inspector about Poetry"), published in 1926. Following the venerable Russian literary tradition that extends from Gogol and Dostoyevsky, Mayakovsky satirised the pompous bureaucrat with caustic humour. In a photomontage on the front cover, the author stares out at the reader while the tax inspector points an accusing finger at him. Both figures hold paper in hand, but, as Mayakovsky points out in the poem, they deal in different currency. Says the poet to the inspector:

A rhyme is
A bill of exchange
In your jargon....

A poet is forever
In debt to the universe.
He pays his percentage
In pain and anguish.

Mayakovsky taunts his relentless persecutor with the prospect that the poet will ultimately prevail by virtue of his unique contribution to the future.

In keeping with Mayakovsky's tone of light-hearted banter, Rodchenko's cover does not show Mayakovsky in direct physical confrontation with the tax inspector. Instead, the poet seems to ignore his antagonist as he unfolds a piece of paper — presumably his poem — and turns toward the reader, as if enlisting his or her approval. The rear cover has become a virtual icon of the Revolutionary period: a photomontage comprising a photograph of Mayakovsky's head topped by a globe which is being circled by three aeroplanes.

The romantic theme of aviation also dominated the front cover of "LEF", No. 3, and "Let: Avio-stikhi" ("Flying: Aviation Verses"), both published in 1923. In the latter, a black aeroplane flies straight upward, as if breaking forth from all earthly bounds (here represented by the book cover). The bold red and white lettering of the title is composed of the same mechanically precise style of the aeroplane itself. "Avio-stikhi" is printed below, within a triangle whose downward-pointed apex forms a visual counterpoint to the rising nose of the plane.

One of the most dramatic examples of this fascination with flying appears in Rodchenko's logo design of 1925 for the "Federatsiia" Publishing House, in which two semi-circular forms containing the words "Federatsiia" (Federation) and "Izdatel'stvo" ("Publisher") surround a central vertical form that can be taken to represent both a pen and a rocket ship blasting off — an allusion to the artist's conviction that both the printed and "designed" word possessed the power of a rocket. Rodchenko and his contemporaries believed that print was all the more potent when combined with mechanical imagery (aeroplanes, industry, skyscrapers, radio towers) since advanced technology was a crucial component of the Soviet self-image during the 1920s.

A favourite symbol of modern progress was the Eiffel Tower, which was hailed in Russia as a pioneering triumph of industrialisation and a harbinger of the new urban technology. In 1923 Mayakovsky composed a poetic address to the Eiffel Tower entitled "Parizh" ("Paris"). Calling for a revolt against the decadence of Paris, Mayakovsky invited the personified tower (referred to in the text as a "Bolshevik") to remove itself to the USSR.

The bridges,
maddened by the traffic hell
will rise from the river banks
of Paris...

Come, tower!
To us;
You —
there,
are much more
needed!
Steel-shining,
smoke-piercing,
we'll meet you.

By inviting the Eiffel Tower to soar above the spacious vistas of Moscow, Mayakovsky was metaphorically expressing his compatriots' utopian vision of a new society supplanting the outworn relics of Old Russia. Nevertheless, Mayakovsky's fascination for city life was ambivalent, being tinged with the alienation and paranoia of the isolated individual:

I furrow Paris —
so terribly alone,
it's terrible — nobody
Around me —
autos fantasise a dance,
around me — ...

In 1925, Mayakovsky completed a second work entitled "Parizh", a book of poems that included "Gorod" ("The City") and "Verlen i Sezan" ("Verlaine and Cézanne"), exuberant verses in the enthusiastic vein of the 1923 poem. Rodchenko's cover for the later book consists of an aerial photograph of the Eiffel Tower, seen rising above the crowded city. Similar bird's-eye-views of cities and clusters of modern buildings, which appeared frequently in Soviet illustration during the 1920s, were especially prized, not only because they provided an urban-contextual view of buildings, but also because they implied the use of an aeroplane.

Two other major book covers of the 1920s, Rodchenko's designs for "Biznes" ("Business") and "Geroi Tekhniki" ("Heroes of Technology"), were also composed around aerial city views although here it was New York rather than Paris that provided the paradigm of modernity.

"Biznes", published by the Literary Centre of Constructivists under the editorship of Kornelii Zelinsky (b. 1895) and Igor Sel'vinsky (1889-1960), is an anthology of ideological, critical and fictional writings, and a noteworthy product of the Centre's intention to emphasise technological demands in its revolutionary activity. In his essay, "Konstruktivizm i Sotsializm" ("Constructivism and Socialism"), Zelinsky explains that the title of the anthology is a transliteration of the English word "Business' (which in Russian is "delo"), which he cites as the "lifestyle" of contemporary American capitalism, manifested in the "hooting machines" of industry that strain man's energy in order to generate profits. True progress, however, can only be approached through "Socialist business," organised according to Constructivist principles of collectivity and necessity.

Rodchenko's cover design duly alludes to Zelinsky's ideas concerning the great physical and urban potential of a business centre.
The large scale and bold placement of the anthology's title above the photomontage, and the publisher's name and date below it, recall the printed agitprop devices (posters, commercial signs, political slogans) that were highly visible in Soviet cities during the 1920s.

The detective story with an American theme or hero was a popular extension of the Russian mania for urban America. More or less the equivalent of an American dime-store novel, Marietta Shaginian's "Jim Dollar" saga in "Mess Mend: ili Ianki v Petrograde ("Mess Mend: or a Yankee in Petrograd") is an exciting mystery series that combines Russian enthusiasm for the vigorous pace of American life with typical Soviet satire aimed at American capitalism and bourgeois lifestyle. Rodchenko's variously coloured photomontages for the "Mess Mend" series are among the most imaginative productions of the 1920s.

A different photomontage illustrates the theme of each number in the "Mess Mend" series. All of the covers are dominated by images of mystery and danger, such as a sinister black hand, a ticking bomb, or human figures poised in tense confrontation. The individual components of the montages, and their juxtaposition on the cover, tend towards the bizarre and the incongruous: for example, a colossal dinosaur, a modern pocket watch, and a man's head, all roughly the same size. A varied assortment of machines, vehicles, buildings, animals and human beings is assembled to create a composite view of the modern world. The seemingly irrational relationships of scale, disjuncture of anatomy, and frenzied activity presented on each cover convey the excitement, intensity and dynamism of "Mess Mend". As the film director, Lev Kuleshov (1899-1970 remarked, "In detective literature, and more so in the American detective scenario, the fundamental element of the plot is an intensity in the development of the action, the

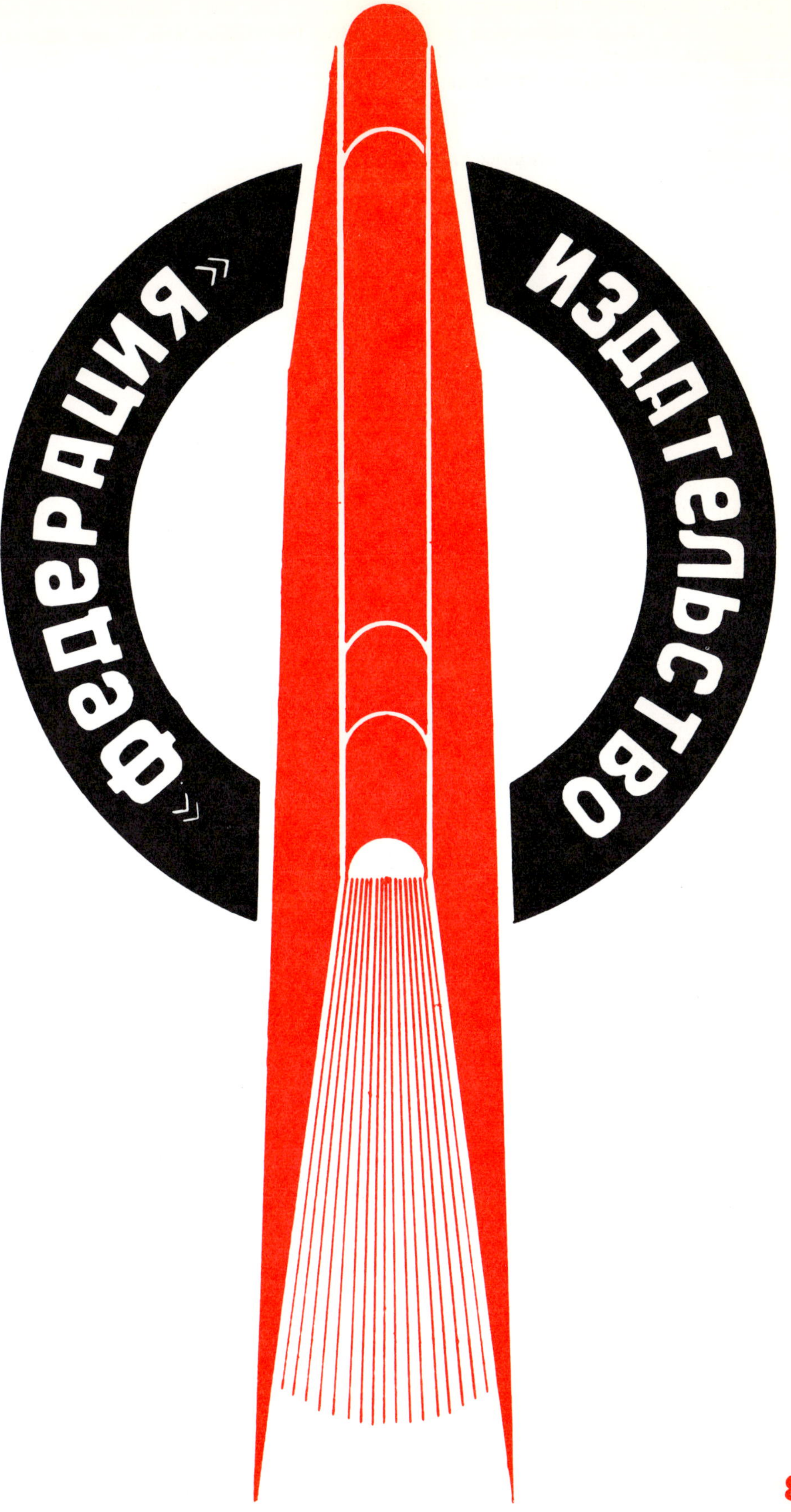

Logotype for "Federatsiia" publishing house, 1925

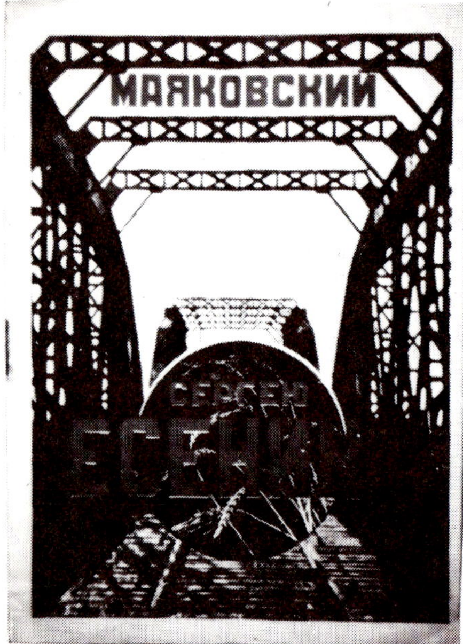

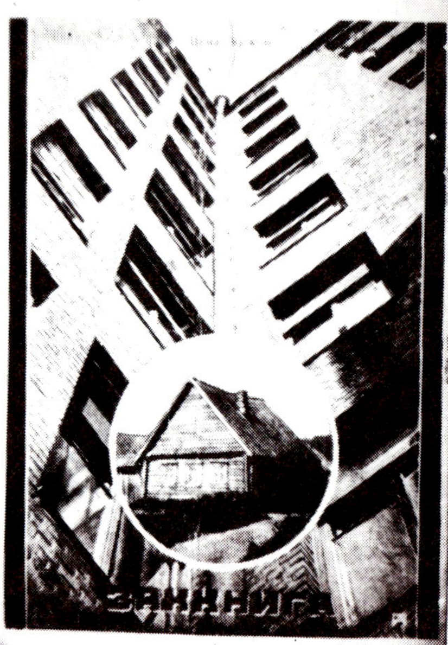

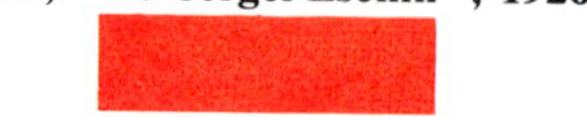

Left: Front and back cover of V. Mayakovsky's poem, "To Sergei Esenin", 1926.

Opposite page, left to right: Covers of Mayakovsky's "Syphilis", 1926; Ehrenburg's "Materialisation of Fantasy", 1927; and Mayakovsky's "A Conversation with a Tax Inspector about Poetry", 1926.

dynamism of construction...."

The rear covers of this "Jim Dollar" series are equally complex, functioning as independent typographical designs as well as relating thematically to the text. The back cover of Number 10, "Vzryv soveta" ("Explosion of the Soviet") illustrates this point. A large clockface and question mark enforce the suspense created on the front cover's photomontage of a Soviet meeting and a ticking bomb. The varying scale, typeface and placement of the title lettering that surrounds the clock enhance the sense of expectancy.

In his use of Constructivist lettering, non-objective elements, spatial dynamism, photography, photomontage, and bold colour, Rodchenko joined Lissitzky in creating a graphic revolution that exploited the printed letter or word both as an independent unit of design and a narrative element.

Rodchenko's design for Mayakovsky's "No. S" (an abbreviation for the Russian, Novye stikhi — "New Verses") presents the title lettering in a bold and emphatic manner. Large scale and contrasting backing colours transcend any purely verbal function and identify this typography as significant graphic design in its own right. Lissitzky's design of the front cover of Mayakovsky's book Khorosho! ("Fine"), a poetic celebration of the tenth anniversary of the Revolution, employs the same typographical approach: precise lettering, boldly printed in black and red with white. However, the letters are arranged so that they hover on an undifferentiated white background, thereby suggesting the indeterminable spatial extension that Lissitzky had formulated in his "Prouns" as early as 1919. In contrast, Rodchenko's red and black rectangles provide his letters with a solid backdrop, against which they appear as bolder, more autonomous graphic elements. The fact that the title had already been abbreviated by Mayakovsky may well have influenced Rodchenko in his decision to treat it primarily as typographical, rather than a narrative, image.

With these innovative designs, Rodchenko and Lissitzky extended the traditionally passive experience of typography to include kinetic and dynamic elements. This new dimension is especially evident in Rodchenko's cover designs for Nikolai Aseev's (1889-1963) 1923 publication of "Izbran: Stikhi" ("The Choice: Verses") and for Mayakovsky's "Tuda i obratno" ("There and Back") published in 1930, the year of the poet's suicide. In the earlier composition, Rodchenko opposes the colours and directions of the collection's title and the author's name. "Izbran" is written in orange letters that can be read only by turning the book ninety degrees to the right, whereas the black letters of "N. Aseev" are superimposed onto the title and read vertically down the front cover. This manipulation of the visual experience through a kinetic reaction — whether real or implied — is a basic principle of Constructivist design.

Mayakovsky's poem is bound within one of the most striking covers ever produced. Four black pointed elements, arranged vertically, dominate both covers. Two horizontal red bands that run across the covers unify the four black "arrows", thereby integrating them into the book's basic horizontal format. The front cover is further enlivened by the title typography: a connective "i" (and) relates "tuda" (there) and "obratno" (back) both narratively and visually, its assymetrical, curvilinear form contrasting with the otherwise rigid lettering, and establishing a continuous rhythm that leads the eye both vertically and horizontally.

When the Soviet Union made its "international début" at the 1925 Exposition Universelle des Arts decoratifs et industriels in Paris, it was Rodchenko's cover for the USSR's decorative arts catalogue that introduced new Russian design to an eager audience in the West. Rectangular panels in red, black and grey form a Constructivist background to the bold red letters "URSS" rendered even more prominent by the clarity of their forms and diagonal alignment. In his designs for Sergei Tret'iakov's (1892-1939) "Den Shi-Khua: Bio-Interview", published in 1930, Rodchenko demonstrated that Constructivist graphics and typography could be continued effectively from the cover throughout the text. Dedicated to the new China, Tret'iakov's book recounts the author's own experiences in the Far East as if in a tour conducted by a guide named "Den Shi-Khua". Rodchenko emphasised the book's numerous documentary photographs with non-objective configurations of horizontal, vertical and diagonal lines that clearly separate illustration and text while reflecting geometric design-elements that appear within the pictures. These linear forms also appear independently, as Constructivist clichés at the beginning and end of each chapter. When used for chapter headings, these designs surround bold-face type in order to command visual attention (the letters recall "LEF's" typographical design in everything but their small scale). At the conclusion of every chapter, the linear patterns are set with graphic precision en page along rhythmic, sometimes diagonal, axes characteristic of Russian avant-garde art.

Even as late as 1930, the heritage of Constructivism — geometry, clarity, and rhythm — remained a vigorous element in Rodchenko's book design.

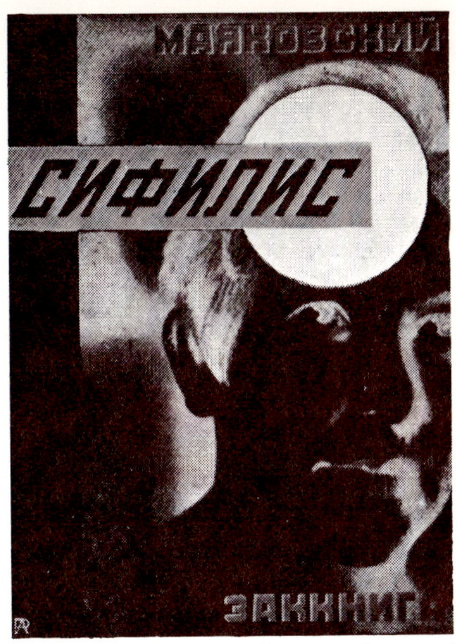

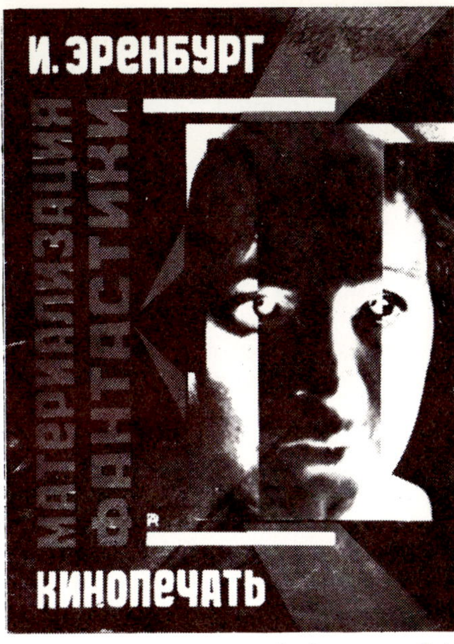

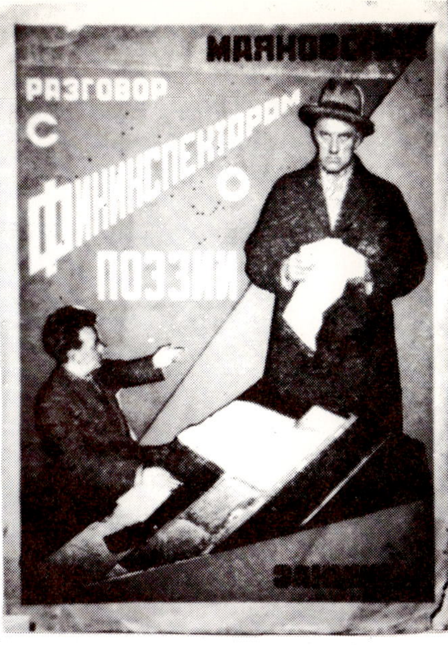

Photomontage and superimposed exposures marked many of Rodchenko's book covers of the 1920s. For example, an undated photograph from that period shows both a frontal and a profile view of a man. This double exposure relies on tonal contrasts as well as variations of pose to distinguish the two images. The result is an extended physical and psychological definition of the subject, which, according to the Formalist critic Viktor Shklovsky (b. 1896) approaches the fourth dimension. Rodchenko used underexposure and photomontage in his cover design for Mayakovsky's "Siflis" (Syphilis) of 1926 and for Il'ia Ehrenburg's (1861-1967) "Materializatsiia Fantastiki" (The Materialisation of Fantasy) of 1927. The cover portrait for "Siflis" is so heavily underexposed that it appears to be a photo-negative. The forms are seen as black shadows and bright light rather than as solid shapes, an eerie, unnatural effect that is reinforced by the superimposition of a disc of light across the head, over which Rodchenko has projected a horizontal band containing the title. The choice of title was no doubt motivated by Mayakovsky's anti-bourgeois stance; also, "siflis" rhymes with Tiflis, the home of "Zakkniga" Publishers and a hotbed of Russian avant-garde activity following the Revolution.

On the cover of "Materializatsiia Fantastiki", beams of light cross a portrait head, transforming it from an anonymous face into the subject of Rodchenko's design. The luminous rays, which are printed in red, seem to emanate from the title printed to the left of the illustration, also in red. Rodchenko thus demonstrated the "materialization of fantasy" (i.e., the function of film itself) in this static pictorial suggestion of the cinematic process.

Along with other revolutionary artists in Russia, Rodchenko considered film an essential medium for Soviet psychological and social expression. Film was regarded first by the Russian avant-garde and later by Soviet officialdom as the only art form appropriate to modern life. As early as 1913, Mayakovsky claimed: "The theater moves towards its own destruction and must hand over its heritage to the cinema. And the cinema industry, branching away from the naive realism and artifice of Chekhov and Gorky, opens the door to a theater of the future — linked to the art of the actor." Beginning in 1922, Rodchenko designed titles for the "Kino-Pravda" documentaries on the USSR, directed by Dziga Vertov (1896-1954). Ehrenburg's theoretical history of film offered Rodchenko another opportunity to manifest his pronounced affinity for cinematographic techniques.

Three-dimensional cut-out figures and animals that Rodchenko designed for Tret'iakov's children's book "Samozveri" further extend these principles of spatial dynamism and movement. The almost sculptural, angular forms of the characters aggressively challenge the two-dimensional quality of the book, and the plays of their shadows en page energizes the background and projects the book-space into an almost theatrical setting.

Rodchenko also designed film posters and used cinematic effects in his own photography, an aspect of his work that was strengthened by his friendship with Vertov and his acquaintance with Kuleshov and Sergei Eisenstein (1891-1948). He also designed books for "Kino-pechat" (The Film Press), which had published "Materializatsiia Fantastiki", and in 1936 collaborated with his wife Stepanova on the cover and layout of a volume on the Soviet cinema, produced by VOKS, the Russian agency for publication and distribution of information on the Soviet Union abroad. In this later book, photographs are printed on the covers and interior in the form of filmstrips. On the front endpaper a portrait of Lenin is repeated several times within a film-strip format over which a red flag has been montaged. A die-cut fold-out photograph of a cinematographer's conference includes a "see-through" opening that reveals a portrait of Stalin from a photograph on the following page. A tissue overlay with a silver-leaf profile of Stalin also contains his pronouncements on the importance of cinema, printed in red. The lightweight paper acts as a recessive foil for the tactile qualities of the silvered illustration and the red typography. The assymetrical placement of typographical chapter headings and photographs en page make this book one of the latest-known examples of an innovative format derived from the Constructivists' experimental approaches.

Nowhere are such techniques more evident than in one of the most extraordinary productions of the 1930s: the publication of English, German, French, and Spanish editions of the periodical "SSSR na stroike" ("USSR in Construction"). Edited by Maxim Gorky (1868-1936) and a collective board, the magazine was organised to present the varied facets of the Soviet Union, covering such topics as the outlying republics, individual industries, and the military. Rodchenko and Stepanova collaborated on the design of several issues between 1933 and 1940. Geometric photo-formulations emphasize their subjects: for example, a triangular photograph shows a horse pulling a tractor, which is aligned against the frame of the hypotenuse, thereby conveying a sense of motion and distance from the photograph onto the page (No. 8, 1936); and a photograph of runners is set in page diagonally, as a visual expression of the subjects' dynamic activity (No. 11-12, 1938). These photographs are accompanied by large-type captions, whose messages are exclamatory and optimistic in the tradition of "LEF" and "Novyi LEF".

Enlarged or telescopic views and unexpected vantage points of photographs that appeared in many of Rodchenko's periodical designs reflect Rodchenko's experiments in photography from the mid-1920s on. Although the stress on so-called "factography" promulgated in the later issues of "Novyi LEF had been extended during the 1930s into official pressure for straightforward reportage, Rodchenko nevertheless continued to produce book designs that portrayed Soviet life through artistic means. Of special note is the exaggerated perspective in his photographs and montages for "Novyi LEF" and "USSR in Construction". Here Rodchenko used worm's-eye and bird's-eye views in order to manipulate the reader's visual experience. By removing the subject from its logical context, Rodchenko focuses attention on the integral formal elements of the image. For example, the repetition of apartment balconies or trees emphasises the intrinsic rhythm of ordinary objects and also suggests the cinematic process. Serial images of this sort — reminiscent of film strips — alternate in Rodchenko's work with close-up views of human objects, observed with the intensity of a "camera-eye" that embody his personal interpretation of the Soviet vision of a future constructed with human resources.

Rodchenko did not suffer the harsh fate encountered by many of his avant-garde compatriots, whose work was condemned outright — or cruelly ignored — for "incomprehensibility to the masses". Because of the clarity of his typographic design, and the factual basis of his photographic experiments, Rodchenko's work was more adaptable than the non-objective art of Tatlin, Malevich (1878-1935), and others, to increasingly stringent official demands for artists to produce "a true historically concrete depiction of reality...combined with the task of ideological transformation and education of the workers in the spirit of Socialism".

Although many of Rodchenko's photomontages manifested suspect experimental or "artistic" aspects, and therefore were not thought suitable for a popular readership in Russia during the 1930s, many of his photographs were suitable for various propagandistic books and journals, notably "USSR in Construction". By 1940, when Rodchenko and Stepanova designed a special issue of "USSR in Construction" devoted to Mayakovsky, Rodchenko's career as a book designer had virtually come to an end. He continued to produce photographs and posters, yet these were far less adventurous and innovative than his earlier works. Ironically, he also returned to painting, the art which he had abandoned in 1921 in favour of industrial design and "Comfut" (Communist-Futurist) publications.

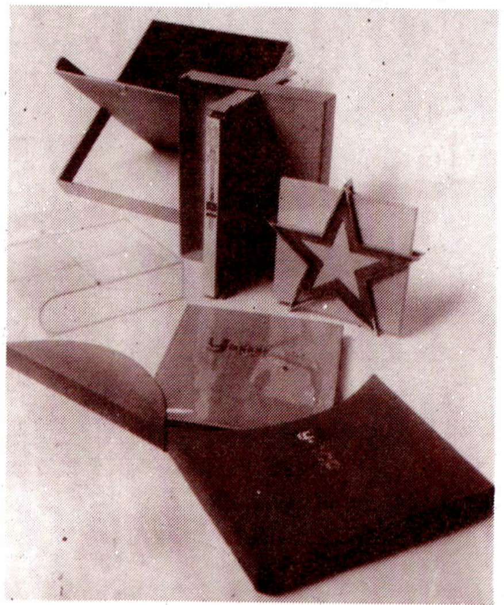

Box and cover for the photo album, "Ten Years of Soviet Uzbekistan", designed with V.F. Stepanova, 1933-35.

Opposite page: Photomontage of Mayakovsky on back cover of "A Conversation with a Tax Inspector about Poetry"

As early as 1923, in the premiere issue of "LEF", Ossip Brik had written: "Rodchenko is patient. He will wait; meanwhile he is doing what he can — he is revolutionising taste, clearing the ground for the future nonaesthetic, but useful material culture." Rodchenko had, indeed, revolutionised taste, guiding it towards more functional, proletarian, and Constructivist concepts. Ultimately, however, reactionary cultural policies and the imposition of Social Realism as the one official style, following government decrees of 1932-34, effectively suppressed Constructivism. Even though he was denied proper credit for having achieved a revolutionary artform, Rodchenko's contribution to twentieth century design remains significant, not only within the context of Soviet design, but as a progenitor of principles which have formed our own artistic heritage in the West today.

а 25 к.

PHOTOGRAPHY VERSUS PAINTING

Ossip Brik

This article first appeared in "Sovetskoi Foto", No. 2, 1926

Ossip Brik (1888-1945), a writer, critic and theoretician, was a leading exponent of Futurism and a founder member of OPOYAZ, the Formalist group. He helped form the LEF group and was a leading supporter of Productivist art.

Photography pushes painting aside. Painting resists and is determined not to capitulate. This is how the battle must be interpreted which started a hundred years ago when the camera was invented and which will only end when photography has finally pushed painting out of the place it held in daily life. The photographers' motto was: precision, speed, cheapness. These were their advantages. Here they could compete with painters. Particularly in the case of portraits. Even the most gifted painter cannot achieve the degree of faithful reproduction of which the camera is capable. Even the quickest painter cannot supply a portrait within minutes. The cheapest painting is more expensive than the most expensive photograph. After portraits landscapes were tackled, reproductions, genre pictures. And all had the same advertisement: precision, speed, cheapness. The painters recognised the danger. The success of photography was enormous. Immediate steps had to be taken. A stronger counter-attack mounted.

Cheapness and speed could hardly be fought. The camera works more cheaply and quickly. Precision can be disputed. So this was where the attack was centred.

Photography is not coloured. Painting is. This means that painting reproduces an object more faithfully and is without rival in this respect.

This is how the painters argue. And the consumer had to be convinced of this. But the painters were wrong and many are still wrong today.

It is true that in life we do see objects in colour. And a painting reproduces these objects by means of colours. But these are different from nature, not identical with her. Painting cannot transpose real colours, it can only copy — more or less approximately — a tint we see in nature. And the problem is not how talented a painter is, but is basic to the very nature of his or her work. The colour media with which a painter works (oil, watercolour, size) have a different effect on our eyes than the rays of light which give diverse colours to objects. However much the painter tries s/he cannot go beyond the narrow limits of the palette. S/he cannot give a picture those colours — either in quality or in quantity — which objects possess in reality.

Photography does not yet reproduce exact colouring, but at least it does not falsify an object by giving it the wrong colours. And this is an advantage not to be underestimated.

The most sensitive and progressive painters have long since grasped that precision of colour reproduction is not at all easy and that the principles of painterly colouring are not identical with those of reality. So they declared: "Precision is not the ultimate aim."

The painter's task certainly does not consist in showing an object as it is but rather in recreating it in a painting according to different, purely painterly laws. What do we care for how an object looks? Let observers and photographers deal with that, we — the painters — make pictures in which nature is not the subject but merely an initial impetus for ideas. The painter not only has the right to change reality, it is virtually his duty to do so; otherwise he is not a painter but a bad copyist — a photographer.

Life cannot be represented in a painting, it would be senseless to imitate it; that means it must be recreated on canvas in a separate, painterly way. This is the idea behind the theories and schools of painting which have emerged since the middle of the 19th century under the names of Impressionism, Cubism, Suprematism and many others. The painters' repudiation of the idea of reproducing nature marked a decisive divide between photography and painting. They had separate tasks which could not be compared. Each fulfills its own task. The photographer captures life and the painter makes pictures. A photograph transmits no colours at all; a painting gives a consciously different, non-real colour to an object. The situation seems clear. But here, in Soviet Russia, an interesting artistic phenomenon can be observed, namely the attempt by the painters to regain lost positions and to strive for the reproduction of reality in line with photography. This is reflected in the activities of the AKhRR (Association of the Visual Artists of Revolutionary Russia) The social roots of this phenomenon are quite obvious: Firstly an immense need for a visual record of the new life. Secondly a lot of painters who abandoned their style because nobody wanted to buy their pictures, and thirdly far less artistically cultured buyers who do not distinguish between an exact reproduction of an object and an approximation. The attempt by the AKhRR to resurrect the so-called painterly realism is completely hopeless. One of the representatives of the AKhRR said in a discussion: "As long as photography is not sufficiently advanced in this country realistic painting is necessary." This "as long as" shows up in a nutshell what the work of the AKhRR means. As long as we do not have enough automobiles we will have to go by horse-drawn carts. But sooner or later we shall go in automobiles.

The photographer captures life and events more cheaply, quickly and precisely than the painter. Herein lies his strength, his enormous social importance. And he is not frightened by any outdated daub.

But the photographers themselves do not realise their social importance. They know they are doing a necessary, important task, but they think they are only artisans, humble workers far removed from artists and painters. The photographer is enormously impressed by the fact that the painter does not work to commission but for himself, that paintings are presented in large exhibitions with varnishing days, catalogues, music, buffet food and speeches, that long essays giving an exact analysis of composition, structure, brushwork and colour scale are written on every picture, every painter, and that such exhibitions are regarded as cultural events. All this confirms him in the idea that painting is true art, photography merely an insignificant craft.

This explains every photographer's

The AKhRR was an abbreviation for "Association of Artists of Revolutionary Russia". Founded in 1922, its aim was to promote realistic art which depicted the everyday life of the proletariat and peasantry. Its members returned to the traditions of the nineteenth century realist painters and declared their opposition to Leftists.

dream to achieve a painterly effect in his photographs. It also explains the attempts to take artistic photographs and to work on them "so that they look like reproductions of paintings".

The photographer does not understand that this chasing after painterly attitudes and the slavish imitation of painting destroys his craft and takes away the forcefulness on which its social importance is based. He moves away from faithful reproduction of nature and submits to aesthetic laws which distort this very nature. The photographer wants to attain the social recognition which the painter enjoys. This is a perfectly normal wish. But it is not fulfilled by the photographer following the painter, but rather by his opposing his own art to that of the painter. If the photographer follows the main principle of his craft, which is the ability to capture nature faithfully, he will as a matter of course create things which will have just as strong an effect on the spectator as the painting of an artist, whoever he may be.

The photographer must show that it is not just life ordered according to aesthetic laws which is impressive, but also vivid, everyday life itself as it is transfixed in a technically perfect photograph.

By battling against the aesthetic distortion of nature the photographer acquires his right to social recognition, and not by painfully and uselessly striving to imitate models alien to photography.

This is not an easy path, but it is the only true one. It is not easy because neither here nor in the West is there even the beginning of a theory of the art of photography, the art of how to make highly accomplished photographs. All that is being written or said on the subject is reduced either to a series of technical tips and prescriptions or to hints on how to achieve painterly effects, how to make a photograph not look like a photograph.

And yet some artists and painters do exist who have abandoned painting in favour of photography; people who understand that photography has its mission, its aims, its own development; there are some among them who have already achieved certain results in this field.

What is needed is that these people somehow exchange their views, tell each other of their experiences, unite their powers in a common effort, a common battle against the painterly element in photography and towards a new theory of the art of photography which is independent of the laws of painting. The experiences of those people who have previously been painters are particularly interesting in this context.

Former popes and monks make the most convinced campaigners against religion. Nobody knows the mysteries of churches and monasteries better than they. The best fighters against painterly aestheticism are former painters. Nobody knows the secrets of artistic creation better. Nobody can expose the falseness of artistic reproduction of reality better. They have consciously moved away from painting, they will consciously fight for photography. One of them is A.M. Rodchenko, once a brilliant painter, today a committed photographer. His photographic works are little known by the general public because they are mainly experimental. The public wants definitely finished products, but for the professional photographers, for those who take an interest in the development of a photographic art, an acquaintance with Rodchenko's results is indispensable.

His main task is to move away from the principles of painterly composition of photographs and to find other, specifically photographic laws for their making and composition. And this must after all interest everybody who does not see photography as a pitiable craft but as a subject of enormous social relevance, called upon to silence painting's chatter about representing life artistically.

PHOTOMONTAGE

Varvara Stepanova

This article, written in 1928, first appeared in "Fotografie", Prague, 1973

A group of artists on the left artistic front has given its attention to the problems of productional art. This shift of interest has dictated a change in the basic method of work, in the use of technique and media to express documentary truth. This had led us to use photography as a viable method of communicating realities.

In photography — more than in other forms of communication — images must transmit the phenomena of the external world. And this places considerable responsibility on the artist. Periodicals, newspapers, book illustrations, posters, and all other types of advertising confront the artist with the urgent problem of how to record the subject in documentary terms. An approximated design cannot fulfill this challenge, this need for documentary truth. The mechanical complexity of the external forms of objects and of our industrial culture forces the artist concerned with production — the Constructivist artist — to move from his imperfect methods of drawing a subject to the application of photography.

And so photomontage was born. Photomontage — the assemblage and combination of expressive elements from individual photographs. In our country the first photomontages were created by the Constructivist A.M. Rodchenko in 1922 as illustrations to I.

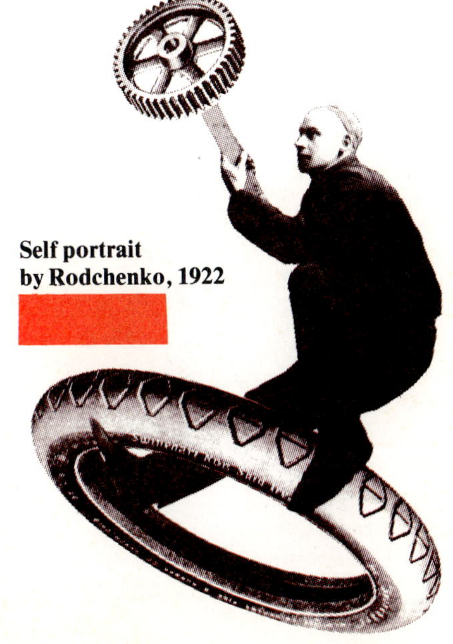

Self portrait by Rodchenko, 1922

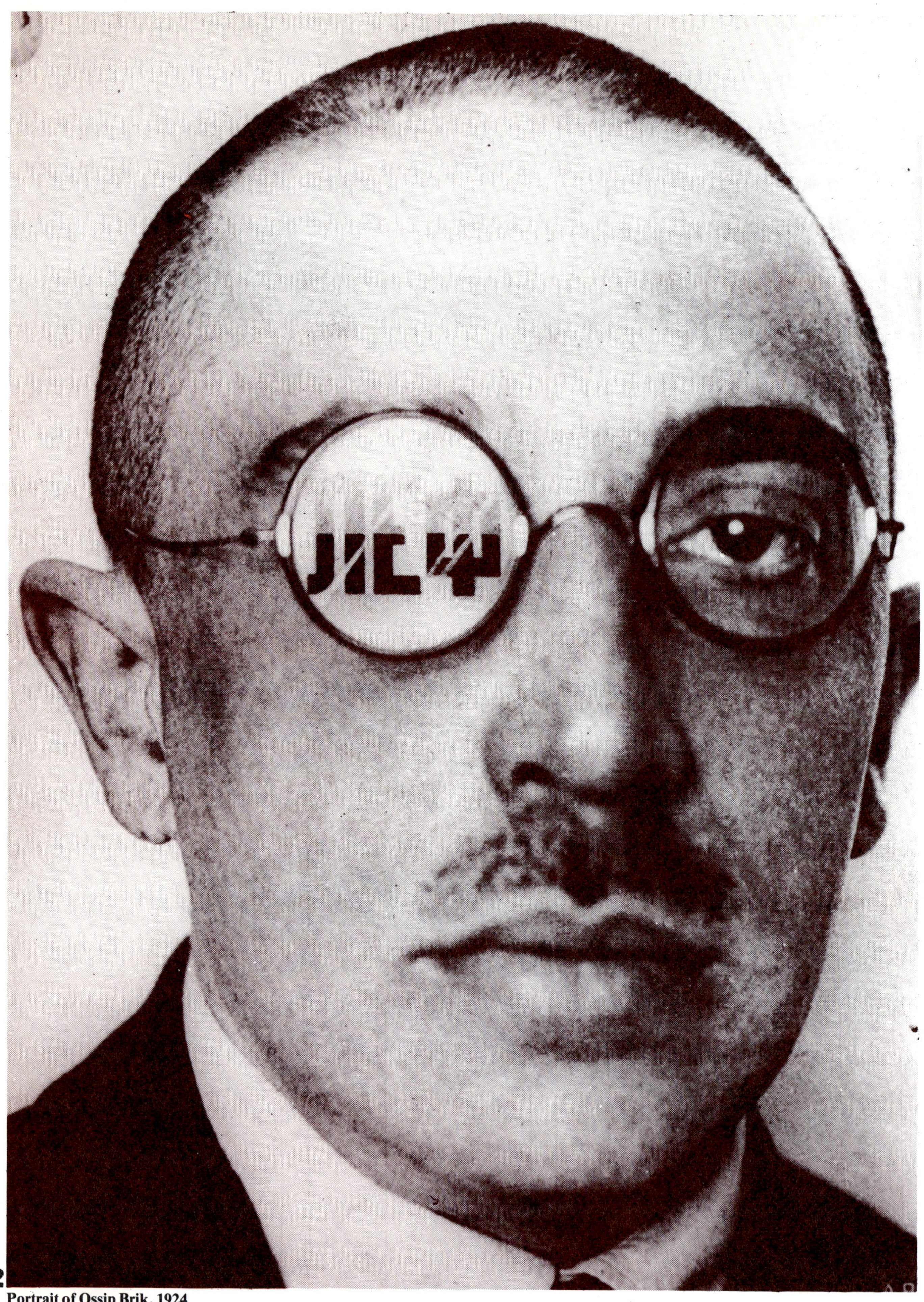

Portrait of Ossip Brik, 1924

A. Aksenov's book "Gerkulesovy stolby" ('The Pillars of Hercules').

The need for documentary truth is characteristic of our era, but it is not confined to mere advertising as some suppose. We now know even poetry needs it. The first great work in photomontage that played a definite and necessary role in our book illustrations, book covers, and posters was V.V. Mayakovsky's book ("About This", 1923) with photomontages by Rodchenko. From that time on, photomontage — as a new art form, replacing drawing — has expanded greatly and permeated the periodical press, propagandist literature, and advertising. Because of its great potential, photomontage is becoming very popular and very necessary. It is catching on quickly in workers' clubs and in schools where photomontage on walls can make ready response to any topic of urgency. In particular, photomontage is used extensively in political campaigns — from anniversary celebrations and parties right down to the decoration of offices and rooms.

All our Soviet publishing houses... have accepted photomontage as one of the most common methods of typographical layout for book covers and posters. Photomontage is found even in film posters. The years 1924-26 witnessed a general upsurge of interest in photomontage on the part of the Soviet press.

Within its short life, photomontage has passed through many phases of development. Its first stage was characterised by the integration of large numbers of photographs into a single composition, which helped bring into relief individual photo-images. Contrasts in photographs of various sizes and, to a lesser extent, the graphic surface itself formed the connective medium. One might say that this kind of montage had the character of a planar montage superimposed on a white paper ground.

The subsequent development of photomontage has confirmed the possibility of using photographs as such. The photograph, the photographic snapshot, is becoming increasingly self-sufficient. [Of the distinguished works of this period one should single out Istoriya VKP (b) History of the All-Union Communist Party (Bolsheviks)], published by the Communist Academy in 1926. This incorporated a poster format with Rodchenko's photomontages, although the individual snapshots are not fragmented and have all the characteristics of a real document. The artist himself must take up photography. He searches for the particular shot that will satisfy his objective but montaging someone else's photographs will not fulfill his needs. Hence, the artist moves from an artistic montage of photographic fragments to his own distinctive shooting of reality.

This was the path of A.M. Rodchenko, the first photomontagist. From 1924, Rodchenko worked with his camera. Instead of the conglomerate photomontage, he now used a montage of individual photographs or a series of individual photographs. The value of the photograph itself came to assume primary importance; the photograph is no longer raw material for montage or for some kind of illustrated composition but has an independent and complete totality.

In the final stage of photomontage we note that virtually every artist who has some connection with the polygraphic industry has equipped himself with a camera. Photography is the only medium that can provide him with the traditional method of drawing while allowing him to fix and record the reality around us.

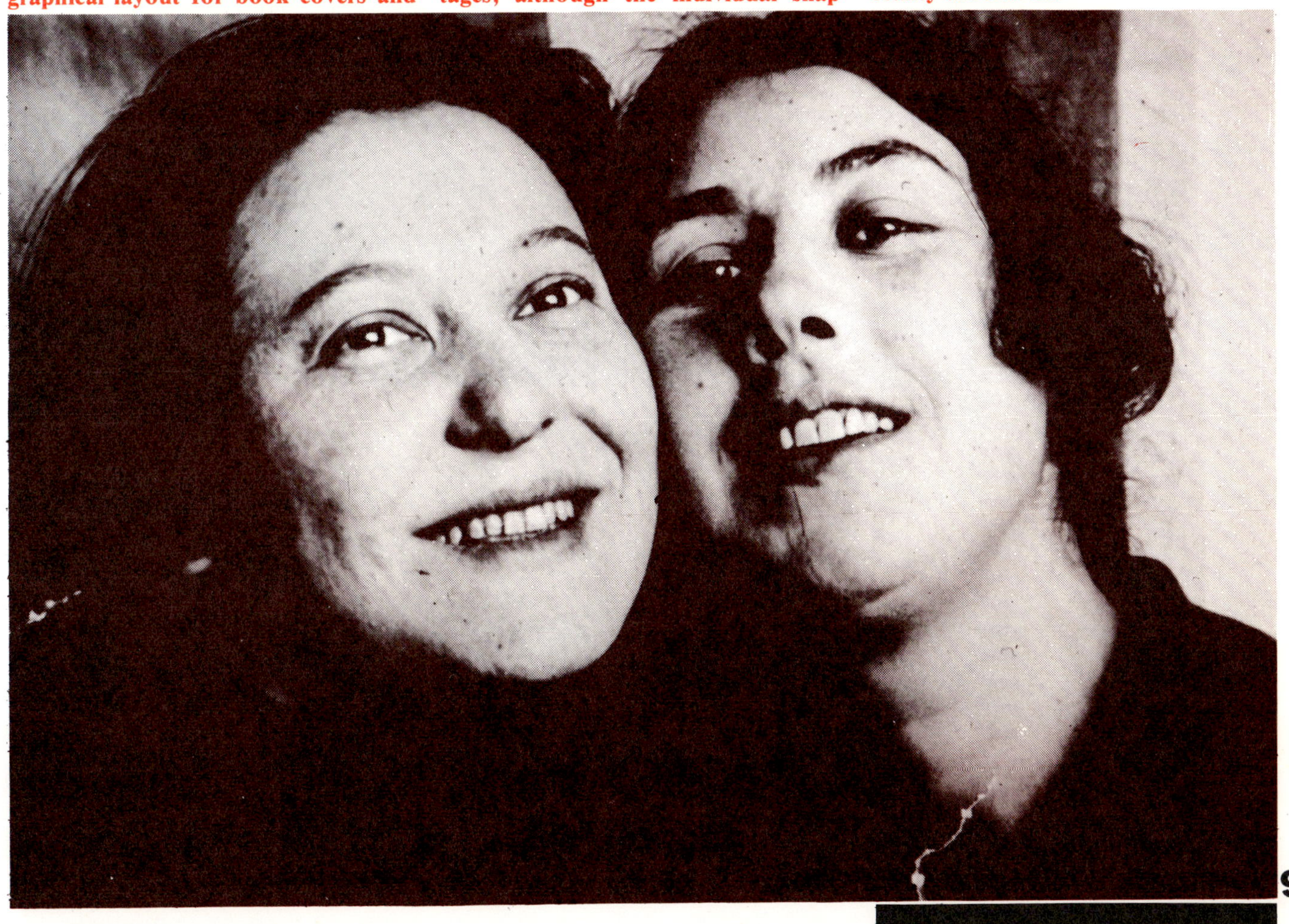

Portrait of V.F. Stepanova and L. Popova, c. 1923

Varvara Fyodorovna Stepanova (1894-1958), was an artist, graphic designer and illustrator. She was married to Alexander Rodchenko.

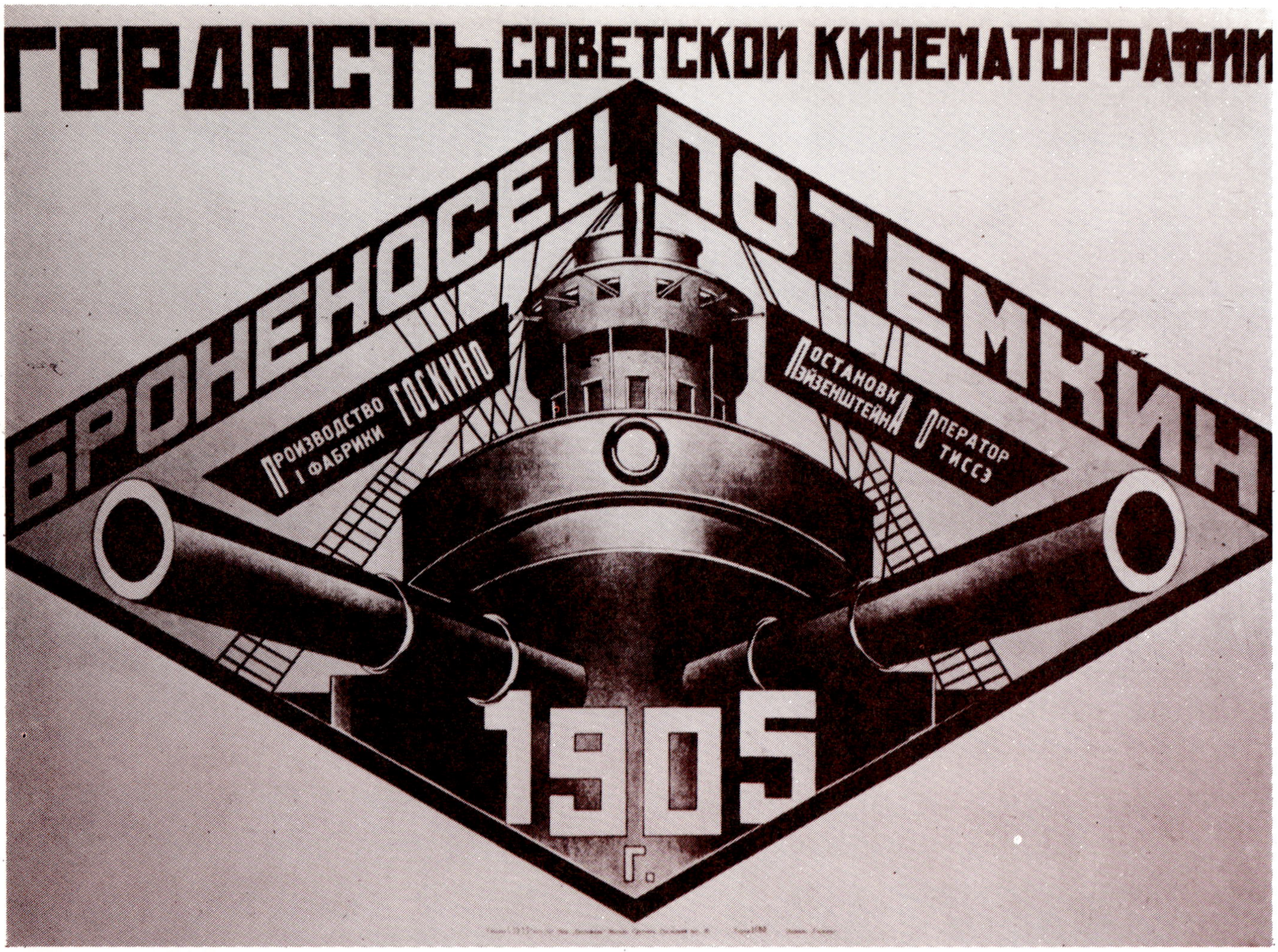

Poster for Dziga Vertov's film, "Kino Glaz" (Cinema Eye), 1923.

Top: Poster for Sergei Eisenstein's film, "Battleship Potemkin", 1925

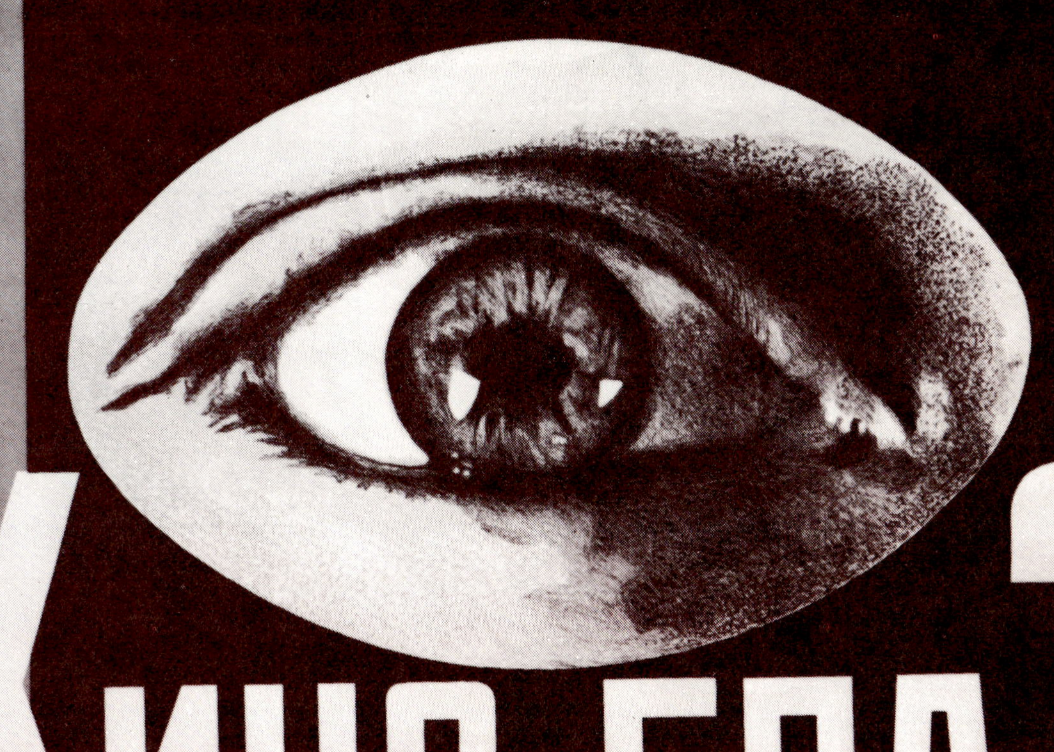

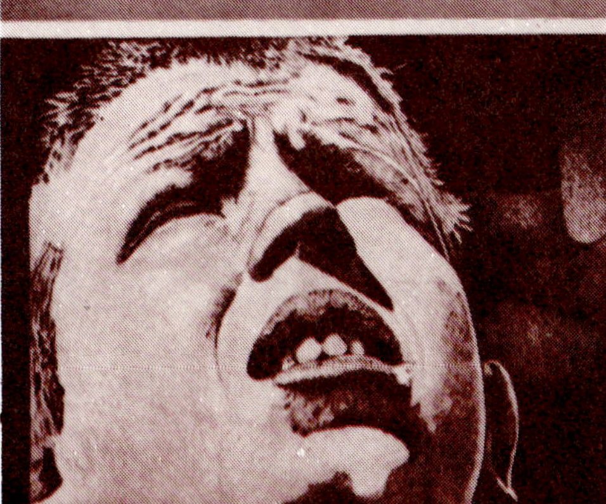

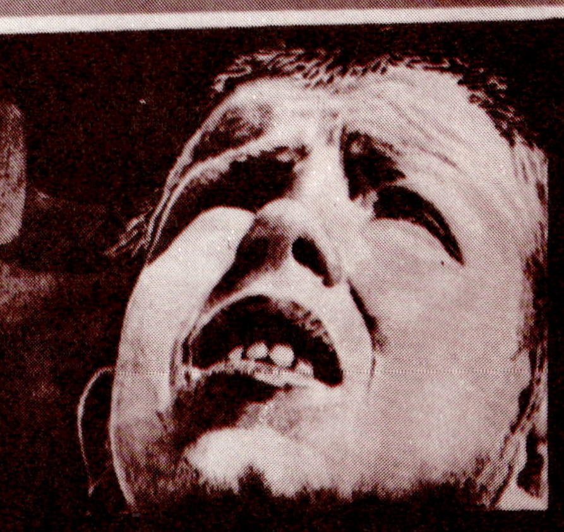

Poster for ''Kino Glaz'', 1924

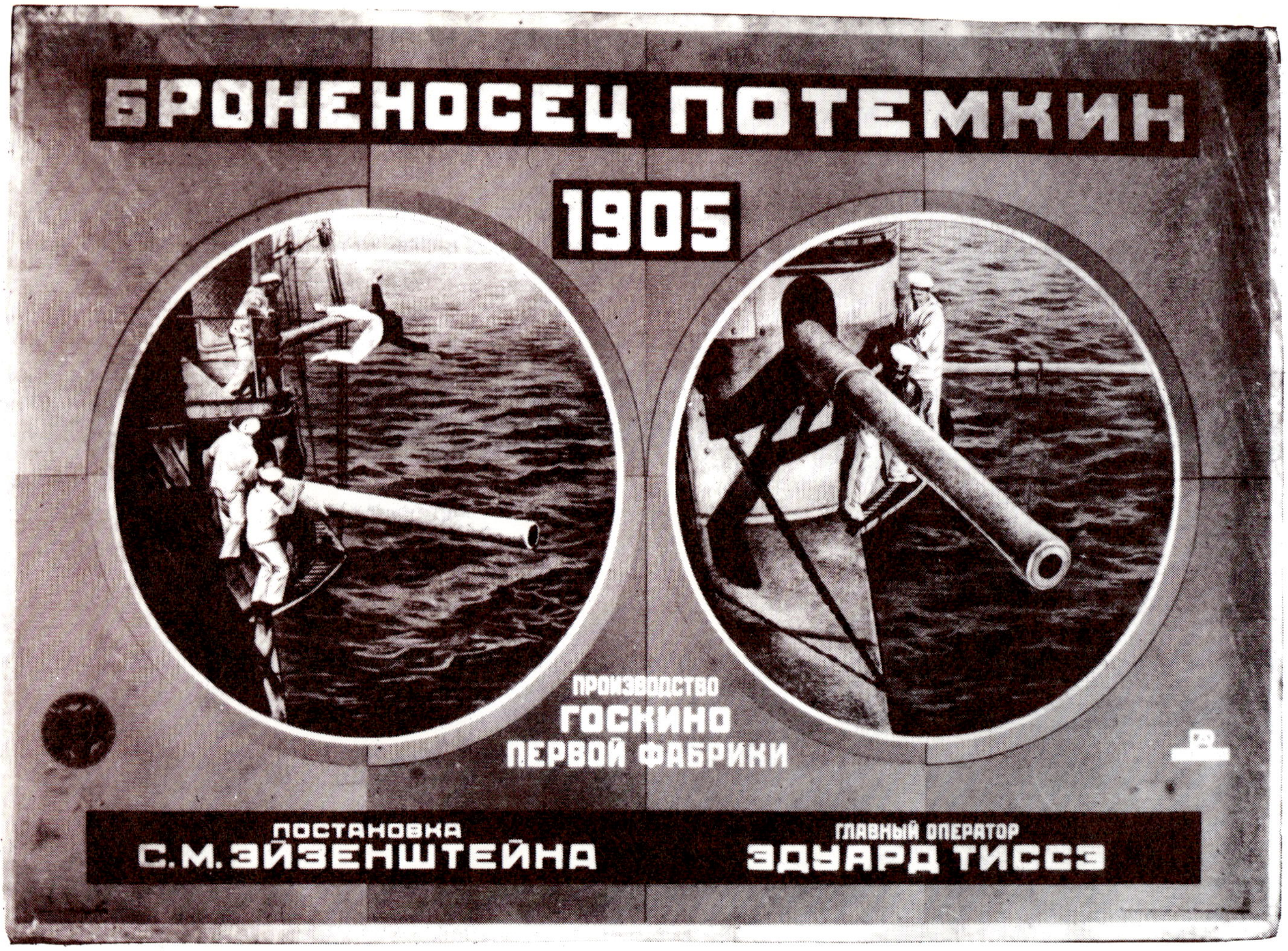

БРОНЕНОСЕЦ ПОТЕМКИН
1905
ПРОИЗВОДСТВО
ГОСКИНО
ПЕРВОЙ ФАБРИКИ
ПОСТАНОВКА
С.М. ЭЙЗЕНШТЕЙНА
ГЛАВНЫЙ ОПЕРАТОР
ЭДУАРД ТИССЭ

Poster for "Battleship Potemkin", 1925

Right: Poster for galoshes, 1923. Text by Mayakovsky written in Persian reads: "Amongst the Eastern peoples the camels wear the best galoshes"

Opposite page: Poster for Dziga Vertov's film, "One Sixth of the World", 1926

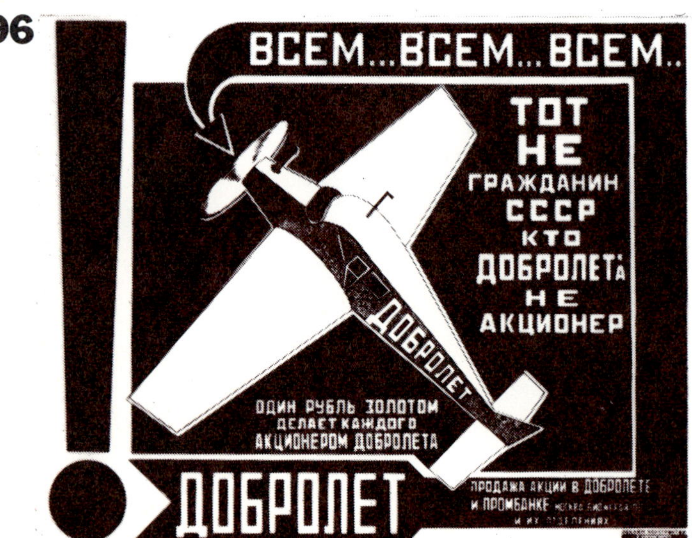

N.E.P. poster to promote the purchase of shares in "Dobrolet" [The State merchant air service], 1923

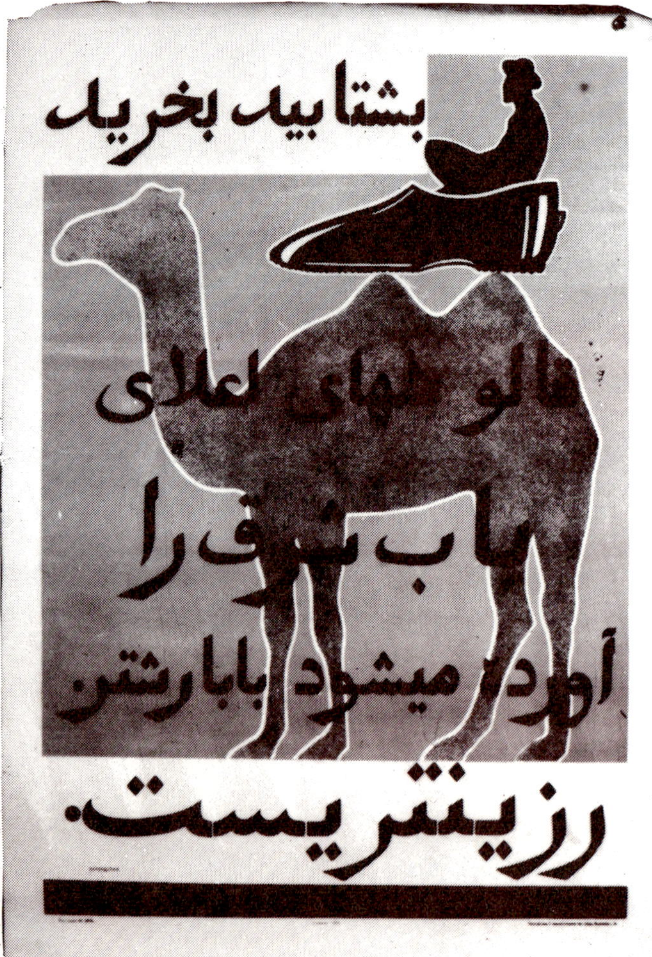

ШЕСТАЯ ЧАСТЬ МИРА

АВТОР-РУКОВОДИТЕЛЬ
ДЗИГА ВЕРТОВ

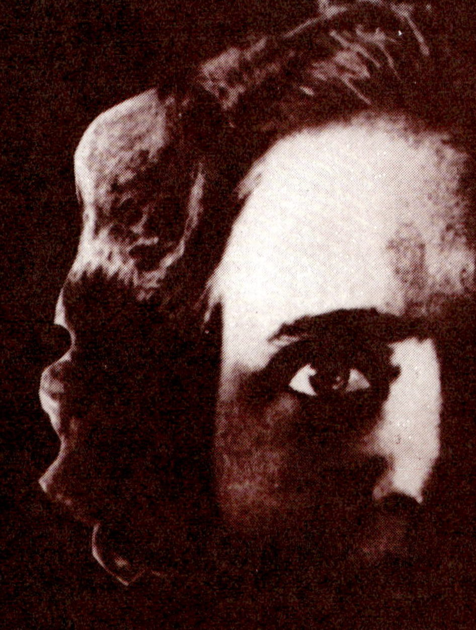

1 выпуск.

ПРОИЗВОДСТВО
ГОСКИНО

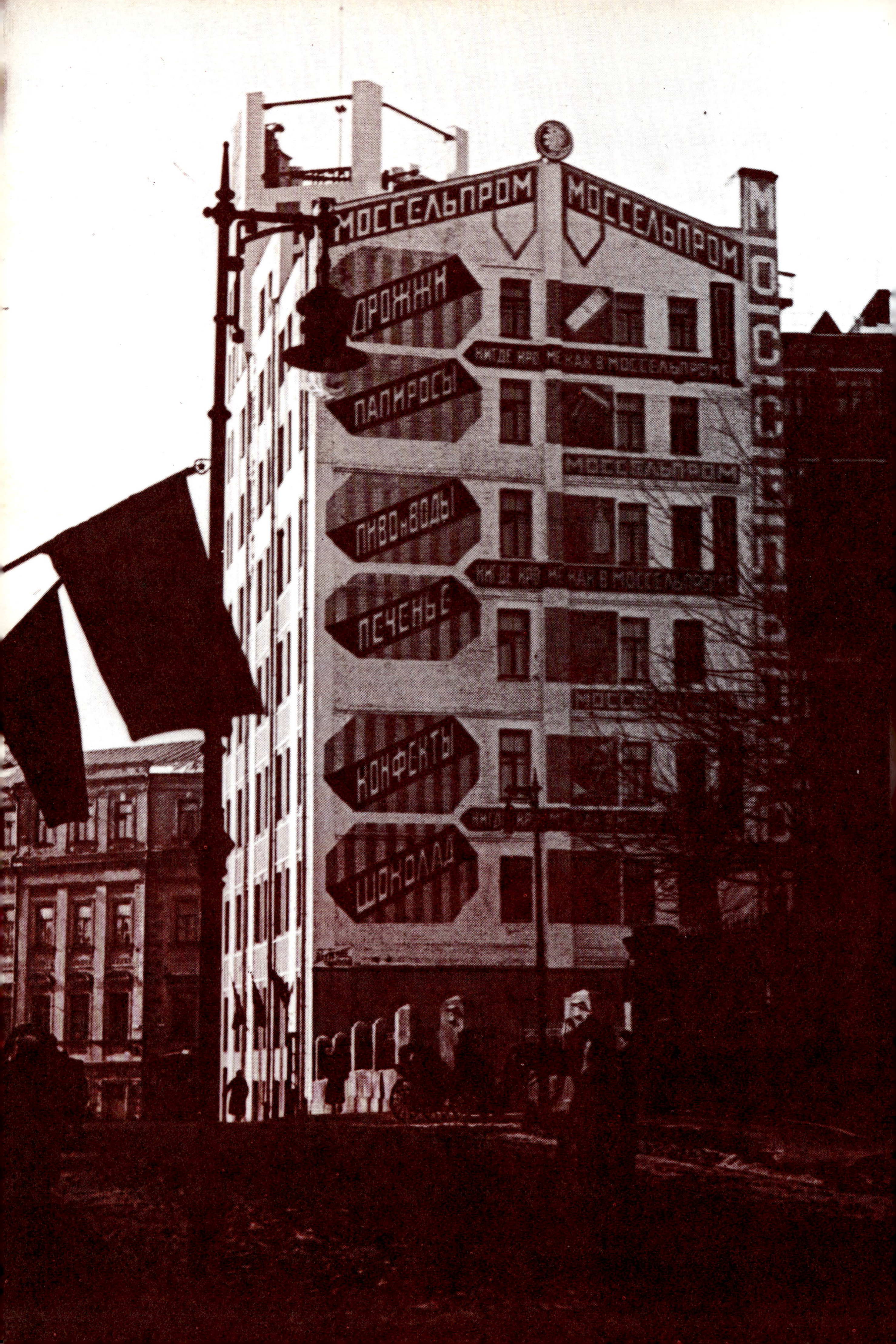

МОССЕЛЬПРОМ
МОССЕЛЬПРОМ
ДРОЖЖИ
НИГДЕ КРОМЕ КАК В МОССЕЛЬПРОМЕ
ПАПИРОСЫ
МОССЕЛЬПРОМ
ПИВО и ВОДЫ
НИГДЕ КРОМЕ КАК В МОССЕЛЬПРОМЕ
ПЕЧЕНЬЕ
КОНФЕКТЫ
ШОКОЛАД

Below: Drawing, writing and dining table designed in Rodchenko's studio at Vkhutemas, c. 1924.

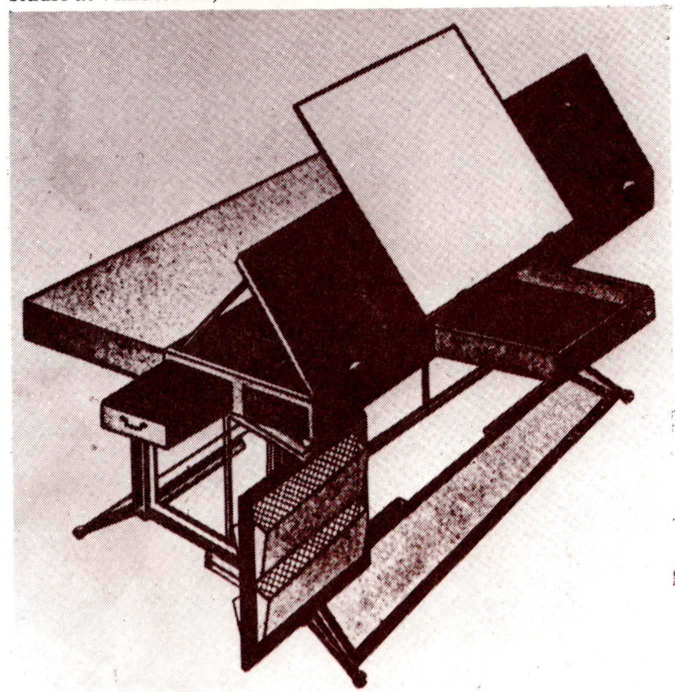

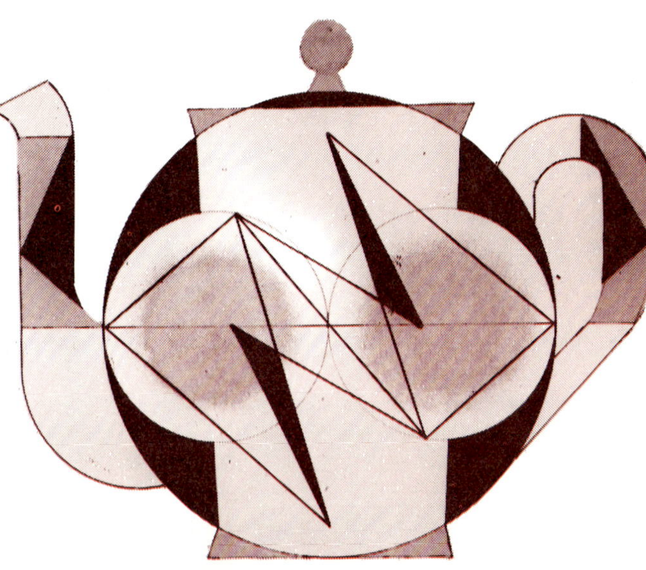

Above: Design for a teapot, 1922

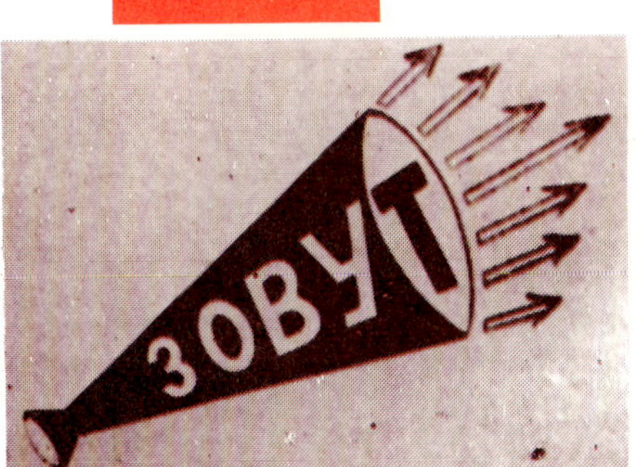

Above: Film title "Zobut" for "Kino Pravda", 1923.

Opposite page: Painted advertisements by Rodchenko on the Mossel'prom store, Moscow. Photograph taken in 1925

Below: Design for film title of Dziga Vertov's newsreel, "Kino Pravda", 1923

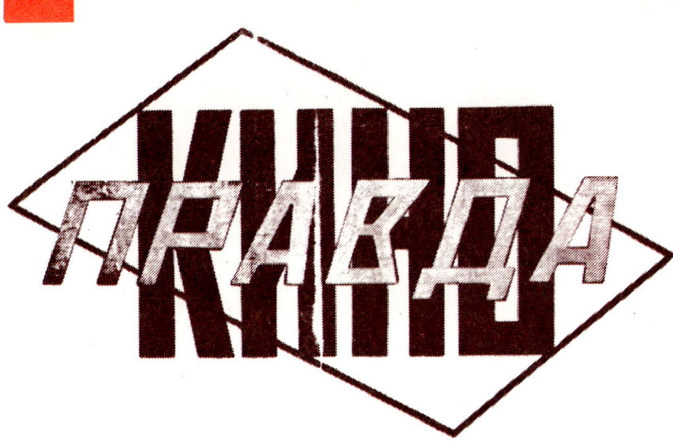

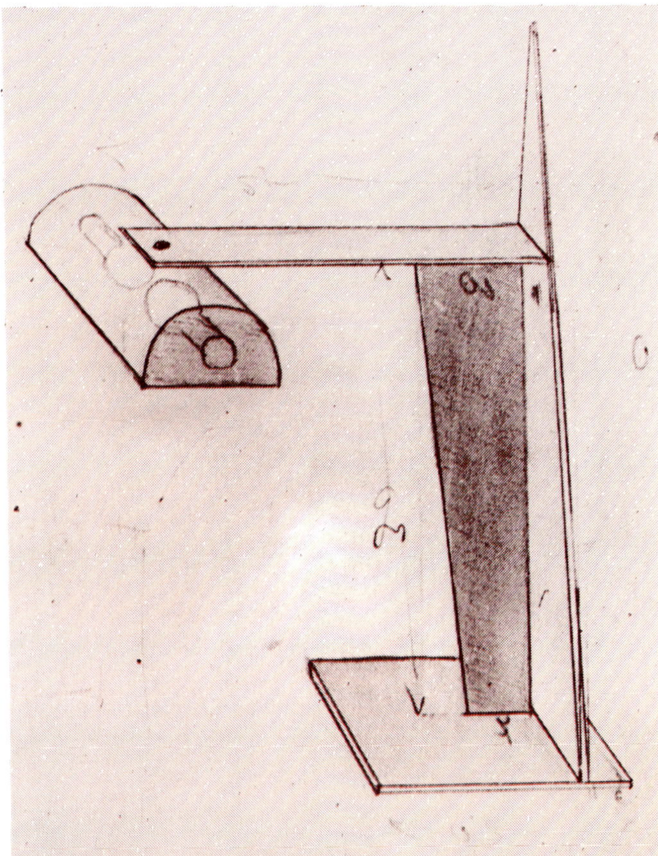

Above: Design for a table lamp, 1929

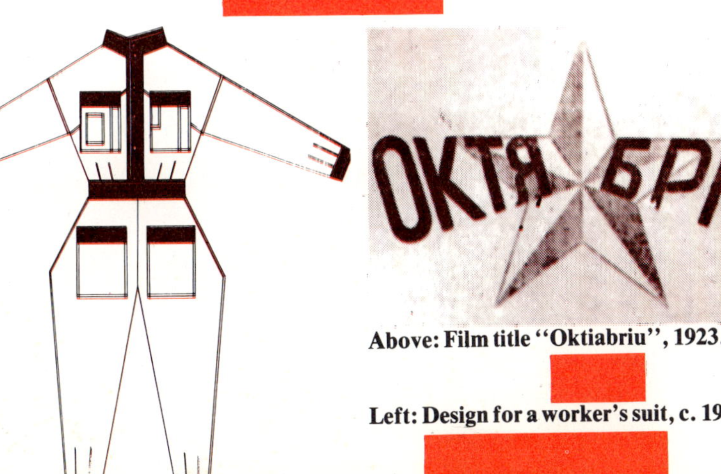

Above: Film title "Oktiabriu", 1923.

Left: Design for a worker's suit, c. 1921

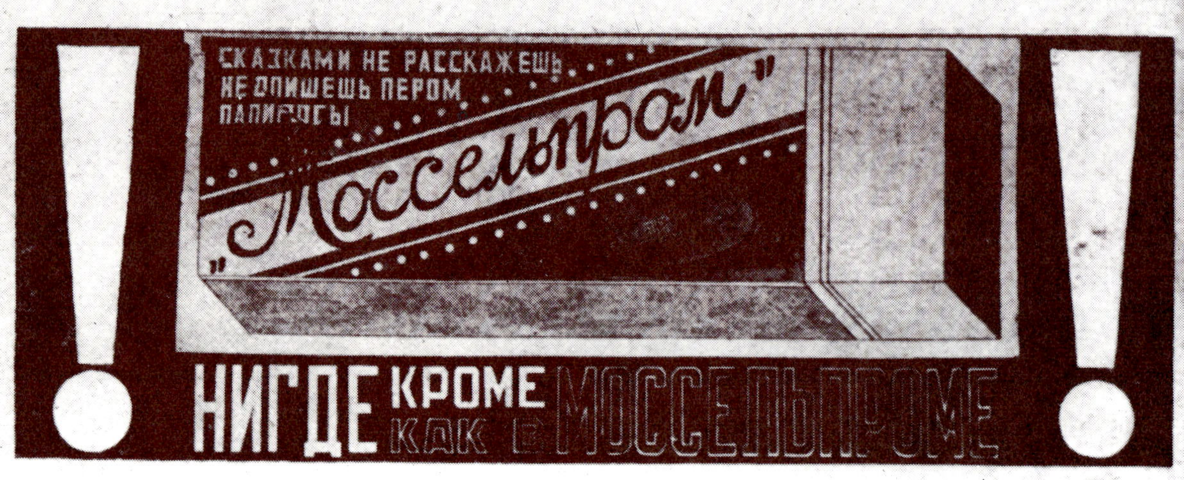

Full-page cigarette advertisement for Mossel'prom, 1923

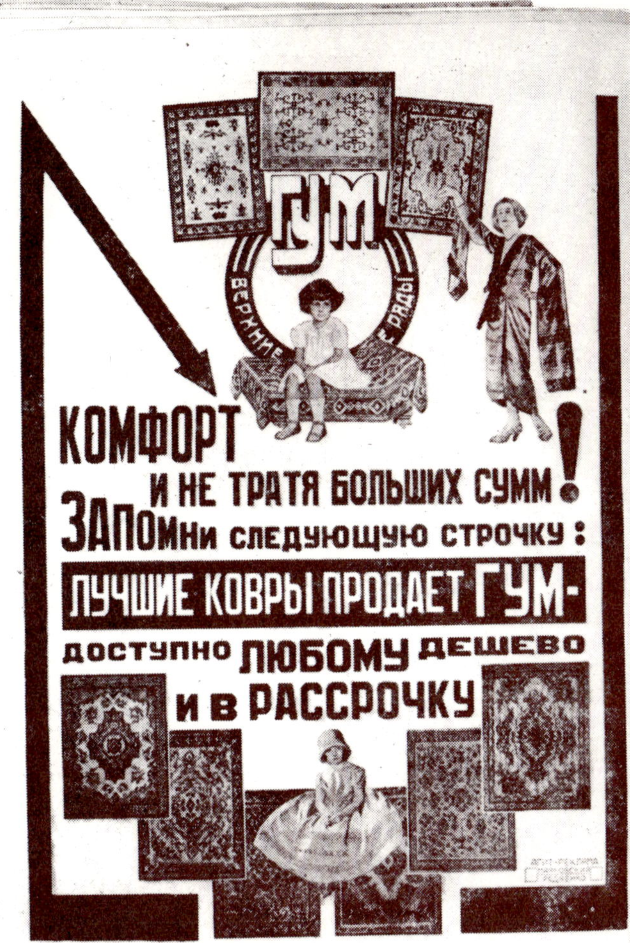

Full-page carpet advertisement for GUM, 1923

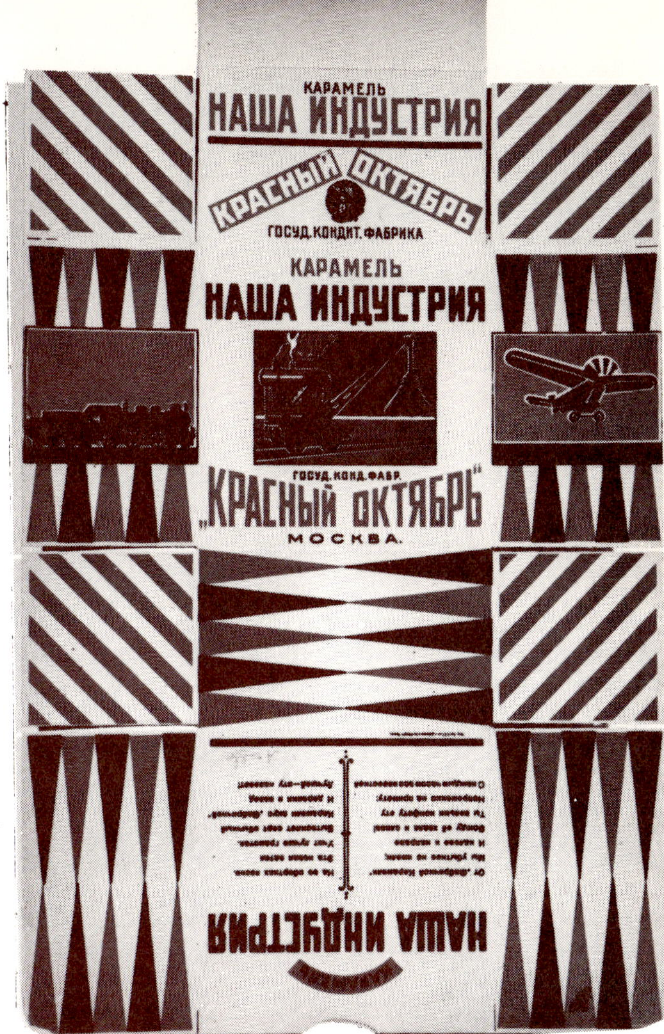

Packet design for "Our Industry" sweets, 1923

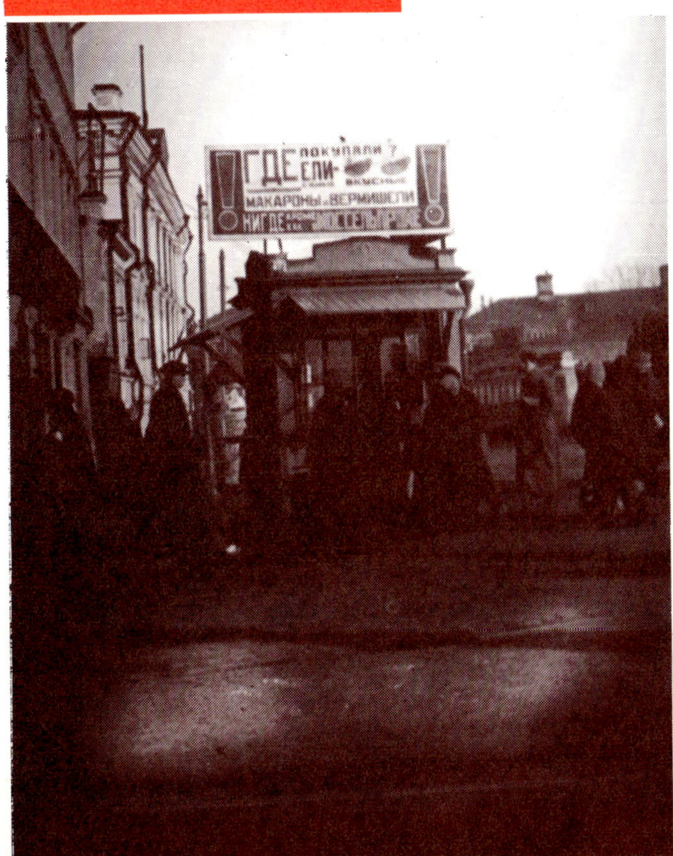

Poster advertising food in Moscow, 1925

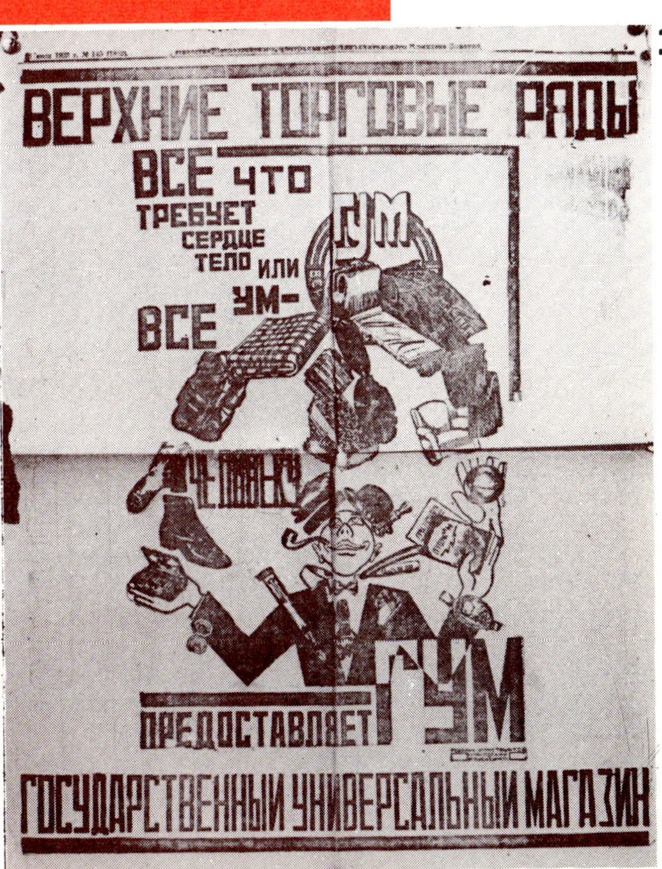

Full-page newspaper advertisement for GUM, 1923

WORKING WITH MAYAKOVSKY

Alexander Rodchenko

These recollections, written in 1940, first appeared in "V Mire Knig", No. 6, Moscow, 1973

I exhibited 57 works at the XIX State Exhibition. The exhibition was opened on 2 October 1920 in the "Salon" on Bolshaya Dmitrovka. Mayakovsky was at the Private View.

From that time I began to visit Vodopyany Lane, near Myasnitsky Gates; my friendship with Aseev and others also dates from then.

From the first Mayakovsky called me "old man" and I him Volodya, although he was only two years younger than me.

1923. Volodya wrote "About This"; he read the poem for the first time in Vodopyany. The room was light blue and five-sided bounded by a stove, a table, Lilya Yurevna Brik's bed and a piano. As always there was a great crowd of people and some sat on the bed. I made a notice, "No sitting on the bed". I also made a lamp for the light out of plywood and tracing paper.

A.V. Lunacharsky and N.N. Aseev were there. I don't remember who the others were.

Volodya read with unusual animation.

After the reading there was a short discussion. Anatoly Vasilevich commented approvingly.

I began work on the photomontages for "About This".

I did the cover and eleven montages.

I then began work on advertisements for the society "Dobrolet". I made badges and a poster. "Anyone who is not a shareholder of Dobrolet is not a citizen of the USSR."

One evening we were sitting in a small café on Tver Boulevard — Volodya, Aseev and I. They began to mock the Dobrolet verses, knowing that I had done the poster but supposing that the lines had been written by some bad poet. I took offence and upbraided them for not writing texts for advertisements and said that I had written that text and that it had turned out that way by chance; I had simply shortened and rearranged the text I had been given.

I do not know if this spurred Volodya on or if he was already thinking of doing it and therefore noticed the poster but shortly afterwards he asked me to do the posters for GUM: "English Tobacco", "Moser Clocks", "Dutch Butter" and others.

Our joint work began. This was our stamp: "Advertisement Constructors Mayakovsky-Rodchenko". We both worked with great enthusiasm.

The texts, written by Mayakovsky on various scraps of paper, were noted down at the piano in Vodopyany Lane.

I would go to the Brik's apartment on Vodopyany Lane, (it was a few doors away from my home), and wait while Volodya wrote the texts, standing at the piano. Sometimes he would walk about the room beating out the rhythm with his hand and then again lean on the piano and begin to write.

Arriving from dachas, towns and villages
No need to wear out shoes searching — immediately
In GUM you'll find everything, precisely what you want quickly and cheaply.

....Work on Soviet advertisements — the creation of our new type of advertisement — went at full speed.

Volodya would write the texts in the evening and would take or deliver orders during the day.

I and two students from Vkhutemas would draw until morning.

This was stock-jobbing, not done for money but in order to promote the new advertising everywhere.

All Moscow was decorated with our work.... The Mossel'prom signs. All our kiosks... The Gosizdat (State Publishing House) signs — "black, red, gold"... Rezinotrest, GUM, Ogonek, Chaiupravlenie.

We made about 50 posters, 100 signs, wrapping papers, dust covers, wrappers, illuminated signs, advertisement drums, illustrations in magazines and papers.

Our work over several years on this would alone fill a book.

In the evening Volodya himself would draw illustrations and posters for advertisements.

Here is a note:

"Rodchenko,
Come round at once with a drawing pen, without delay. V. Mayakovsky."

I go and it turns out he needs to write a text or draw something. He did not like squaring up and measuring, he liked to do everything by hand, to draw everything straight off with a pencil, afterwards to outline everything in ink and then paint it.

It obviously came to him easily and he worked with pleasure. It was a relaxation for him and he became jovial and easy-going. Volodya had a very serious attitude to the work on the Soviet advertisements. He even compiled a price list of every advertisement in the Union, these were ratified, and a tariff was set on everything in them: text, design, artistic realisation. I made an album of our works to show to clients.

In the morning he would go and take orders, note down the print run and thematic specifications. Often there was a large quantity of accounts, of boring books, which he would read and then write down the numbers, themes, etc.

I would arrive at 7 or 8 in the evening. Sometimes he finished writing the texts while I was there, sometimes they would already be ready. With the text would be a drawing, he could not help doing one, although each time he would say "I drew this but of course you don't need it; I did it just to make it clear."

After I had the measurements and titles of the works, I would go home and at once get down to sketching. The boys, students from Vkhutemas, would come and having set everything up in my studio, set to realising the designs. I made the sketches, oversaw their realisation, executed the crucial bits myself and established the proportions.

Sometimes we worked until dawn. At 11 in the morning I would take the posters to Volodya or he would call for them. In the evenings the same thing would be repeated plus sometimes a revision. The number of works was always increasing and I collapsed from lack of sleep, fell ill with anaemia and nervous disorder; it was necessary to cut down on work. Volodya enlisted Levin and Lavinsky and began to do a lot himself.

Wherever he was — in institutions, publishing houses, editorial offices, — he always drew in friends to help.

Volodya usually delivered the work. I was with him on only two occasions. Firstly because I did not know how to take or deliver orders and secondly because I didn't have the time...

I remember him delivering the posters to Chaiupravlenie. One of the posters "stuck", i.e. raised a doubt in someone. Someone said, "Why doesn't the Chinaman have a plait?" On the poster the Chinaman was drawn full face,

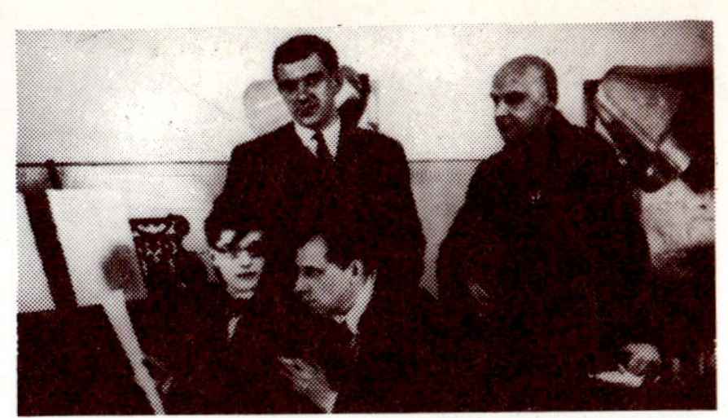

Left to right: Shostakovich, Mayakovsky, Meyerhold and Rodchenko. Photo by A. Temerina, 1929

walking with raised arms and in his hands tea — chests in an arc in the air from one hand to the other. The Chinaman looks up at them as if he were juggling. Volodya answered: "There is a plait but it is at the back, if you turned his back, the plait would be visible. Another man asked "Why do the chests stay in the air like that? It's unreal." Volodya, "The Chinese are famous as jugglers". Laughter. The poster was accepted.

Working on photomontage I began to be interested in photography — something would have to be copied, enlarged, made smaller.... I bought myself two cameras — one 134 x 18 with a triple extension and a Dagor lense and the second a camera for reproductions and a pocket-size Kodak.

I did not have an enlarger and I constantly looked for one in shops. In the shop BEKA on Tver Street I found a suitable enlarger — I put my hand in my pocket — there were 180 roubles and I needed 210. Having hastily paid 180, I said that I would bring the rest immediately. I ran out of the shop and wondered, walking along the street whom I could borrow the money from. From the Briks, from Volodya? But they would only be home in the evening.

And suddenly there he was right in front of me. "What's up old man? You look very crushed." Immediately without explaining anything I said, "I need three chervontsy!"[1] Volodya gave them to me and I hastily hurried back away from him. I went into the shop, paid and dragged the lamp home, resting on the windowsills of shops.

Sadly I thought: "You idiot not to have taken more from Volodya for a cab..."

I dragged it up to the 8th floor. An agitated Varvara Stepanova met me. It seemed Volodya had telephoned to ask what was wrong with me. He had met me in a state, I had asked for three chervontsy and, having taken them, run off somewhere without saying anything...

It is only a small incident but it has stayed in my memory... Volodya's attitude to his friends was very sensitive, attentive.

Volodya was always looking, observing. He was interested in everyone. He did not retire into his shell. There was always a crowd of people at his house and the crowd always grew, it didn't diminish.

On my first visit to Mayakovsky's dacha in Pushkino in 1924 I had a small camera 6.5 x 9 called a Tenax with a 4.5 lens.

It was Sunday. Varvara and I arrived at 12.00. Thirty people were already there. Tea and other things were on the table.

There were people in the rooms, on the balcony, in the garden — everywhere. Some were playing gorodky,[2] amongst them was Volodya, who hit with his left hand.

The whole crowd sat down to lunch. While the ice cream was being eaten Volodya went out. I also left to have a look at the garden and take photographs. I caught sight of the ice cream man on the back porch. Spooning out several portions and placing them on the floor. Scottie (the dog), it seemed, adored ice cream and Volodya was making sure that the ice cream man actually gave Scottie the ice cream that had been ordered for him in full.

Of course I arranged everyone in a group: Mayakovsky, Lavinsky, Grinkrug, Shklovsky, Levidov, Aseev, Levin, Kol'tsov. I put one chair on top of another and poured magnesium into the ashtray. I put out the light and focused by the light of a match. Everyone sat in darkness. I lit up and took my place by Mayakovsky. While the ribbon was burning, Volodya said "Mind you don't burn the house down!" There was a terrible noise — and the photograph was taken.

The room was full of smoke, the windows open.

Once Volodya asked me to print a photograph of Lenin. I had reproductions of photographs in the Lenin Museum. I brought him two, one of Lenin's head photographed while he was speaking and the other of Lenin standing on a lorry on Red Square. He hung them in his room on Lubyanka Street. The photograph of Lenin talking hung on the wall until the last.

Obviously once when he was looking at this photograph he wrote the poem, "A Conversation with Comrade Lenin".

1925 Volodya was a member of the International Paris Exhibition of 1925 Committee at the Academy of Arts and at his request I was commissioned to produce the "Workers' Club" as an exhibit for the International Exhibition in Paris. I also had to make copies of the posters we had done for Mossel'prom, GUM and Rezinotrest.

They accepted the club, both model and designs but due to a shortage of time, they decided it should be completed in Paris. So I had to go to Paris.

In addition to the Club I had to see to the painting of the inside and outside of our stand, devise a layout for the three rooms in the Grand Palais and see to its execution and the distribution of the exhibits.

In short, there was much to be done.

I left in March 1925 and set to work. Every day in Paris from ten until six I was at our stand and at home as well I sketched the designs. I worked for three months.

Volodya also arrived in Paris, he was about to go to America. We spent several evenings together. He showed me Paris, introduced me to Elsa Triolet-Aragon and Léger.

Ehrenburg also showed me Paris. I already knew his wife, L. Koznitseva from Moscow. She had studied under me in Vkhutemas.

The Ehrenburgs sometimes asked "Why is art necessary?' because I always said that when I saw only art and no technology.

At that time I only acknowledged technology.

Volodya soon left for America. It seems he wasn't at the opening of the exhibition.

Unexpectedly we were assigned three rooms in the Grand Palais. We did not have the money to set them up and didn't even know if we had enough exhibits. The Grand Palais had already been in use for a long time housing exhibitions and therefore the walls were dirty, tatty, with holes where nails had been and in the floor as well. The light from above came through dirty window panes.

One problem came up: how to set it all up cheaply, quickly and originally.

This is what I thought up: light shelves of plywood, walls papered and then painted and the floor... the floor coloured with a mixture of soot and glue. I put screens on their sides and painted them — grey, white, red. There was no inscription proclaiming USSR or the colour red to be seen as you entered from rooms belonging to other countries, Poland for example but as you moved across the room you were enveloped more and more in red and then saw the fiery inscription USSR where you had entered.

Well visitors carried the black floor and its black soot into other stands on to light blue and gold carpets... There were complaints but that did not help, we pleaded that we had no money. Finally they laid down strips of carpet for us at their own expense.

Volodya and I were awarded a silver medal for the advertisements and I was also given two medals for the theatre and the interior. We would have received the gold medals but at that time France's relationship with USSR was not very good and she did not encourage agit-prop.

I put a large number of books and magazines in the Workers' Club. Every day the public stole them and we silently replaced them. The Committee pointed out to us that we had few guards and therefore people stole things. But we asked what we could do, we were poor. Then they gave us an "agent".

...An order came from Comrade Krasin that all of us, workers on the stand, who had come from Moscow, should be properly dressed.

Our Government Commissar, Pyotr Semeonovich Kogan bought a top hat for the opening of our stand and the opening of the exhibition. It lay in a wonderful hatbox. But the opening was postponed and in the meanwhile Kogan's children jumped from a chair on to the hat and put it away again in the box. When it was time to go to the opening the top hat now had the appearance of an ordinary hat. But Pyotr Semeonovich did not lose his head and never put it on but always carried it in his hand.

Stepanova and I were invited to a reading of the "Bedbug". I don't remember who was there but I think it was on Taganka.

I remember in particular how Mayakovsky began the reading of the "Bedbug". It was so unexpected and so original...

The rehearsals were already in progress and for the first parts set in the present day Kukryniksy had made the designs. But for the future, set in 1979, designs had not been made at all.

But Volodya, apparently, persuaded Meyerhold and asked me to design it. I quickly devised a scheme and while his assistants built it I hurriedly made designs for the costumes, there were a great many of them.

Meyerhold did everything himself and therefore he liked young unknown artists, whom he could lead.

But he knew that this was not the way to handle me and gave me complete freedom of action and did not cross me in anything. Only, during the last days when construction was brought out of the studio and was housed temporarily in the auditorium, he stated that it was very gloomy and that it wouldn't do. When some of the finished costumes were shown on the set he declared that they would not fit in at all.

But I observed calmly: Let's see it all on the set this evening and then we can argue about this and decide it.

The workers began to mount the set and, having arranged everything, I went home to lunch. A rehearsal with set and costumes was set for that evening.

I arrived late on purpose and when I walked into the hall the rehearsal was already in progress. Volodya was the first to come up to me, he shook my hand and said "Thank-you" and that he was very pleased with everything.

I remarked gloomily that Meyerhold wasn't satisfied.

Volodya said that, on the contrary, he was delighted.

Meyerhold also congratulated me as if nothing had happened earlier that day.

14 April 1930... I had been in the planetarium, where I was organising an anti-religious exhibition, since morning. Varvara telephoned me and said "Volodya has shot himself".

— What, is he...?

— Yes, dead.

It was strange and absurd — were we guilty of it?

Perhaps, partly, we were

But he was so strong!

And he suddenly crashed down, as if struck by lightning.

But how could this be?

And still fleetingly, "perhaps not completely... perhaps there's still hope..."

But when I went into the dining room and saw the people, the faces and that strange silence...

Hey!
Gentlemen!
Conivers at
sacrilege
butchery
crime —
most awful of all;
have you seen
my face
when
I'm
absolutely calm?[3]

...He lay in his tiny room, covered with a blanket, slightly turned to the wall.

Slightly turned away from everyone, so strangely silent. And this arrested time... And this dead calm.

I took five photographs and went home burdened by that dead silence.

Days of sorrow began... everyone wanted portraits. A terrible mood, to sit here in a darkroom with Mayakovsky continually appearing on a plain piece of paper in front of you.

It was brutal... but for him, necessary.

Varvara laid out the "Literaturnaya Gazeta" dedicated to the memory of the great proletarian poet.

And the last lay-out was completed, it showed the grave in the Union of Writers on Povarskaya.

But here not without a struggle; I fought with flowers...

They wanted to heap him with flowers, they brought more and more... Suddenly everyone began to bring flowers — all the organisations, editorial offices, printing houses....

I wanted to preserve a certain severity, a hatred of vulgarity.

I was continually taking flowers away...

Again I felt this emptiness in the guard of honour, the absurdity of death...

But how many people — the people kept on walking by, there was no end to them...

This was the man who said he "drew no response from crowds".

....When they brought the coffin, the police could not hold back the crowd, people broke through from side streets the whole time and continually upset the proceedings.

They hung up flags and Mayakovsky's verses on the buildings.

If Volodya had seen that, he would have understood that he was not alone, that he had a response, that he was loved, that he was needed.

But he swayed slowly on the lorry, on the iron platform built to Tatlin's design by Vkhutemas students, dully rumbling and severe.

He floated past slowly
The most alive of the living
The energetic commander of the new revolutionary front of the arts.
The great proletarian poet of the USSR.

1. One "chervonets" is a ten rouble note.
2. Gorodky is a game played with skittles.
3. From "A Cloud in Trousers" a poem written by Mayakovsky in 1913.

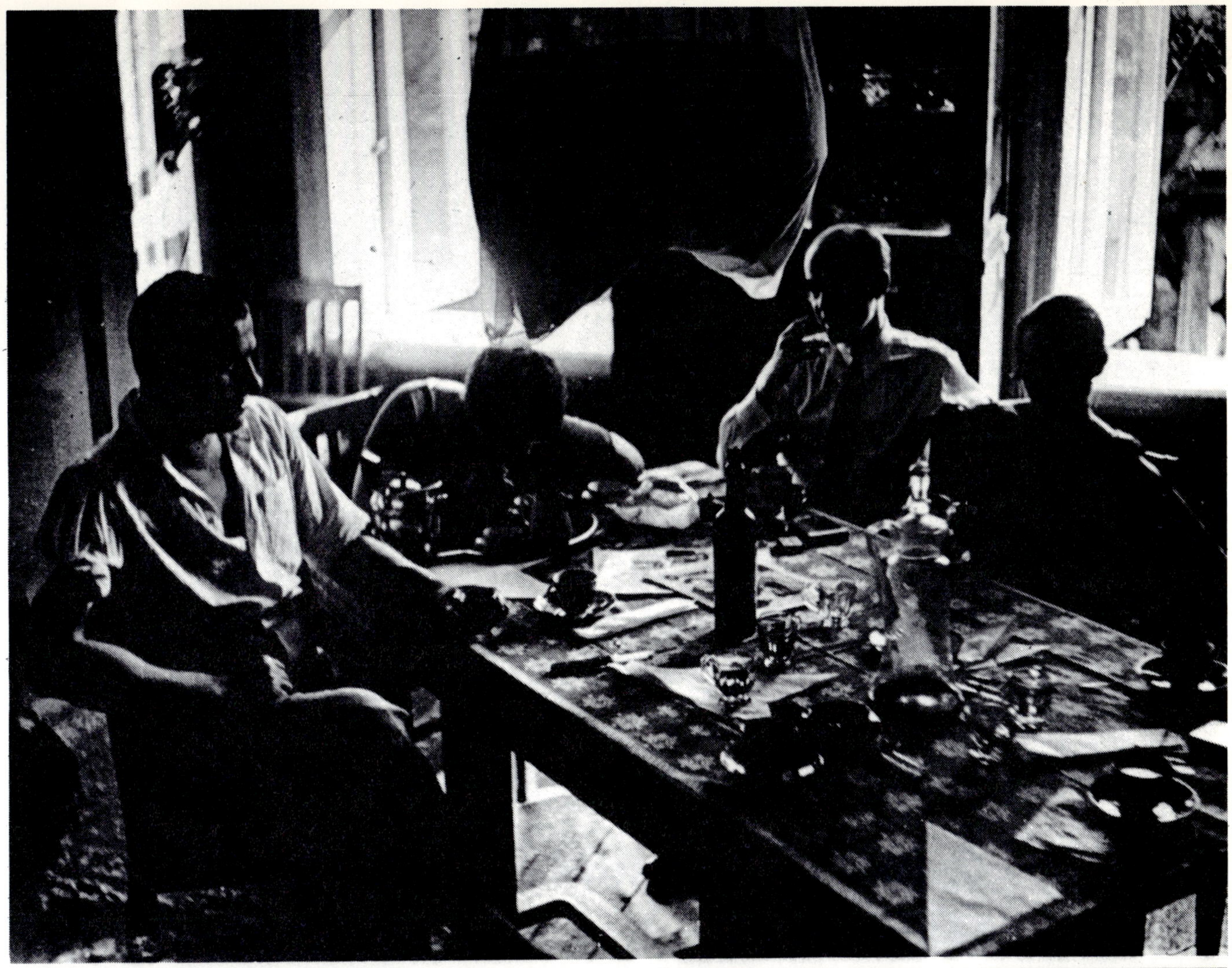

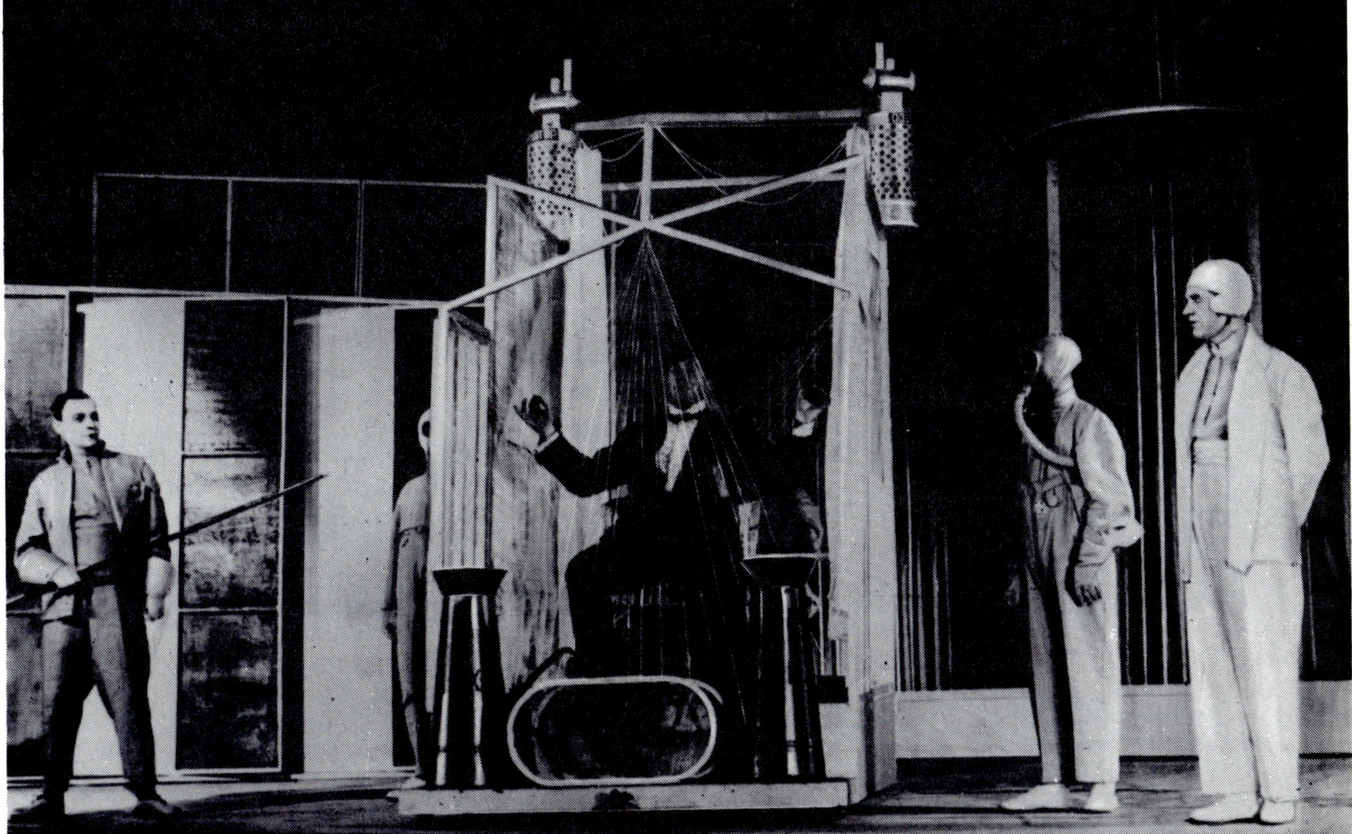

Stage set for Mayakovsky's "Bed Bug", 1929.

Top: Mayakovsky's flat, 1928; Left to right: Mayakovsky, Stepanova, El Lissitzky and Lilya Brik

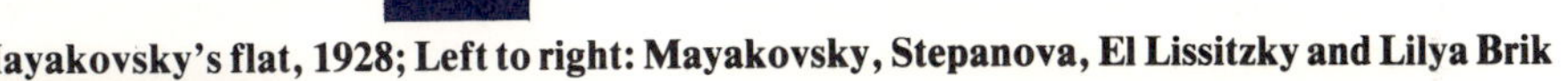

VKHUTEMAS

Svomas, Vkhutemas, Vkhutein: In 1918 the old Moscow Institute of Painting, Sculpture and Architecture and the Stroganov Art School were integrated to form the Free Art Studios (Svomas). This was renamed Vkhutemas (Higher State Art-Technical Studios) in 1920 and then Vkhutein (Higher State Art-Technical Institute) in 1926. Vkhutein was disbanded in 1930.

Recollections by one of Rodchenko's former students, G. D. Chichagova

Galina Chichagova (1891-1957) studied at Vkhutemas under Rodchenko and later graduated in typography. Worked with her sister Olga, and illustrated a large number of children's books. She contributed to the International Press Exhibition in Cologne, 1928.

In August 1920 my sister, Olga Chichagova, and I decided to join the art studios.

It was rumoured that the so-called "Free Studios" were being reorganised, that the teaching programme was being revised and that new, progressive artists were being drawn in as teachers.

By 1 September the lists of students who had been accepted had been put up in the hall of the new building of the former Stroganov Institute on Rozhdestvenka (now Zhdanov Street).

It turned out that I had been accepted and had been put in Rodchenko's studio. I had not heard of that artist's name nor of the names of the other teachers, for example, Drevin, Udal'tsova, Baranov-Rossiné, etc.

My sister, Olga Dmitrievna, had been enrolled in Baranov-Rossiné's studio.

There were eight studios or disciplines on the foundation course and a different teacher taught painting in each discipline. For example, Discipline No 5: Construction. Teacher: Alexander Mikhailovich Rodchenko. Problems of this discipline: the clear definition of form, precisely placed on a plane or in space.

As so, the first lesson. A man walked into the studio, he looked from his appearance like a combination of pilot and motorist. He was wearing a beige jacket of military cut, Gallifet-breeches of a grey-green colour, on his feet were black boots with grey leggings. On his head was a black cap with a huge, shiny, leather peak. His face was very pale and had regular features, his lips stood out by their brightness from the pallor of his face. The shining eyes were dark, outlined with thick eyelashes.

I immediately saw that this was a new type of man, a special one. His way of talking and his behaviour towards us was not that of a professor. Having examined us (there were twenty of us), without any preamble, he silently set about composing a still life out of the things he had brought. We saw that these things echoed the colour of his clothes: beige and black, shiny and black, matt, several shades of grey

None of the things that everyone was used to see in contemporary painting was in that still life. There were no bright materials, ruddy apples, richly and ornamentally decorated plates. Here is a description of what he made: in the background was a piece of plywood, a little distance away was a black, lacquered square. To the right a bent figure cut out of aluminium. Here stood a rolled up piece of white paper. To the left near the front was a grey photographic developing tray shot with blue and in the foreground a glass ball frosted on the inside.

The still life stood on a tall, wooden stand at eyelevel.

Rodchenko's apartment consisted of two rooms. The first room was small with windows looking onto a narrow street. The second room was very big and had windows overlooking Volkhonka. The apartment was evidently an official one since Rodchenko was chairman of the purchasing commission of pictures by contemporary artists for museums in Moscow and its periphery. The big room, it seems, was intended for meetings of the commission and served at the same time as his studio.

I remember on one of the visits, Rodchenko, perhaps at our request, showed us some of his works. But we saw a great number of his works at the exhibition I would like to describe here.

The exhibition of painting in 1920 in which Rodchenko, Kandinsky and other artists participated, was put on in the exhibition rooms on Dmitrovka (now Pushkin Street). Few of us had had the opportunity to see painting like Rodchenko's before. We had all visited the Morozovsky Museum on Prechistenka, (now Kropotin), and the Shukinsky Museum in Maly Znamensky Lane, (now Gritsevets Street) many times. We loved Cézanne and Picasso very much but were little acquainted with abstract painting. The room, where Rodchenko's pictures were, was very big. Strength and deeply considered problems could be felt in these huge, coloured, pictorial canvases. It was especially interesting for us, the students from discipline 5, to look at his painting. We could already understand his works since we worked in that plane. Nobody who has not seen Rodchenko's paintings of that period can imagine how strong the impression they create is. There was something thrilling, staggering in them.

We all went to that exhibition together and of course to the private view. I do not remember if the catalogue was printed. On the wall by the entrance into Rodchenko's room hung a typewritten text setting forth Rodchenko's views on contemporary and future art. On the last day of the exhibition Rodchenko took down that text from the wall and gave it to me. I quote some of his declarations:
"The art of the future will not be the cosy decoration of family homes. It will be just as indispensable as 48-storey skyscrapers, mighty bridges, wireless, aeronautics and submarines which will be transformed into art."

These words, which seemed in those times unrealisable even in the distant future, have been confirmed in our time. In actual fact artists now work successfully on the construction of the indispensable things around us. They work in industry; in a very short while not one thing will be produced without the participation of artists of the stamp of Rodchenko.

WORKING WITH RODCHENKO

Zakhar Bykov (born 1898), graduated from the Stroganov Institute in 1917. Studied at Vkutemas 1923-28. For eight years he directed work in industry and then worked for the Arts Committee of the Academy of Architecture, USSR. Rector of the Moscow Higher Institute of Industrial Art, (formerly the Stroganov Institute), since 1955. Correspondent member of the Academy of Architecture of the USSR, Honoured Worker for the Arts, RSFSR. Professor.

Recollections by Zakhar Nikolaevich Bykov

I had taken seven courses in metalwork at the Stroganov Institute before I went to Vkhutemas. From 1918-21 I was in the Red Army and was demobilised "to complete his studies", as it was put in my papers, at Vkhutemas.

At Vkhutemas I met my old friends from the Stroganov Institute, N. Prusakov, L. Zharova, K. Kozlova, N. Alexandrov, P. Glushkov, A. Naumov, P. Zhukov and others.

We applied to the board of Vkhutemas, (to P. Novitsky), for permission to work independently and to set up a studio "without a supervisor". This they allowed us to do. There were ten people in our group and we were assigned a huge room on the top floor overlooking Rozhdestvenka Street as a studio. We worked together amicably and enthusiastically. We made up a large library using our own books, picked up quite good props and invited in a model.

During the day we painted, drew, built things and in the evenings sitting around the stove we would read and argue a lot about art.

In 1923 N. Prusakov and L. Zharova transferred to the textile department, K. Kozlova and A. Naumov to the fine art department and the others to the department of graphic design. As a metalworker and a Stroganov engraver I transferred to A.M. Rodchenko's studio. He was at that time the head of the metal-working department and already had a group of eight men under him. I immediately "found myself" in his studio. Being a metal-worker I had mastered all the skills: assembly, relief work, engraving, filigree work, soldering, beating and other techniques. In the Stroganov I had studied drawing, watercolour painting, modelling and composition but having had the training had found no creative outlet.

What should one do in a new Soviet VUZ? (Institute of Higher Education) Where should I direct my skill? In which field should I work?

I had not yet worked this all out clearly for myself and the simple wish to do everything in a new way was not enough. For me and all the group, Professor Rodchenko was the man who taught us to understand the contemporary situation in a creative and concrete way. He indicated and revealed anew our place in production art. As a man with advanced ideas and creative ability in many fields, he taught us a lot.

I formed a close relationship with Alexander Mikhailovich from the very beginning. I spent a lot of time in his studio. He acquainted us with the programmes, lectures and notes that had been drawn up. It was while we were still students that Rodchenko recruited me and two of his pupils, Prokhor Zhigunov and Nikolai Sobolev, to do the artwork on the advertisements which he and Mayakovsky produced.

The work was organised in this way. In the evenings after studying we three would usually go with Rodchenko to his apartment. He would ring up Vladimir Mayakovsky who would read out the text of the new poster. Rodchenko would write down the text and in front of us immediately and very quickly sketch outlines in black, blue and red crayons on paper, usually squared, from the pile that always lay on his desk. He drew them straight off without making any corrections. Very occasionally if the first draft did not please him he would make a second and sometimes a third. I still have some of these drafts. On the reverse side of the drawing he immediately wrote the name of the person who should realise it. Explanations and remarks about colours were given verbally. I worked with Rodchenko on advertisements, dustcovers, labels and posters for several years and learnt a great deal.

I still have drafts for the following posters:

1. All that we have left from the old world are the cigarettes "Ira".
2. All smokers everywhere always prefer "Red Star".
3. Don't tell fairytales, a pen will never describe "Mossel'prom" cigarettes.
4. There never have been such good dummies, suck them 'till you're old.
5. Margarine — attention of the working masses — three times cheaper than butter, more nutritious than other fats.
6. Down with incoherent drunkards. Drink Kayl'bakhovsky beer, drink the beer with the double gold label.
7. Every spice you need from mustard to pickles.
8. Stop! Are you getting hungry? Call in for three minutes — we'll send a twelve course meal for supper.

And others, in all 11 posters.

Alexander Rodchenko would give us paper and materials and having received our brief late in the evening we would leave. We would work through the night and deliver the completed posters by morning.

All the works would be rolled up. Rodchenko would carry them off to Mayakovsky and they would be printed that same day. The whole time we were working there was almost never an alteration or correction. I still remember how Rodchenko could always work at speed, with interest, purposefully, in step with life.

This is what I tell my own pupils about in the Department of Design (established in 1945 at the Stroganov Institute).

ANALYTICAL SEQUENCES

Hubertus Gassner is a critic and art historian resident in Hamburg. He has been involved in the organisation of a number of exhibitions of 1920s Soviet art in Germany and is at present preparing an exhibition of work by Gustav Klutsis to be held in Frankfurt and Oxford.

Alexander Rodchenko's photographic method by Hubertus Gassner

Rodchenko developed from painter to photographer in sudden jumps, yet so consistently that this development can be seen as an example of the fusion of external and internal factors which can govern an artist's work. So the change in Rodchenko's choice of medium is determined as much by the discussion among Constructivists and theoreticians of Productivist art about an art which would be at once avant-garde and socially engaged as by the inner logic of his own artistic development.

Rodchenko's monochrome pictures of 1921 were thought by the contemporary art critic N. Tarabukin to be the ultimate paintings. He thought they were the last flash of light from a dying "Fine Art" and signified the inevitable dialectic abolition of its autonomous power by so-called Productivist art. "Utilitarian-reproductive art" (Arvatov) is seen as part of this Productivist art as much as the construction of real objects for daily use. It is discussed in a book by Tarabukin, published in 1925, called "Art of Today" in which he deals with the design of posters, popular prints, advertisements, books, book-covers and periodicals from a Productivist point of view. In a separate section he discusses the "aims of the reform of photography", saying that this reform entails the abandonment of the naturalistic reproduction of reality, so that stereotyped copying is superseded by an artistic interpretation of reality which is achieved by a process of deformation in the photograph. The manipulation of negatives, positives and of lenses as well as changes of focus and angles are seen as ways of "photographic reform". This reform "is not just an artistic experiment by enthusiasts — as are the experiments in the field of 'fine' art — but is closely connected with the vital tasks of agitational art, that is with the typical manifestations of contemporary artistic culture".

Revolutionary developments in film had already been discussed earlier by the Constructivists, and agitational aims and formal experimentation are even more closely bound up with this medium than with photography. In 1922 Dziga Vertov published the manifesto "We" in "Kinofot", the polemical periodical of Productivist cinematography edited by A. Gan, and headed it with a constructivist drawing by Rodchenko of 1915. The manifesto already touches on all the main issues which were to occupy Soviet avant-garde photography in the '20s. Vertov defines film as "movement art". Its central aim is the organisation of the movement of objects in space.

The impetus which Rodchenko's geometric drawings had on Vertov's art of moving film was not just one-sided; it had repercussions on Rodchenko's own work. He changes his tools: compasses and ruler give way to scissors, the movement of objects is organised in photomontages rather than in abstract constructional drawings. Two of his first photomontages are published in 1922 in the same periodical, "Kinofot", and betray the direct influence of Vertov's manifesto printed two numbers previously.

For Vertov as for Rodchenko the movement of objects which is the specific subject of photography and film could not be reconciled with the interpretation of human psychology as shown in the theatre. The Constructivist artists were not interested in man's emotional upheavals but in his eccentric movements in space. Their fascination with mechanics degrades man to an imperfect machine. "We sometimes exclude man as the subject of film because he is incapable of being guided by his own movements" declared Vertov in his manifesto, and continued: "Our path goes from the wallowing bourgeois via the poetry of machines to the perfect electrical man".

For the Constructivists of that time the incarnation of this future mechanised man was Charlie Chaplin (see Lev Kuleshov on Chaplin). Rodchenko admired the mechanical precision of the movements of Chaplin's body which were adapted to the movements of objects in his films. This "master of detail" as Rodchenko called him "takes up objects, throws them into confusion and then demonstrates their nature by the way he moves himself, by behaving in a confused way". By abandoning the flowing movement of the human body in favour of an edited sequence of partial movements the body comes to resemble the moving parts of an instrument and more generally the technical world of machines. There are two ways to achieve this aim: in the first case the technical world enters man's inner nature, virtually invades him, as in

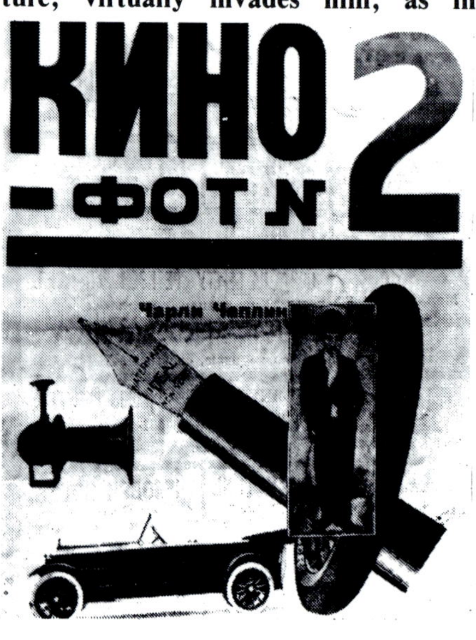

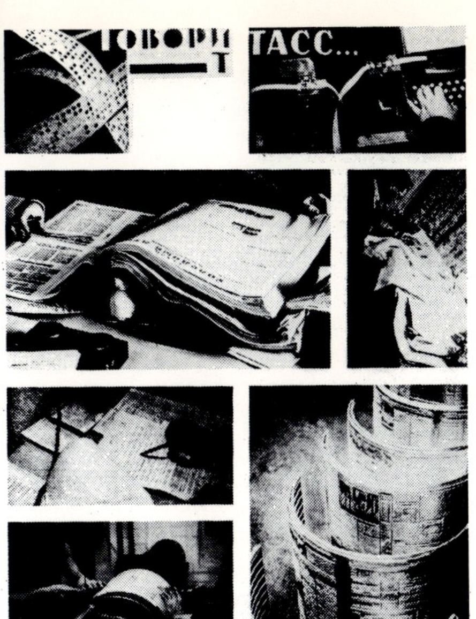

"Tass Speaks...", from the periodical "30 Days", 1929

Chaplin's expressive movements, in Rodchenko's drawings of machine-like human figures of 1919, or in the ten variations on the Chaplin theme which Rodchenko's wife, V. Stepanova, made for his Chaplin manifesto of 1922. Photomontage in which cut-out fragments are reassembled continues this process. In the second case the camera and the person photographed keep their distance. The camera circles round its subject and — by using various angles and focuses — dissects it into a series of separate views which, because they are all different, produce a full image of the subject when taken together, even if they do not add up to a unified image in themselves.

Rodchenko's photographic method is characterised entirely by this second, analytical, approach to the reality which lies before the camera. This is already seen in his first photographs. In his memoirs, "Work with Mayakovsky", he says: "In 1924 I took six photographs of Mayakovsky:

1. Waist-length portrait, with a cigarette (American focus)
2. With a hat, down to the knees
3. With a hat, full-length, showing his hands
4. Head, full-face
5. Sitting, down to the knees
6. Standing, full-length

So the six variant portraits of the man who was then the most famous Soviet poet are not the outcome of different situations — which would have given a narrative character to the sequence — but solely of changes in camera focus. The background behind Mayakovsky remains empty, non-spatial and flat; the figure's sculptural form is clearly set off from it in the various versions.

By excluding all details and descriptive hints of specific circumstances from the subject of the photograph Rodchenko — in a manner typical of the Constructivists — reduces objects to their assumed essence which he believed to lie in their constructional organisation. For him the basic constructional element is the line. Just as the Constructivists Lissitzky and Moholy-Nagy used light in their art to show movement which for them was the substance of all phenomena, so Rodchenko and his pupils used lines. Like his paintings, graphic works and three-dimensional objects, his photographs are linear constructions, now made by means of light and shade, contours of objects, rectangular frame, figures, background and surface contrasts which together create a complex, taut web of interrelations.

In the six Mayakovsky portraits he still uses these formal devices relatively sparingly, even though Constructivist ideas are already behind them. Compared with Moholy-Nagy's striking contemporary portrait photography of the poet which is taken obliquely from below and uses strong shadows, leaving two thirds of the face in the dark, Rodchenko's well-lit frontal and three-quarter views seem almost classical. But there is a development within the series. Mayakovsky's seated figure is put full-length in the centre of the picture and fills it. This photograph is carefully arranged, down to the last details: the slightly oblique position of the parts of the body corresponds to the cross of lines on the back wall, the hand holding the cigarette is at right angles to the hand holding the hat — so that the cross-shape is repeated on different axes — one shoe is shown from the side, the other from the front, and both are the same distance from the front and back of the narrow pictorial space. Yet the pose does not seem stiff and artificial, the relaxed posture and the piercing eyes looking out from under the shaven head create a balance to the formal construction. This photograph belongs to the fine tradition of individual portrait studies by the artist/photographers of the nineteenth century; it is reminiscent of Nadar's and Carjat's photographs of Baudelaire. As in their case the friendship between photographer and sitter has made it possible to achieve a successful synthesis of the various features making up the facial expression of the sitter.

This is the look Rodchenko wanted to capture. In three frontal close-ups which emphasise the contours and size of Mayakovsky's head even more he tries to fix the image of the poet on the plate. The exact symmetry and frontality of these portrait photographs makes the intense facial expression contrast with the rigid composition even more than is the case in the seated portrait. These three shots mark Rodchenko's move away from the norms of traditional portrait photography. They can be seen as the forerunners of the "Pioneer Series" of 1930 in which extreme viewpoints from above or below abstract and formalise faces and figures almost beyond recognition.

These photographs must have convinced Rodchenko that it was impossible to achieve one synthetic photograph in which all the facets of a sitter were combined. In fact the very dissimilarity of several exact, documentary snap-shots of a person shows up how impossible it is to provide a fixed image of a man in one picture. His identity is really always made up of a continuous assimilation of varying experiences and can thus only be portrayed in a sequence. Rodchenko saw how in modern times the unified view of the world and of life was disintegrating and concluded: "Don't try to capture a man in one synthetic portrait but rather in lots of snap-shots taken at different times and in different circumstances!"

The apparent disadvantage of photography — that it can only provide a section, limited in time and space, of an object and not a comprehensive view — is seen by Rodchenko and the other Constructivist photographers as its very strength. Photographic techniques allow the photographer to select and fix individual aspects of reality as often and quickly as desired. Thus an optical analysis is made possible by tracing and comparing varying and contrasting views of a single subject. I will call such a series of snap-shots of a specific subject "at different times and in different circumstances" (Rodchenko) an analytical sequence. I think this is Rodchenko's most important contribution to the history of photography in the twentieth century, much more important than his extreme perspectives from above or below, or the dynamic diagonals of his oblique axes. Both these devices were usually and still are discussed in the context of individual pictures, but they gain their significance only as part of such sequences where they are conceived and shown as one of several possible points of view.

For Rodchenko the importance of this shift from the portrait artist's method of selecting and synthesising to an unfinished series of snap-shots making up a sequence is not confined to portrait photography. He sees it as only one example of a much more basic historical change in the attitude to perception; an example "of the first great clash of art and photography, of the battle between eternity and the moment" (Rodchenko).

The Constructivists in particular are characterised by their analytical attitude towards art and their analytical approach to reality generally. A.V. Babichev, the leader of the "Working Group for Objective Analysis" to which Rodchenko belonged, wrote: "Art is an informed analysis of the concrete tasks which social life poses.... If art becomes public property it will organise the consciousness and psyche of the masses by organising objects and ideas." (1921)

Scientific and visual analysis as an instrument for emancipating the masses by organising mass consciousness: this is an advance into collective intercommunications which a few years later the photographers who used analytical sequences would also proclaim as their aim, thus fulfilling — at least in tendency — Tarabukin's demand for a close connection between photographic experiments and agitational art.

The functional aims of the Constructivist photographers are not just the result of their social engagement but also of their definition of construction. In 1921 the "group for objective analysis" started a discussion on the concepts of "composition" and "construction" in which the most important Soviet artists participated over a considerable length of time. The Constructivists saw these two concepts as the main contrasting principles of traditional and modern art. Composition meant a static order building up a harmonious and hermetic unity in a work of art which remained ineffectively illusionist. Construction meant organising the movement of objects to create new movements. Rodchenko gives an explicitly functionalist definition of construction: "Construction is a system which realises an object by using materials functionally and predetermining the effect." Constructivism is thus seen from the beginning by its leading representatives as movement art in two senses, capturing movement and itself moving, and the transition from painting and drawing to photography is based on this search for dynamic construction and its power to influence the spectator.

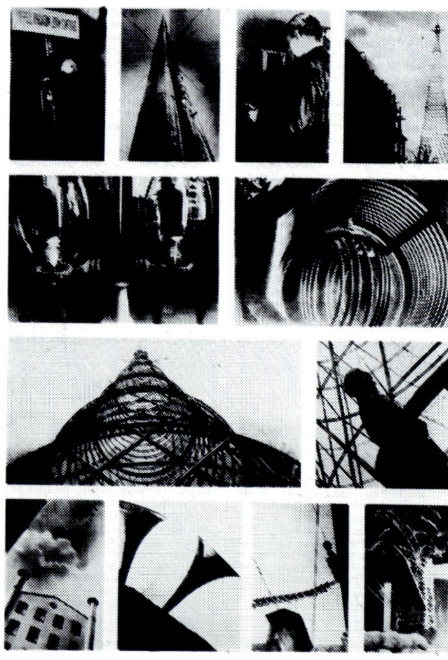

Radio Tower "Komintern", from the periodical "Radio Listener", 1929

Even before Rodchenko personally took up photography he listed the motives which were to make him use photographs in a Constructivist way: documentary photography was conclusively factual; it had a powerful effect on the spectator; and photomontage made dynamic constructions possible. The two last possibilities are already exploited in 1923 in his photomontages for Mayakovsky's poem "Pro Eto" in which he uses newspaper clippings as well as A. Sterenberg's photographs of Mayakovsky and Lilya Brik. The poet and L. Brik look up from these montages at the spectator with wide-open and piercing eyes. This Expressionist device used to intensify the effect is also taken over, as has already been mentioned, in Rodchenko's own first photographic portraits of Mayakovsky, even though their construction is very different from Sterenberg's shots. But Rodchenko abandoned this psychological shock effect in 1924; it cannot easily be reconciled with the Constructivists' stand against psychology and their collectivism, and is replaced by shocking perspectives.

The psychological effect of such unusual angles of vision produced by the unconventional positioning of the camera was examined in R. Arnheim's book on "Film as Art" in 1932, and the author agrees with Rodchenko's arguments about the "navel-perspective". Arnheim says about the photographer who takes a shot of his subject from above or below or tilts it: "By reproducing the object in an unusual, striking view he forces the spectator to pay more attention, to do more than just take note. In this way the object shown sometimes becomes more real, makes a more vivid and compelling impression ... But the new way of photographing objects is not just used as an alarm signal or a trick to entice the spectator. By showing the object from a specifically chosen point of view it can interpret it (more or less profoundly)... The strange and unusual quality of such a point of view is stimulating 'to see an object in a different light'), and through the image itself unknown characteristics of an everyday object are exposed." Virtually the same arguments are used by Rodchenko to defend his choice of perspective against the "navel-followers".

But to avoid misunderstandings Rodchenko stressed that the "new vision" was not dogmatic about taking shots from above and below. The conventional angle was not to be exchanged for another, more effective one, but photographers had to learn through their medium "to show the world from all points of view and to teach the ability to see it from all sides". He was too committed to analytical experiments and disliked systems too much to believe that his choice of perspective was generally and ultimately binding. He explained that his contemporary preference was generally and ultimately binding. He explained that his contemporary preference for worm- and birds-eye-views came from the influence of the urban and industrial environment on human perception.

A photomontage of 1926 for the cover of Mayakovsky's poem dedicated to S. Esenin is an impressive example of this historic change in perception. On the left hand picture Rodchenko fits a circle into his shot of a high-rise building taken from below, and in this circle is a wooden village hut, photographed without perspectival distortion. By its use of perspective this picture convincingly demonstrates how space is perceived differently in town and country. — The photomontage on the right hand side is concerned with the perception of time. Again a circle is fitted into the picture, this time into the receding iron arches of a railway bridge, shot in such a way that the speed of forward movement can be imagined. The circle contains sheafs of corn which seem to move slowly in the wind, symbolising the cyclical rather than linear, movement of nature.

This photomontage of contrasting shots gives a vivid image of the difference between historically and spatially separate ways of perceiving (and at the same time it is a visual metaphor for the simultaneous experience of different ways of life by Esenin, the urban poet of village life). Later Rodchenko tends to present images from a generally urban, industrial point of view. In his photo-sequence "Pushkino-Wood" for instance he shows each "tree taken from below pointing up, like an industrial object — a chimney". In such pictures all points of view are again reduced to one single one, namely the one identified with the era of technology. The usual choice of perspective changes from an instrument of visual analysis to a formal stereotype which hides rather than reveals the subject and shows its movement set in a preconceived pattern rather than in its ever changing form.

But in most cases Rodchenko faithfully follows his own analytical demand: "One has to take several different shots of a subject, from different points of view and in different situations, as if one examined it in the round rather than looked through the same key-hole again and again."

In the early stages Rodchenko usually photographs one object, such as a person, house, town square, glass jug, trees, a machine... from various angles. From 1928 onwards he tends to dissect whole complexes of objects, such as the radio tower, the editorial offices of the telegraphic agency TASS or a car factory, with his camera and put these new views of everyday subjects into a sequence. In these sequences Rodchenko achieves a fourth method of showing movement which still remains the main aim of the constructivists, even if the concept of movement has changed.

This series of dynamically constructed photographs of individual objects in movement which already use the principle of stringing together different moments of movement are followed by the "determining of a fact within a time coordinate", as Sergei Tret'iakov said, "the determining of a process' which he calls the "biography of an object". By telling the spectator about objects these "biographies" should make the objects capable of informing him also about the people who use them. So the photographic sequences of the "factographers" are constructed to show "not the individual human being who passes through the system of objects, but the object which passes through the system of human beings". In 1929 Tret'iakov demanded that "factographic" literature should provide books on subjects like the Wood, Bread, Coal, Iron, The Locomotive, The Industrial Concern , and Rodchenko was the first who optically recorded biographies of such subjects with the camera, usually accompanied by precise information, as in the periodical "Daiesh" (Forward) or in literary essays, as in the periodical "30 Dnei" (30 Days).

With these biographical sequences Rodchenko closely approaches what W. Ranke (with reference to Heinrich Zille's photographs) has called "analytical documentary photography". They show processes which no longer just trace movements of objects, but their development within the framework of the industrialisation and collectivisation of the country. But they lack the critical, or even accusatory ferment which distinguishes most social photographs. They are documents of limited progress, not criticisms of the status quo. — In the early '30s Rodchenko changes from these biographies of objects to photo-reportages which no longer demonstrate the process of perception and the functioning of objects, as the sequences had done, but tell the spectator by means of pictorial stories about the construction and use of new objects by and for the people. In them the literary script has taken the lead, visual analysis has become secondary. One of the best of these photo-reportages by Rodchenko deals with the building of the White Sea canal. The photographer stayed at the building site for two years (1931/2) to take his pictures and thus started the development which Tret'iakov demanded of the "factographic" photographer in 1931, a development "from the photographic sequence to long-term photographic observation". This means that the more or less accidental images of objects in movement are changed into a precise, systematic record of the history of individual and collective lives and circumstances. "We build systematically, we must also photograph systematically! Sequence and long-term photographic observation — that is the method!"

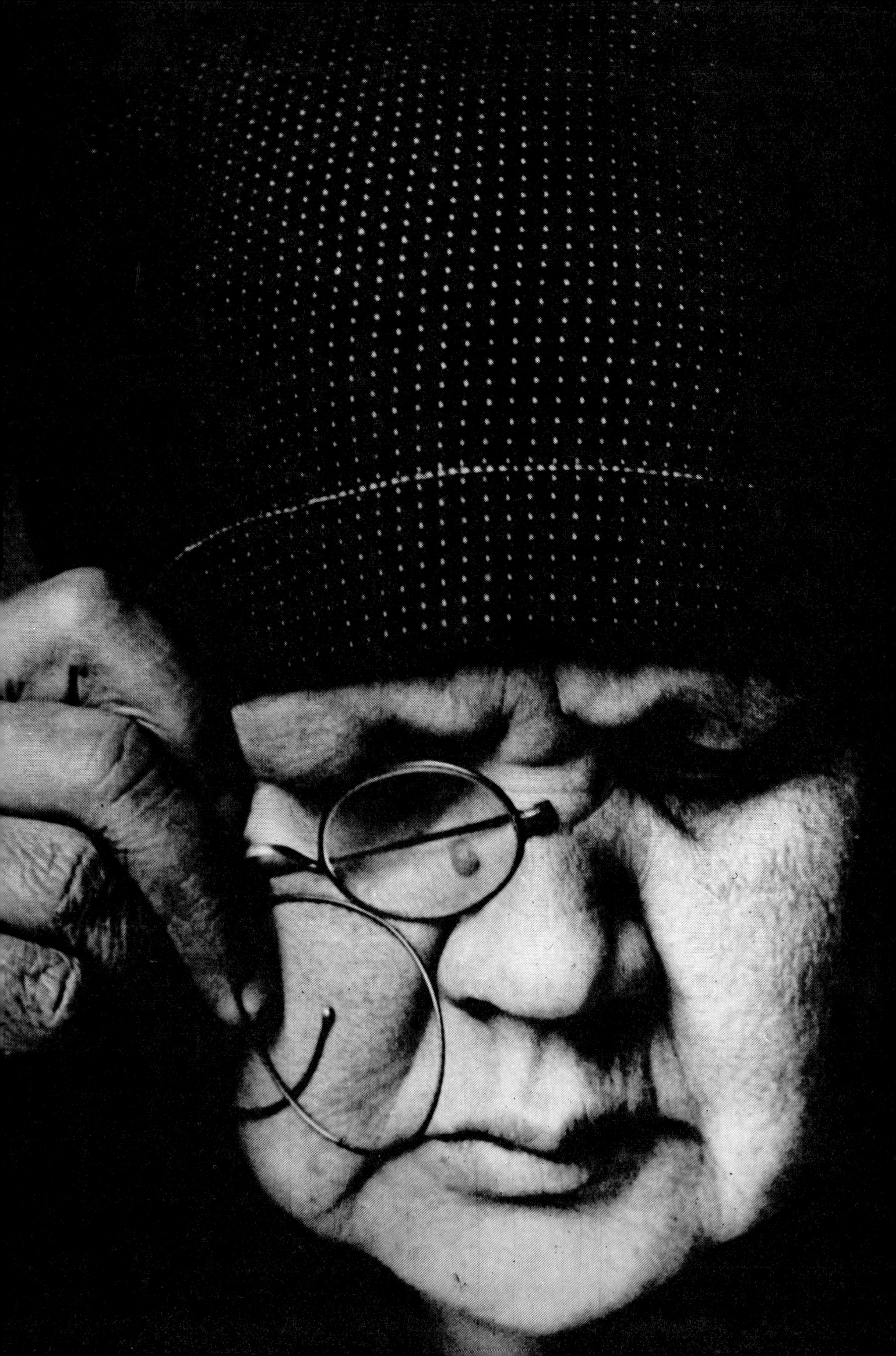

Page 114: Varvara Stepanova, c. 1923

Page 115: Vladimir Vladimirovich Mayakovsky, 1924

Opposite page: Rodchenko's mother, 1924

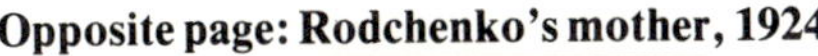

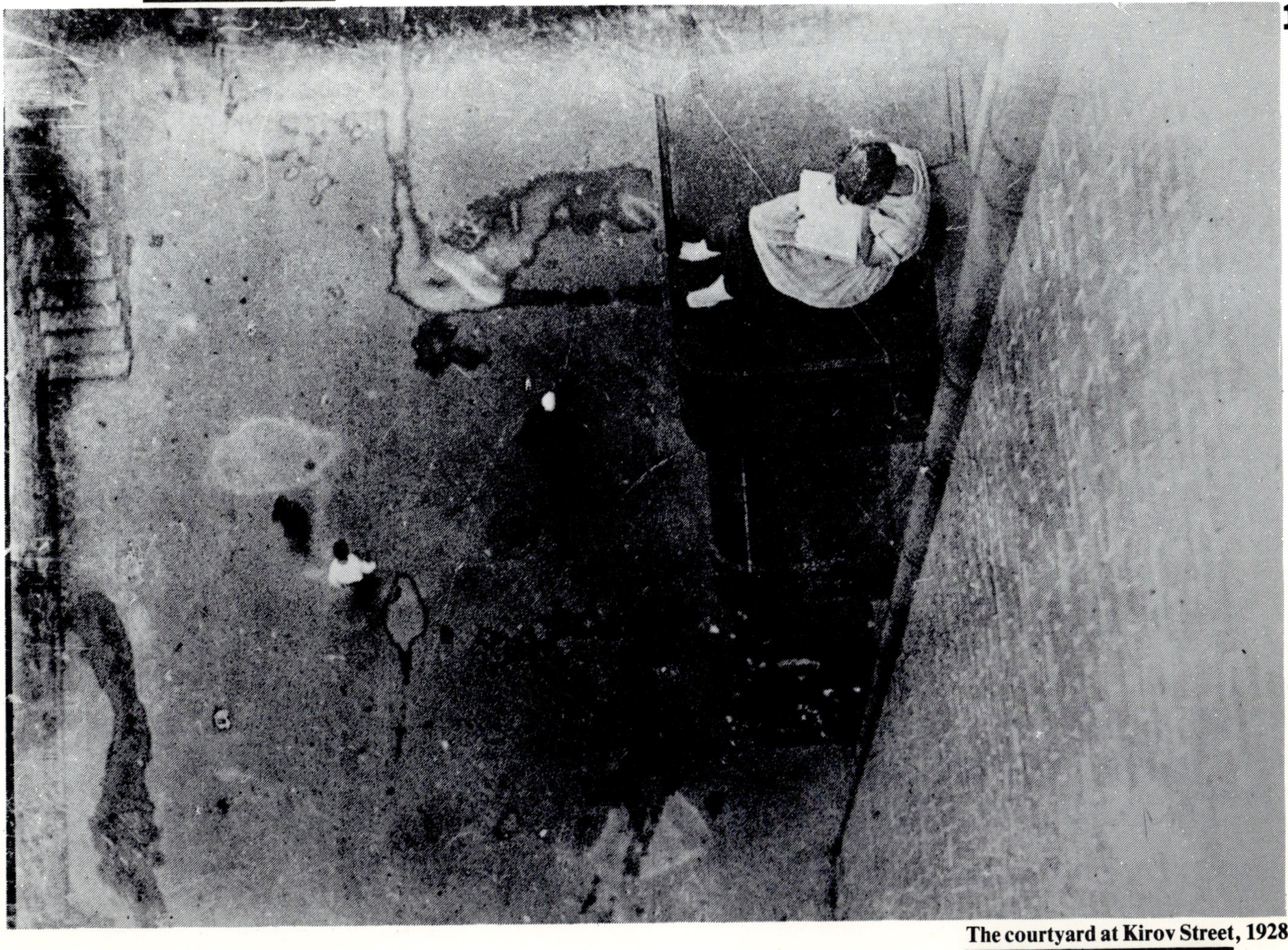

The courtyard at Kirov Street, 1928

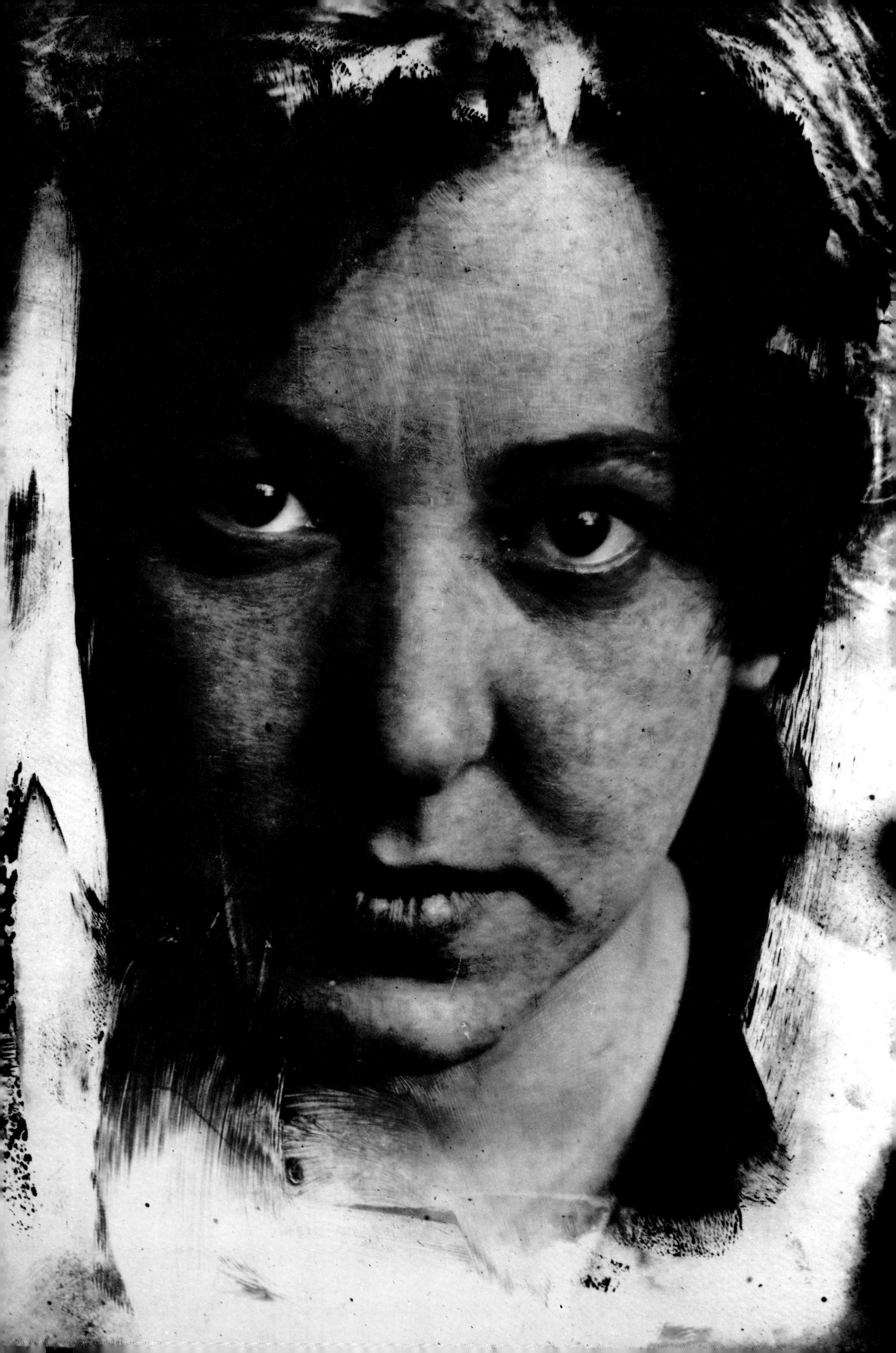

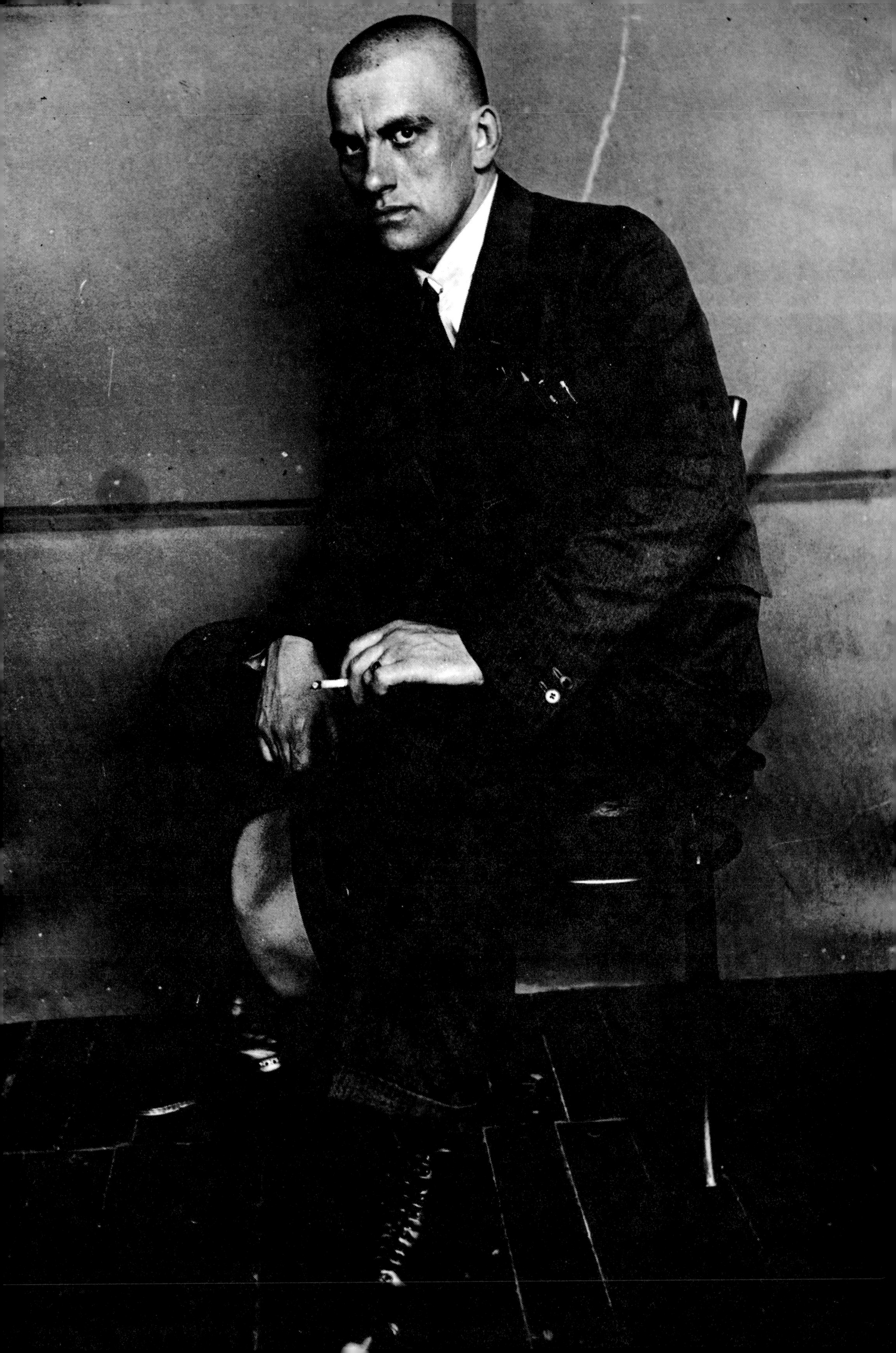

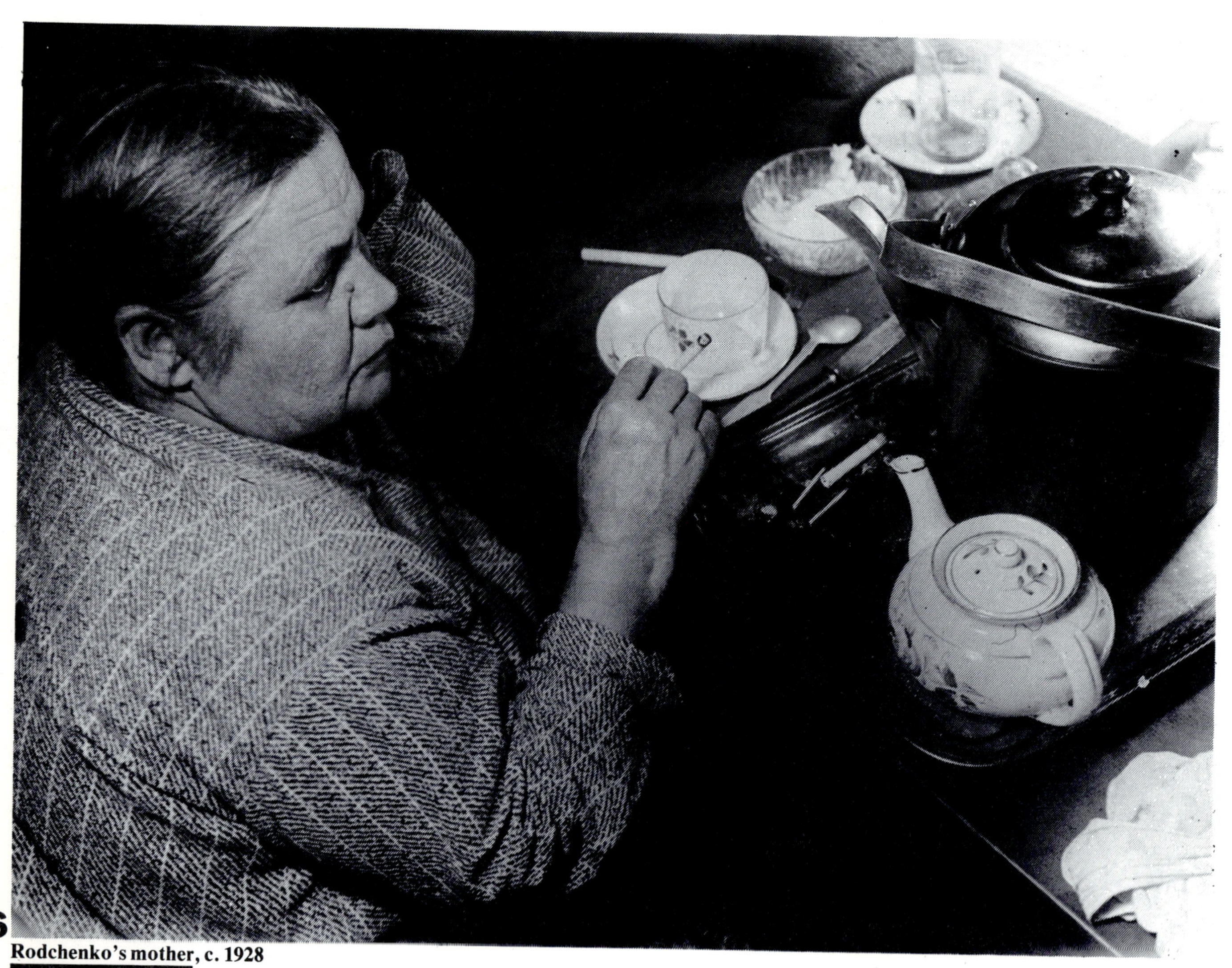

116

Rodchenko's mother, c. 1928

Opposite page: Vladimir Vladimirovich Mayakovsky, 1924

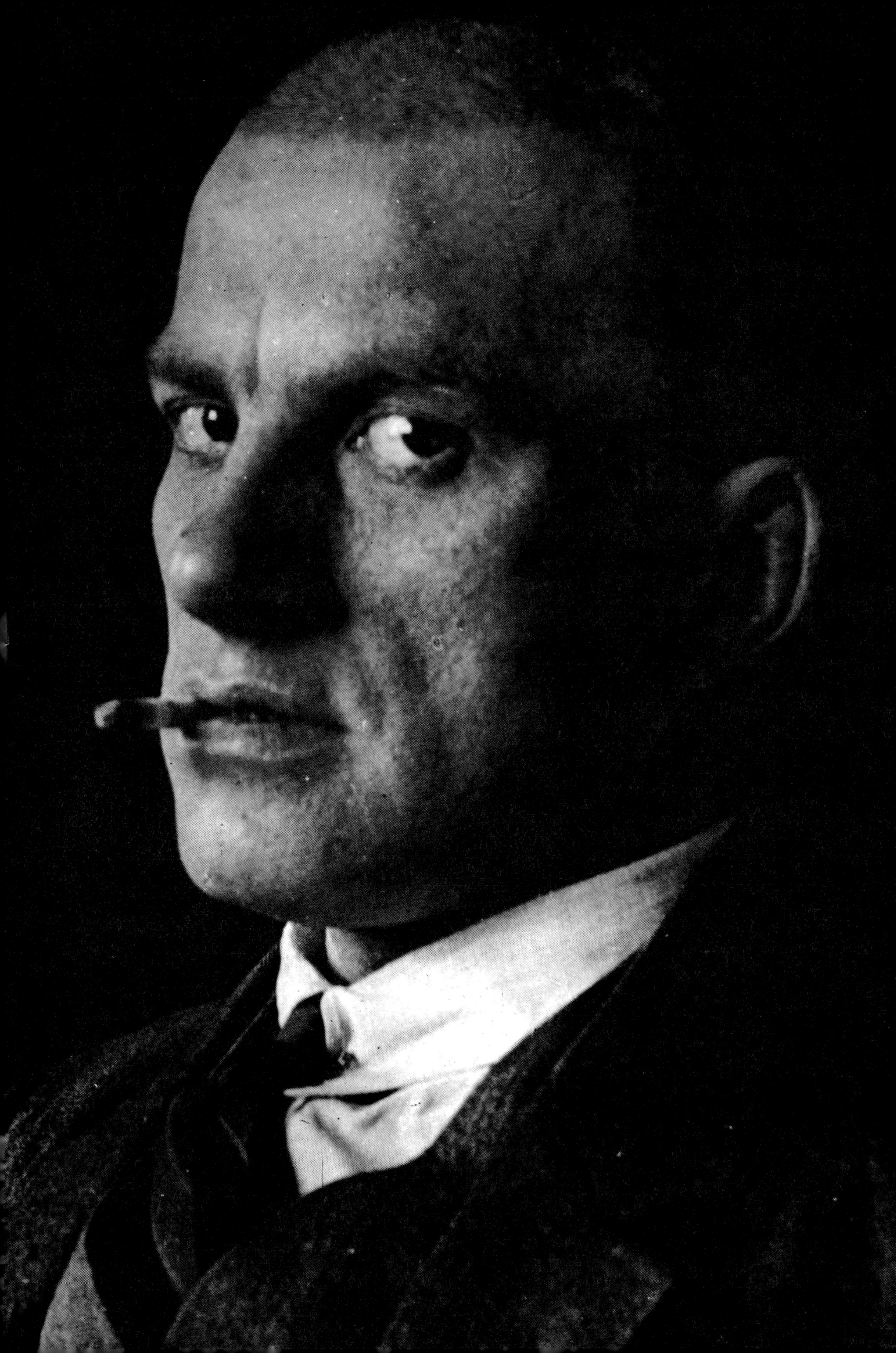

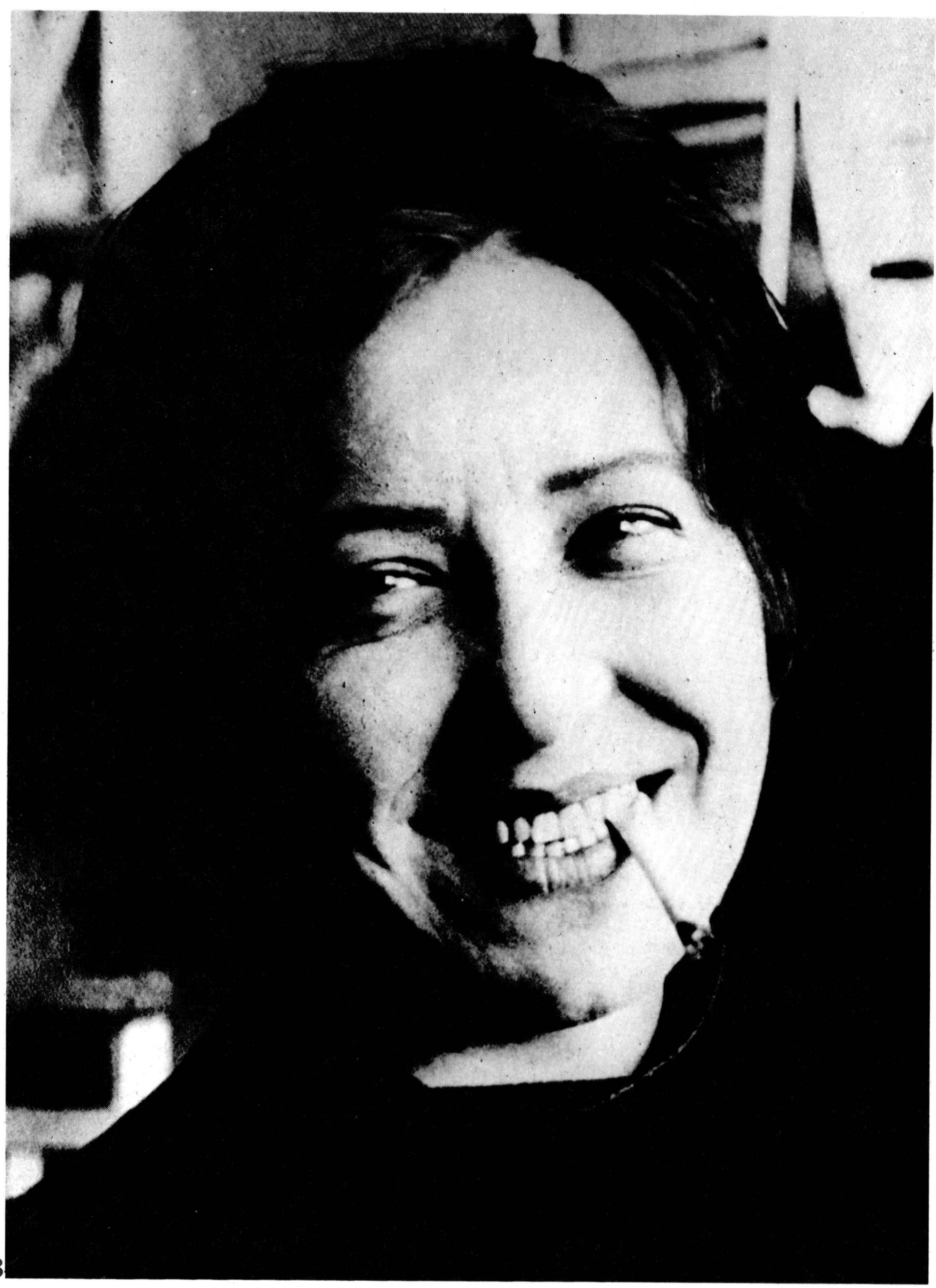

118

Varvara Stepanova, 1924

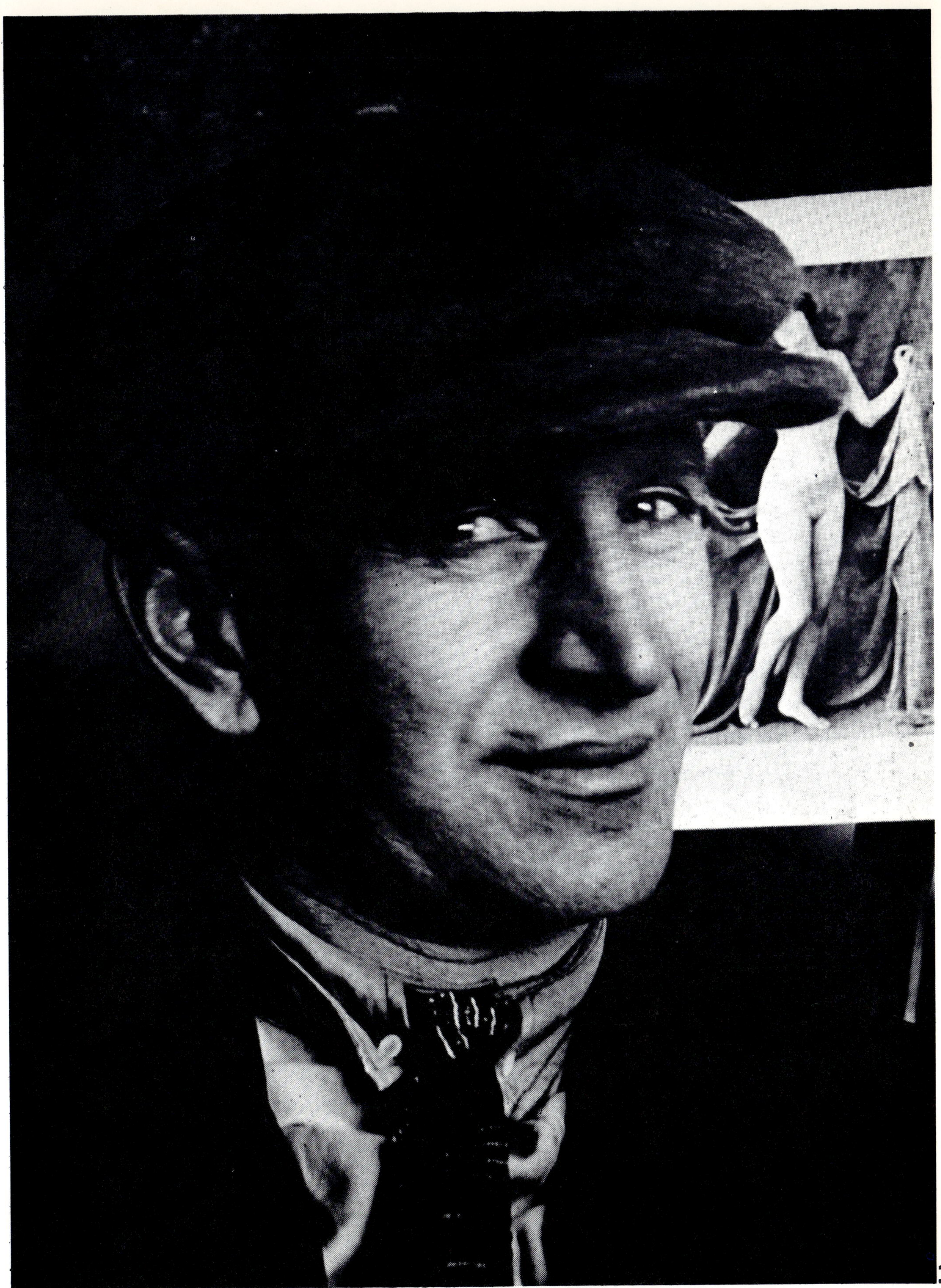

Anton Lavinsky, designer, 1923

Opposite page: Alexander Vesnin, architect, 1924

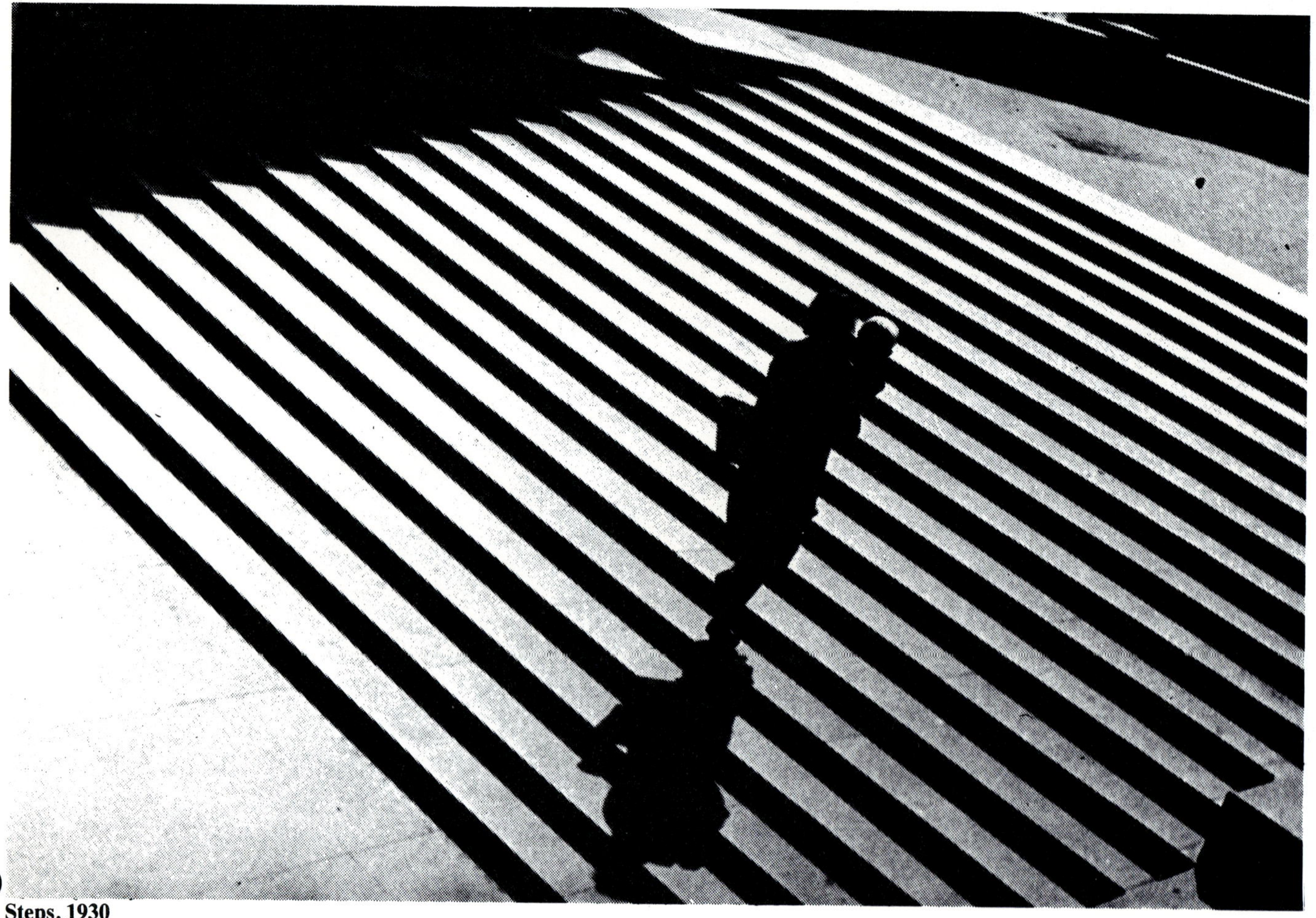

Steps, 1930

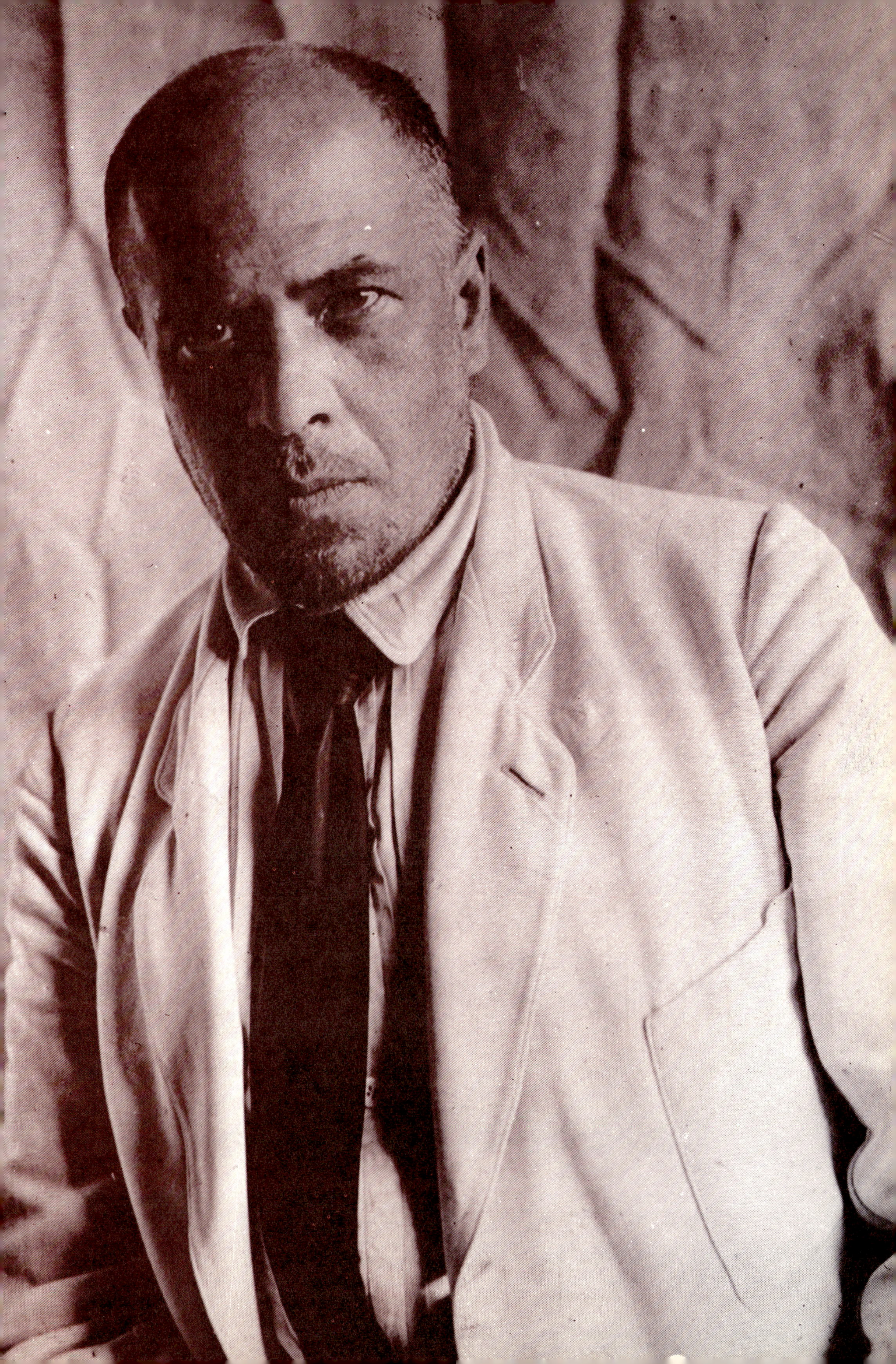

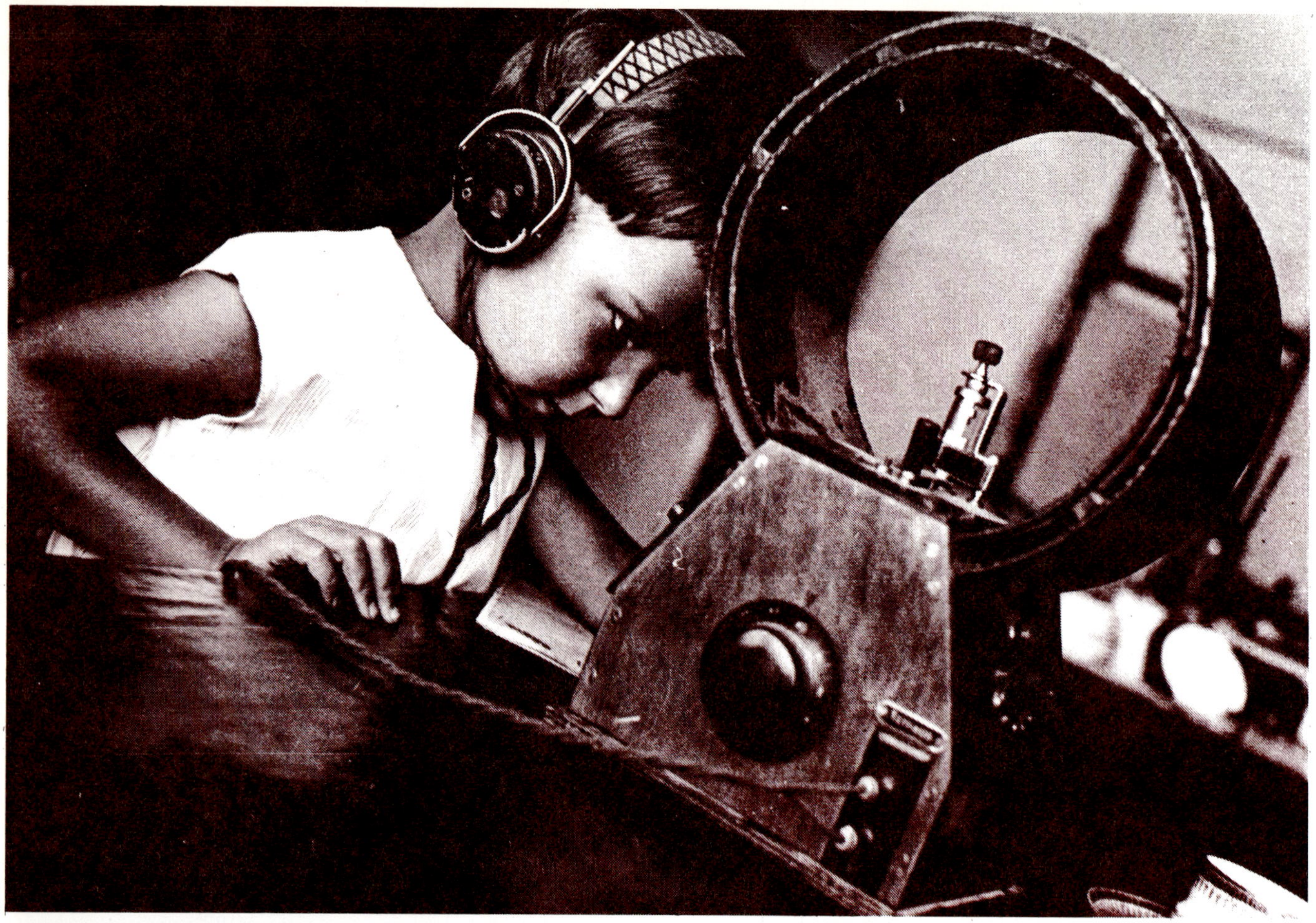

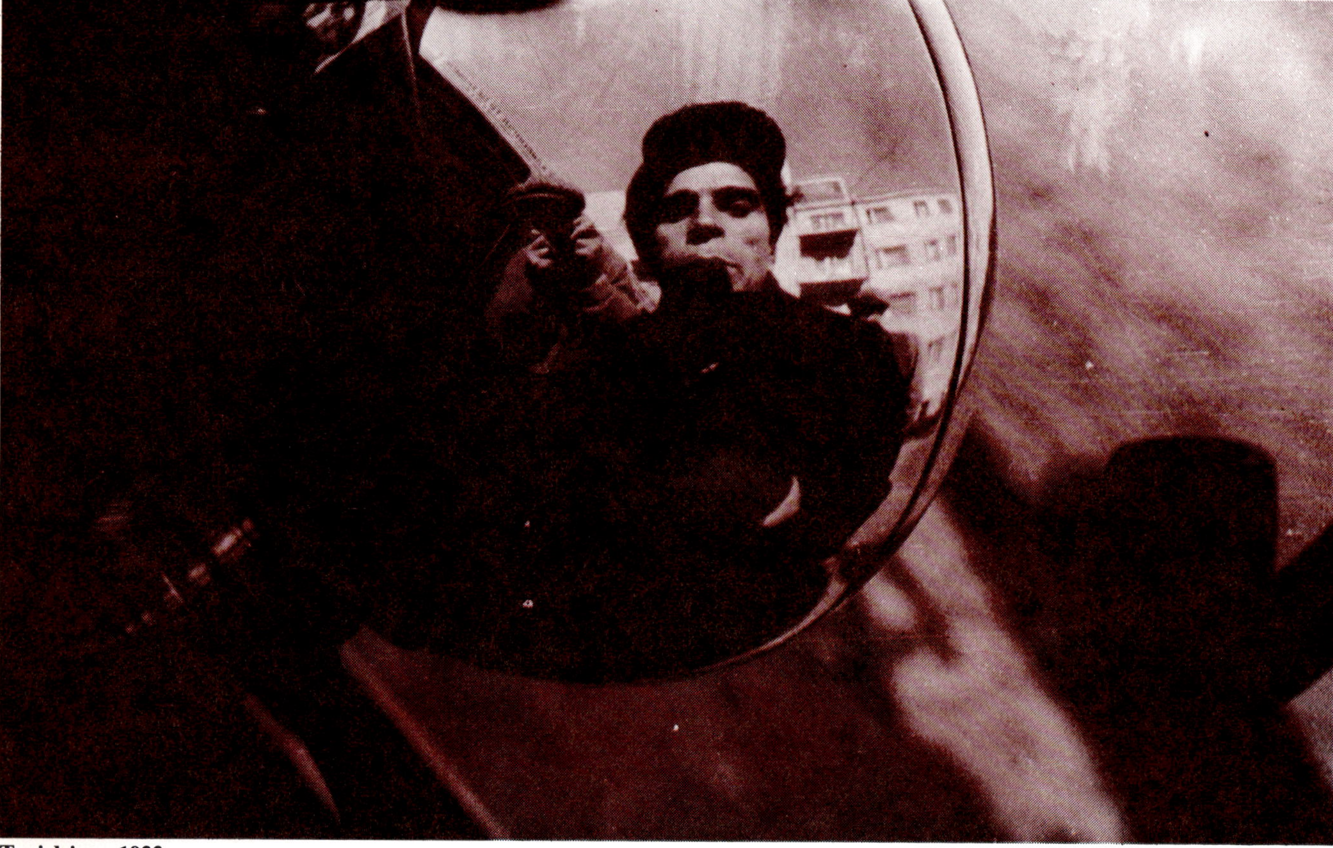

Taxi driver, 1933

Top: Varvara Rodchenko listening to the radio, 1932. Opposite page: Nikolai Aseev, poet and critic, 1930

Page 124: Yevghenya Lemberg, photographer, 1935. Page 125: Sergei Tret'iakov, author and critic, 1928

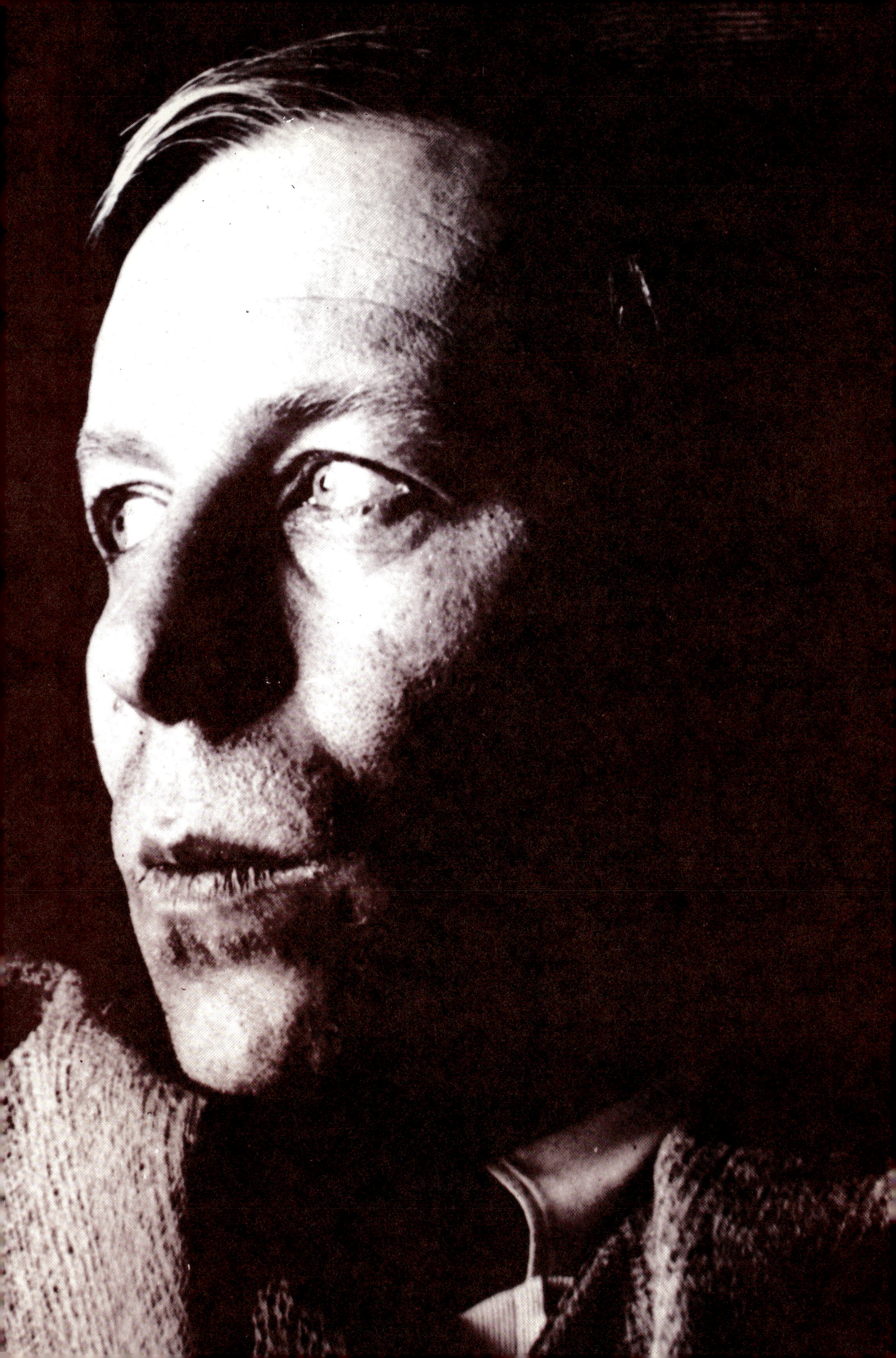

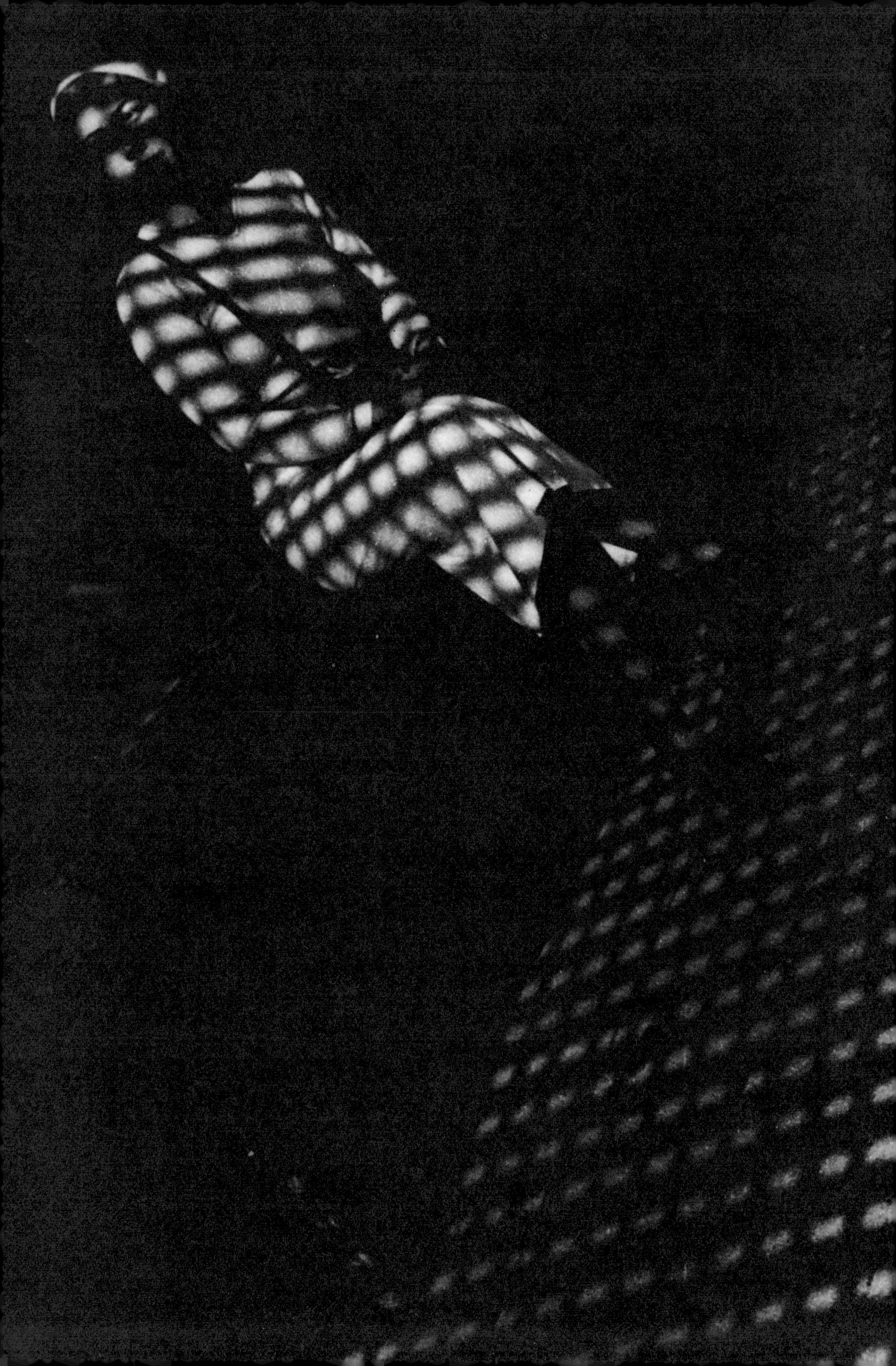

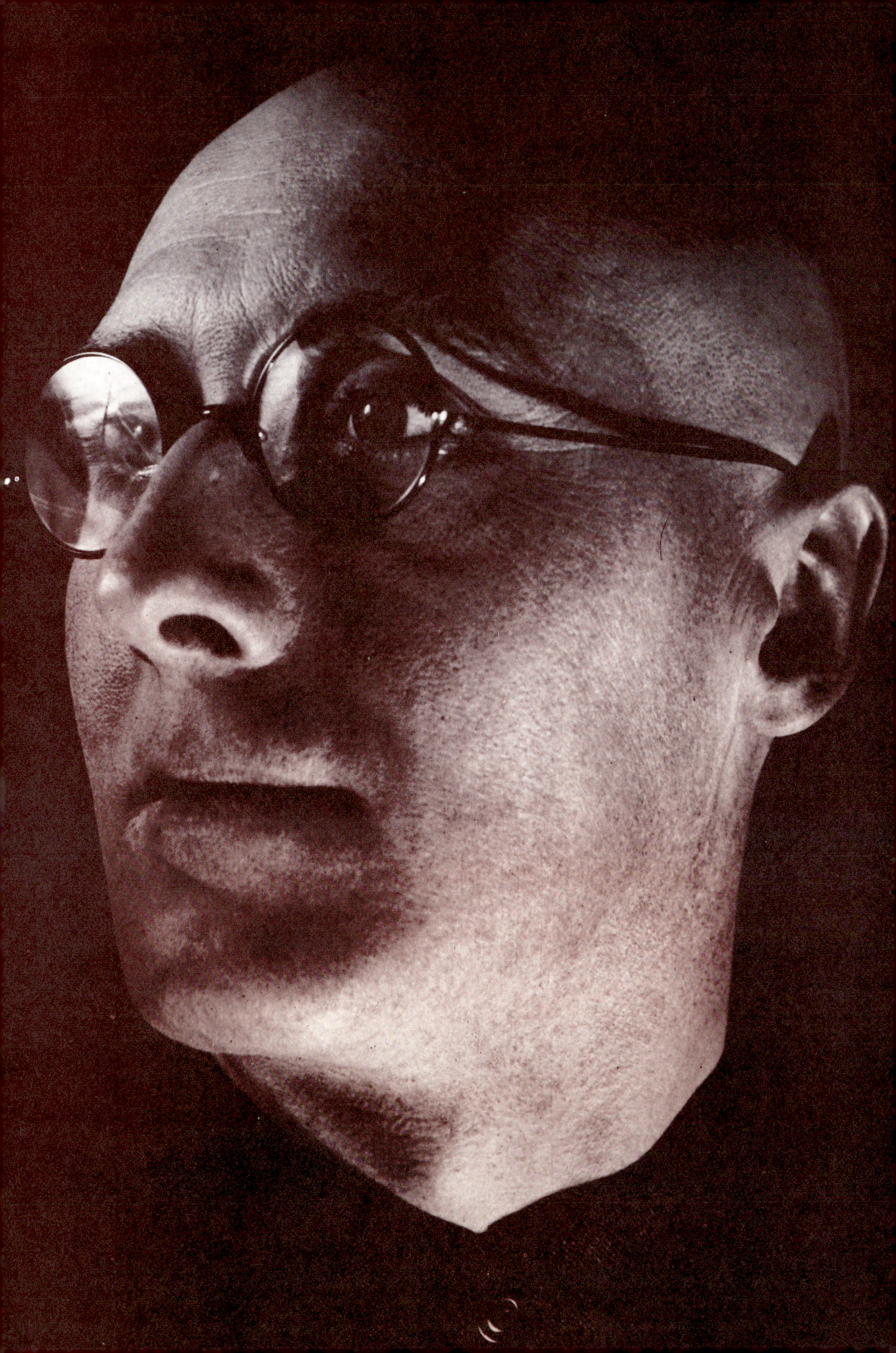

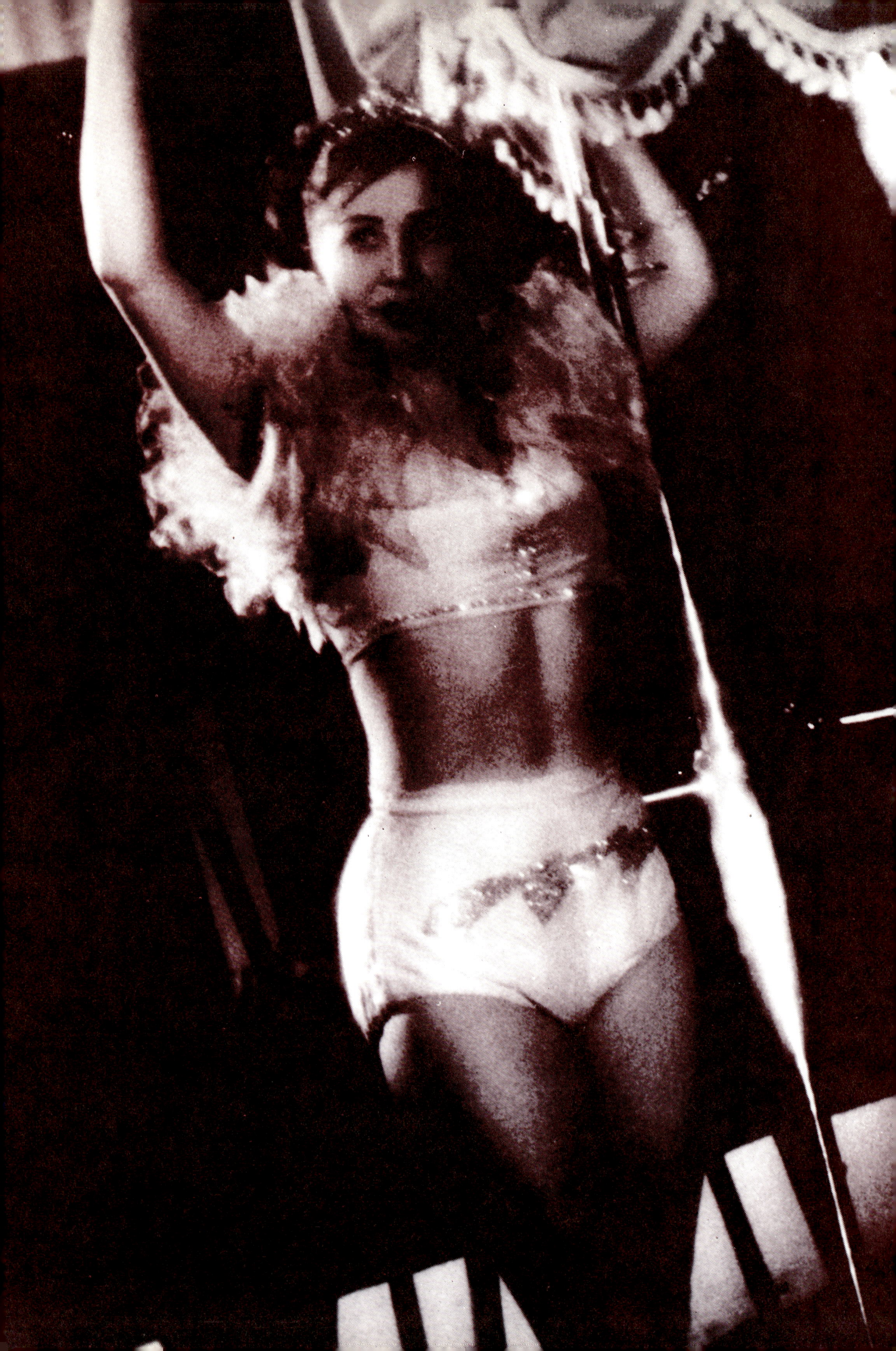

Opposite page: Acrobat, 1937

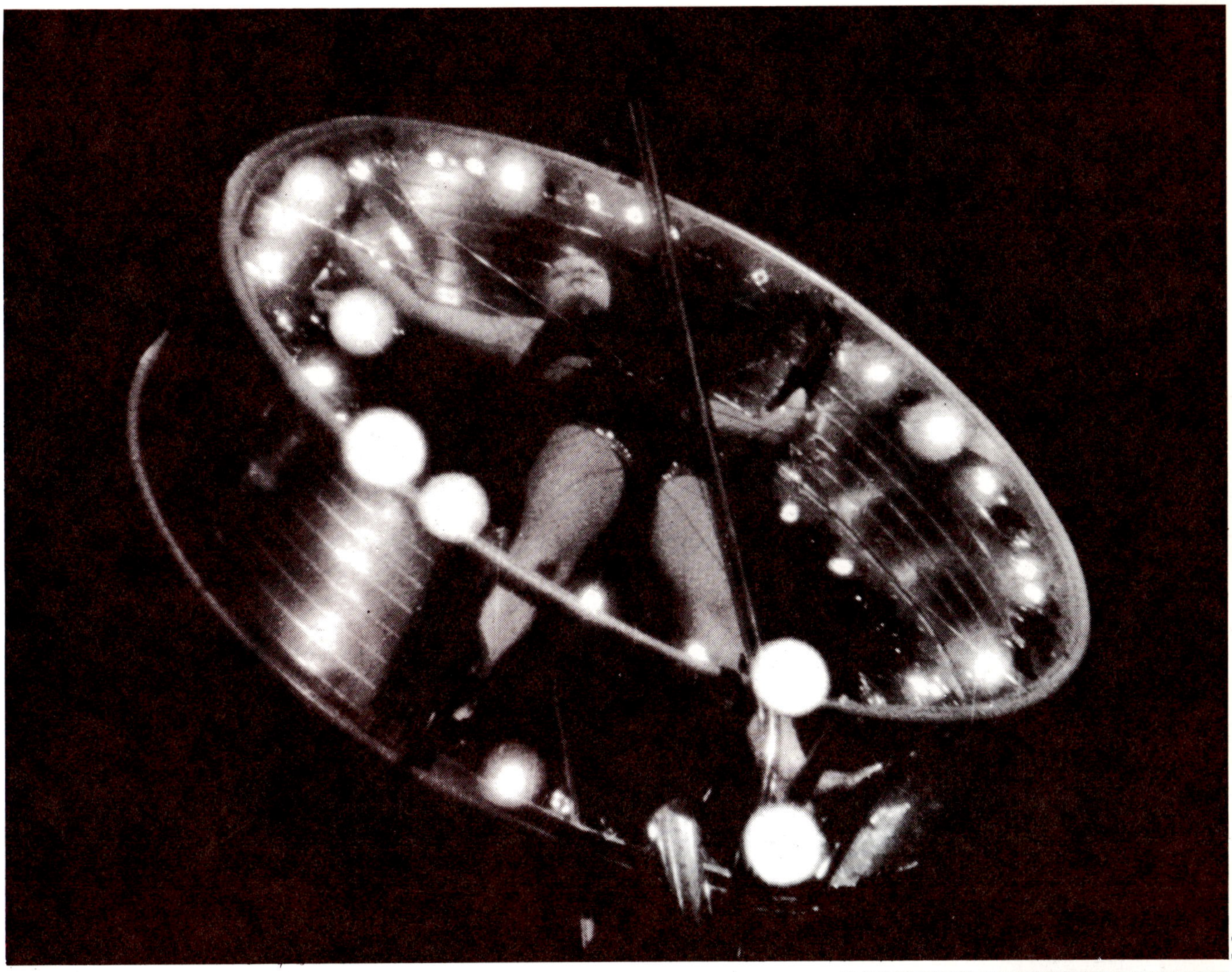

Circus, 1937.

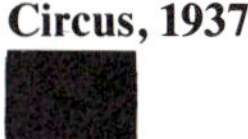

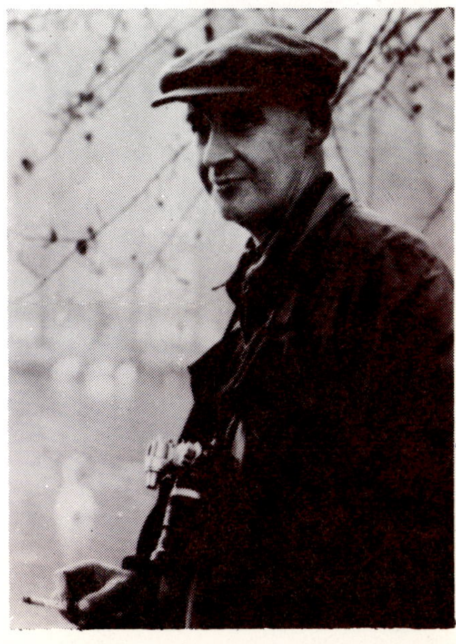

Alexander Rodchenko in 1947. Photograph by V. Kovrigin

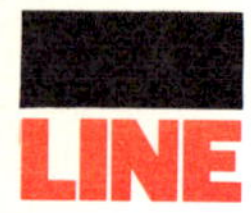

LINE

Inkhuk: Institute of Artistic Culture, Moscow, founded in May 1920; also had affiliations in Petrograd and Vitebsk.

These notes by Rodchenko were written for a lecture given at Inkhuk in 1921

Initially, painting set itself the exclusive aim of painting objects and human beings as if alive — as they are in actual fact — and to the point of total deception or illusion: and it did this so that the spectator would think that this was simply a slice of life and not painting. This entailed a lot of hard work and persistence, but very soon this became inadequate — more important tasks emerged.

What lives should live in the picture ... but it became essential to compose the picture in varying proportions, to compose it differently to how it exists in reality, to distribute its elements in a cleverer, more noble and elevated fashion, to reveal what is important in the subject while more or less concealing everything else, to select colour, shades and overall tone with the utmost harmony and restraint, etc.

Because of the long, persistent work undertaken in order to attain all the effects of painting which rarely moved beyond the same point, an abstracted, "non-living" thing began to appear in the painting: this was something more important, more essential and more professional — "PAINTERLINESS", facture of the surface, all kinds of light effects, Lasierung, lining, fixing, etc. In other words, a painterly approach to the picture was created. Thenceforth the picture ceased being a picture and became painting or an object.

This new approach, "painterliness", has since become an immutable truth and the criterion for any work of painting, particularly for figurative painting.

Why has this fortuitous element been elevated to such permanent heights? Very simple — this is a professional approach to painting. It is the very essence of painting as such.

Painting owes its whole evolution exclusively to form: hardly ever turning back, it has advanced constantly and so consistently and logically that it's as if a straight line can be seen for ever indicating a forward movement.

This line integrates what precedes and what follows into a single organism. Thus, by developing vertically and horizontally, painting utilised all the potentials of its specific character and attained incredible refinements, bordering on Epicureanism.

After exploiting the object in every possible interpretation, from Realism and Naturalism to Futurism, painting reached Cubism and, almost with a knowledge of anatomy, dismembered it — until painting at last freed itself completely from this defence and reached non-objectivity.

After rejecting object and subject, painting began to occupy itself exclusively with its own specific tasks: these expanded and more than replaced the object and its interpretation which painting had excluded.

Subseqently, non-objective art renounced the old means of expression in painting: it introduced new methods of painting, (ones more expedient for its forms — geometrically simple, clear and precise), painting with a flat-edged brush, with colouring, rollers, pressing, etc. The brush gave way to new instruments with which it was convenient, easy and more expedient to work the surface. The brush, which had been so indispensable in painting which transmitted the object and its subtleties, became an inadequate and imprecise instrument in the new, non-objective painting and the press, the roller, the drawing-pen, the compasses, etc. replaced it. (First appeared in the works of A. M. RODCHENKO at the exhibition of the Leftist Federation in Moscow).

Compared to form, colour in painting scarcely evolved. It advanced from grey to brown, from brown to pure, vivid colour and back again; and this interchange was a terribly uniform, monotonous rotation. Pure colour (the spectrum) did exist in paints, but painters killed it by mixing it to get different tones. The tone appeared in painting exclusively because of objectivity, because of the aspiration to transmit nature. Until recent times it existed in painting as a special accomplishment of painterly culture and attained a kind of browny-orange mess, downright ugly.

The Impressionists turned to the spectrum, but again adapted it so as to transmit an impression, the air, light, etc. The Expressionists alighted on colour as a game of coloured spots, as ornamentation.

Non-objective painting cultivated colour as such: it occupied itself with its total exposure, with its processing and conditioning and gave it depth, intensity, density, weight, etc. The ultimate stage in this process was the attainment of monochrome intensity within the confines of a single colour and intensity (no decreasing or increasing). (Works shown at the 1918 exhibition Non-objective Creation and Suprematism, Moscow), can serve as examples of this — works by RODCHENKO (black on black) and MALEVICH (white on white) were exhibited simultaneously).

Lately I have been working exclusively on the construction of forms and the systems of their construction and I have started to introduce LINE into plane as a new element of construction (RODCHENKO's works of 1917-18).

At last the meaning of LINE has been elucidated in full: on the one hand its facetal and lateral relationship, and on the other as a factor of principal construction in any organism in life as a whole — so to say, the skeleton or the basis, the framework or system. Both in painting and in any construction in general, line is the first and last thing. Line is the path of advancement, it is movement, collision, it is facetation, conjunction, combination, section.

Thus, line has conquered everything and has destroyed the last citadels of painting — colour, tone, facture and plane. Line has bid a red farewell to painting) (XIX State Exhibition, Moscow, 1920). Works by RODCHENKO — lines proclaimed in painting for the first time).

In putting line in the forefront — line as an element by whose exclusive means we can construct and create — we thereby reject all aesthetics of colour, facture and style: because everything that obstructs construction is style (e.g. Malevich's square).

Line has revealed a new world-view — to construct essence, and not to depict, to objectivise or to non-objectivise; to build new, expedient, constructive structures in life, and not from life or outside life.

A construction is a system by which an object is realised from the expedient utilisation of material together with a predetermined purpose.

SLOGANS

Vkhutemas 1921

Discipline: CONSTRUCTION. Leader: RODCHENKO

CONSTRUCTION organisation of elements

CONSTRUCTION is the MODERN PHILOSOPHY

ART, like every science, is one of the branches of MATHEMATICS

CONSTRUCTION represents the contemporary demand for ORGANISATION and the utilitarian use of materials.

CONSTRUCTIVE LIFE IS THE ART OF THE FUTURE

ART which has no part in life will be filed away in the archaeological museum of ANTIQUITY

It is time for ART to flow organisedly into life.

A CONSTRUCTIVELY ORGANISED life is above the mystical art of magicians.

The FUTURE will not build monasteries to ROMAN CATHOLIC PRIESTS, PROPHETS and HOLY FOOLS from art.

Down with ART, the shining patches on the talentless life of a wealthy man.

Down with ART, the precious gem in the dirty, dark life of a poor man.

Down with ART, the means to ESCAPE FROM THE LIFE which is not worth living.

Conscious and organised LIFE, the ability to SEE and CONSTRUCT, that is the modern art.

The MAN who has organised his life, his work and himself is the MODERN MAN.

WORK for LIFE and not for PALACES, TEMPLES, CEMETERIES and MUSEUMS.

Work amongst everyone, for everyone and with everyone,

DOWN WITH monasteries, institutes, workshops, studios, studies and islands.

Consciousness, EXPERIMENT...the goal: CONSTRUCTION.

Technology and mathematics there are the BROTHERS of modern ART.

PRODUCTIVIST MANIFESTO

Written by Rodchenko and Stepanova in Moscow, 1921

It is the task of the Constructivist group to direct materialist, constructivist work towards communist ends.

The group tackles this problem by means of scientific hypotheses. It stresses how necessary it is to attain a synthesis of ideological and formal aspects, so that studio work can be directed towards practical activity.

When the group started its work its programme included the following ideological tenets:

1. It is exclusively based on scientific communism which is itself based on the theory of historical materialism.
2. The knowledge of the endeavours of the Soviets has made the group change its experimental activities from abstract (transcendental) to real works.
3. The specific elements involved in the work of this group, that is "Tektonika", construction and "Faktura", provide ideological, theoretical and practical justification for the transposition of the material elements of industrial culture into volume, plane, colour, space and light.

The communist expression of materialist construction is based on these premises.

These three tenets create an organic link between the two spheres of ideology and form.

"Tektonika" has its origins in the structure of communism and the effective exploitation of industrial realities.

Construction is organisation. It uses the ready made substances of things. Construction is shaping, going after extreme solutions, yet it does make allowance for further "tectonic" work. "Faktura" is the name given by the group to carefully chosen and effectively used materials which neither hinder the progress of construction nor limit the "Tektonika".

The material elements are:

1. Materials generally. Knowledge of their origins and changes due to industrial and production techniques. Their nature and their significance.
2. Intellectual materials: Light, plane, space, colour, volume. The Constructivists treat intellectual and concrete materials in the same way.

The group has the following future aims:

1. Ideological aims:

a) To prove the incompatibility of artistic activity and intellectual production through word and deed.

b) To make intellectual production truly participate in the building up of communist culture, as an element equal in value with others.

2. Practical aims:

a) Press activities

b) Production of plans

c) Organisation of exhibitions

d) Establishing contacts with all the productive centres and main bodies of the united soviet institutions which make communist life a practical reality.

3. Propaganda aims:

a) The group is committed to a merciless fight against art in general.

b) The group proves that there cannot be any consistent development from the art forms of the past to the communist forms of constructive building.

Constructivist slogans:

1. Down with art, long live technical science.
2. Religion is a lie. Art is a lie.
3. Destroy the last remaining attachment of human thought to art.
4. Down with the conservation of artistic traditions. Long live the constructivist technician.
5. Down with art which only obscures the incompetence of the human race.
6. The collective art of today is constructive life.

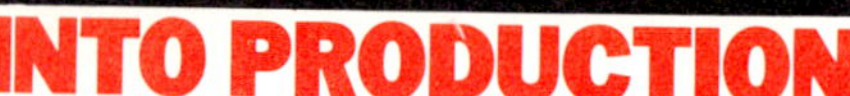

INTO PRODUCTION

Ossip Brik

This article first appeared in "LEF" No. 1, March 1923.

Rodchenko was an abstract artist. He has become a Constructivist and production artist. Not just in name, but in practice. There are artists who have rapidly adopted the fashionable jargon of Constructivism. Instead of "composition" they say "construction", instead of "to write" they say "to shape", instead of "to create" — "to construct"'. But they are all doing the same old thing: little pictures, landscapes, portraits. There are others who do not paint pictures, and work in production, who also talk about material, texture, construction, but once again out come the very same age old ornamental and applied types of art, little cockerels and flowers, or circles and dashes. And there are still others, who do not paint pictures, and do now work in production — they "creatively apprehend" the external laws of colour and form. For them the real world of things does not exist, they wash their hands of it. From the heights of their mystical insights they contemptuously gaze upon anyone who profanes the "holy dogmas" of art through work in production, or any other sphere of material culture.

Rodchenko is no such artist. Rodchenko sees that the problem of the artist is not the abstract apprehension of colour and form, but the practical ability to resolve any task of shaping a concrete object. Rodchenko knows that there aren't once-for-all set laws of construction, but that every new task must be resolved afresh, starting from the conditions set by the individual case. Rodchenko knows that you won't do anything by sitting in your own studio, that you must go into real work, carry your own organising talent where it is needed — into production. Many who have glanced at Rodchenko's work will say: "Where's the Constructivism in this? Where's it any different from applied art?" To them I say: the applied artist embellishes the object, Rodchenko shapes it. The applied artist looks at the object as a place for applying his own ornamental composition, while Rodchenko sees in the object the material that underlies the design. The applied artist has nothing to do if he can't embellish an object — for Rodchenko, a complete lack of embellishment is a necessary condition for the proper construction of the object. It is not aesthetic considerations, but the purpose of the object which defines the organisation of its colour and form.

At the moment things are hard for the Constructivist-production-artist. Artists turn their backs on him. Industrialists wave him away in annoyance. The man in the street goggles and, frightened, whispers: "Futurist!" It needs tenacity and willpower not to lapse into the peaceful bosom of canonised art, to avoid starting to "create" like the "fair copy" artists, or to concoct ornaments for cups and handkerchiefs, or daub pictures for cosy dining-rooms and bedrooms. Rodchenko will not go astray. He can spit on artists and philistines and as for the industrialists, he will break through and prove to them that only the productional constructive approach to the object gives the highest proficiency to production. Of course, this will not happen quickly. It will come when the question of "quality" moves to the forefront: but now, when everything is concentrated on "quantity", what talk can there be of profitability?

Rodchenko is patient. He will wait; meanwhile he is doing what he can — he is revolutionising taste, clearing the ground for the future non-aesthetic, but expedient, material culture.

Rodchenko is right. It is evident to anyone with his eyes open that there is no other road for art than into production. Let the company of "fair-copyists" laugh as they foist their daubings onto the Philistine aesthetes.

Let the "applied artists" delight in dumping their "stylish ornaments" on the factories and workshops.

Let the man in the street spit with disgust at the iron constructive power of Rodchenko's construction.

There is a consumer who does not need pictures and ornaments, and who is not afraid of iron and steel. This consumer is the proletariat. With the victory of the proletariat will come the victory of constructivism.

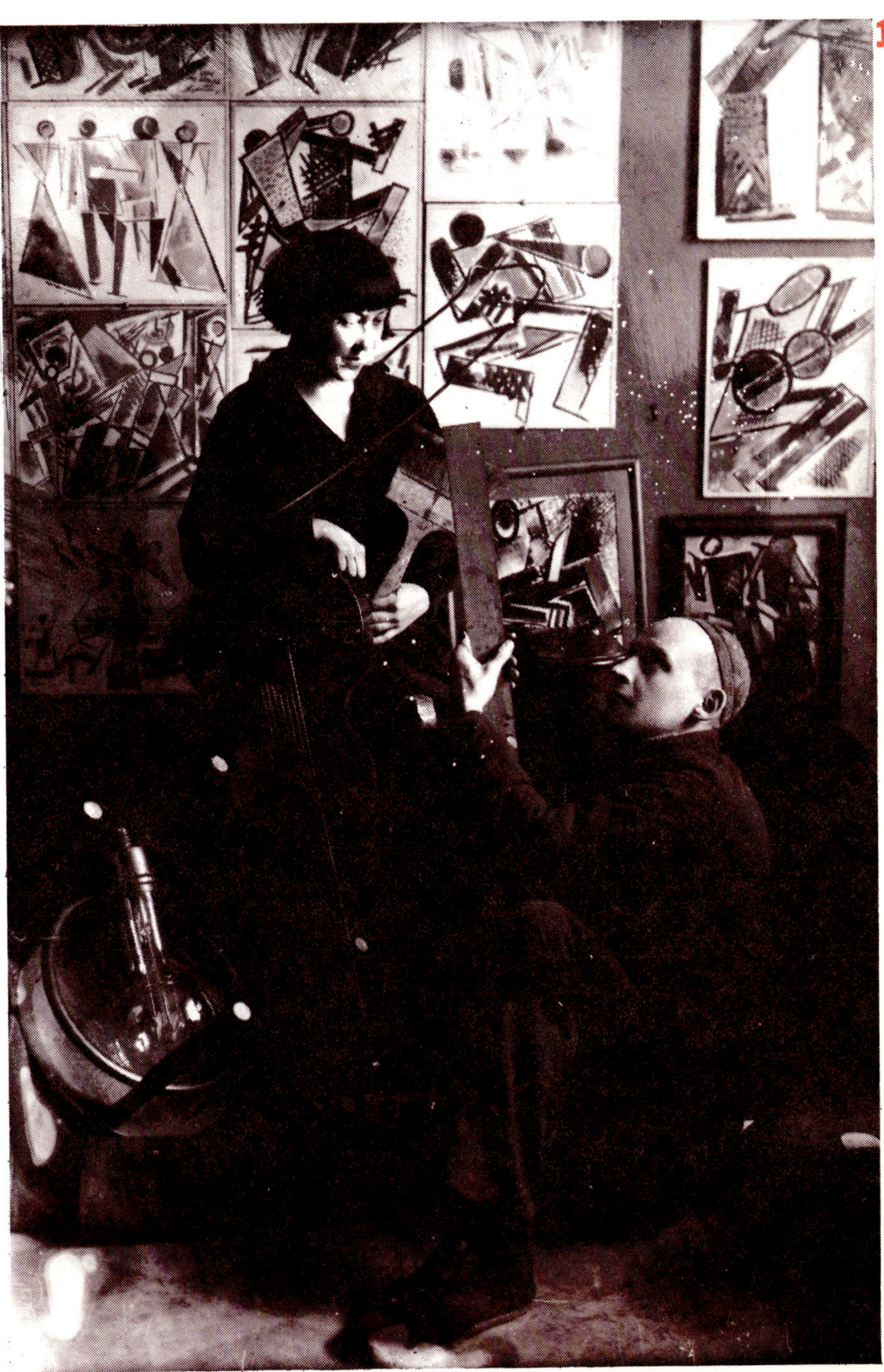

Stepanova and Rodchenko, 1922. Stepanova's paintings can be seen in the background

VLADIMIR TATLIN

Extracts from Rodchenko's recollections, written in 1941, of working with Tatlin on "The Store" exhibition, 1916

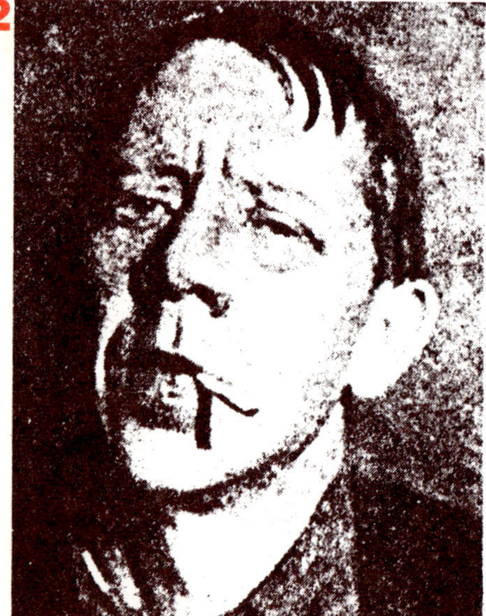

I first met Tatlin at Vesnin's house where I had gone with Varvara (who knew him already) to look for a stretcher. I was living with Varvara in a very small room about 10 metres square and I had just decided to start on a big canvas but I didn't have a stretcher nor money to buy one... When it came to buying canvas I had to be content with cottom which I prepared myself... Tatlin had also come to see Vesnin and I was introduced to him.

...Some time after, Tatlin came round to my place and looked at some work; he liked what he saw and said: "We have organised a group exhibition which will include works by Tatlin, Popova, Udal'tsova, Exter, Pestel, Kliun, Bruni and Malevich to which we will now add those of...Rodchenko. The costs of the exhibition will be shared amongst the exhibitors but as you certainly have not got much money you will pay by working just as I am doing myself! I'm in charge of the administration and the hanging: you will be my helper and what's more you can sell the tickets... ok?"

"Certainly," I replied. And so we then hired an empty shop, 17 Petrovka Street, for a month and began to hang the work. The shop comprised two rooms: one large, the other smaller but going back further. In the first room we hung Tatlin's counter-reliefs and works by Popova, Exter, Udal'tsova, Bruni, Kliun and Malevich. In the second room were Vassilieva, myself, Pestel and later the young Ostetskov who was included in the group. It is in this way that I got my first showing in Moscow.

I showed "Two Figures" a non-figurative work of 150x100cm, several small canvases and some graphic works — also non-figurative. Udal'tsova showed Cubist works, as did Popova, Kliun, Malevich and Pestel. But Bruni showed a broken up barrel of cement and a pane of glass which had been pierced by a bullet, both of which were bound to arouse the indignation of the public. During the day few people came through. Those that did were all of different types but were composed mainly of those who had come in by chance, they either laughed or got angry. On some occasions some of them got interested and even began to admire the work. I tried to give some explanation of the works that were shown with my sketchy knowledge and non-existent comprehension of Cubism. Some visitors saw such works for the first time and tried to understand them. They came back several times, listened to my explanations and thanked me when they understood. Some of them even became enthusiasts. But the one difficulty was in talking about the work of talentless artists, the camp-followers of Futurism. But in this exhibition there were no true Futurists: there were mainly Cubists and abstract artists.

During the Opening Malevich came, and no one knows why, provoked a scandal against Tatlin. I did not wholly understand what had happened but I withdrew my canvases from the exhibition. I liked Malevich's work more than that of the others — except of course for that of Tatlin. They were fresh, original and had no resemblance to anything by Picasso. But Malevich himself, I did not like. He was...not sincere with disagreeably shifty eyes; he was most infatuated with himself and seemed particularly biased in his judgements.

He came up to me and said:
"You are the only painter here, but do you know what you are doing?"
"I don't know."
"Do you know that everything that they've done has been already seen and already made? All of that is out of date. Now we must make new things, something nearer ourselves, something more Russian. That's what I am doing myself: and you already are intuitively doing the same, it's in the air. You should come round and see me." And he gave me his address.

I often went round to Tatlin's house and I respected him greatly, considering him then — as I still do now — as a master. That's why I told him all about this. "You shouldn't go round to see him", he said and I didn't go there.

Vladimir Evgrafovich Tatlin lived at Staro Bassmannoya, on the eighth or ninth floor, in a flat belonging to the railway administration. He had made a studio in the loft which he heated himself. The studio was very strange; it was made with great sheets of plywood which served as partitions. And there he lived, all alone. And as was fitting for a former sailor, everything there was clean and well laid out.

He was then working on designs for Wagner's opera "The Flying Dutchman". He did these without a commission, simply for himself... He was making designs for costumes and architectural details for the sets. I was then astonished by their impressive quantity and by all the variations on a single detail... He was truly a great Russian painter who, although he would have liked recognition, waited... and was prepared to wait. And I am sure that recognition will still come to him. Only true Russian painters can work like this in the shade over the years without their true worth being recognised. They have a great love of work and faith in the future, even whilst remaining unknown, sometimes until death....

A FEW WORDS ABOUT MY FATHER

Varvara Rodchenko was born in 1925. After finishing at the Moscow Institute of Polygraphy she worked on the lay-out of books. She has designed more than 100 books, amongst them:
A series of albums of drawings by S. Eisenstein, 1967-70.
"A Book of Lyrics" by Semeon Kirsanov, 1966.
The Album "Mayakovsky the Artist", 1963.
A monograph on A.M. Rodchenko by L.F. Volkov-Lannit, 1968.
She is a photographer and member of the Union of Journalists and the Union of Artists.

Varvara Rodchenko

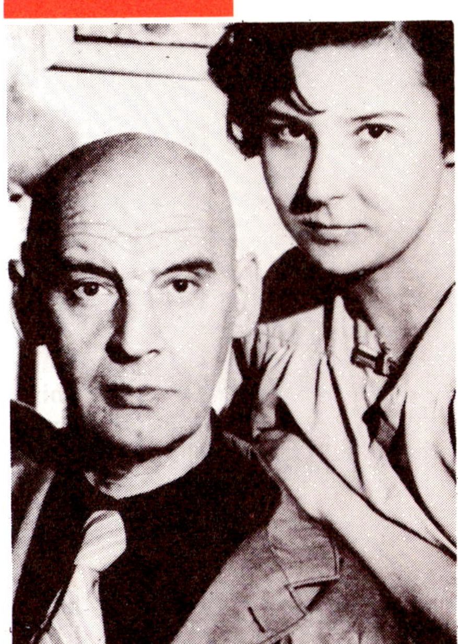

In 1909, when my father was 17, he made a collection of butterflies. This occupation so fascinated him that he copied the names and descriptions of the external appearances of the insects from a "Zoology" of insects into an exercise book. This small calico bound, black book has been preserved. It was called an "Anthology" because later, in 1909-11, Rodchenko liked to note down in it thoughts that corresponded with his frame of mind and pleased him.

In it are quotations from Dante, Rodin, Oscar Wilde, Victor Hugo, Nekrasov and Belinsky, Valery Bryusov and Charles Baudelaire.

"The soul of man is the greatest wonder of the world". Dante

"Not one great artist sees objects as they are in reality. If he did, he would not be an artist." Oscar Wilde

"Reconcile yourself to my muse
I do not know any other tune.
He, who lives without sorrow and anger does not love his homeland." N. Nekrasov

In the "Anthology" the poems and quotations sometimes alternate with tiny pen drawings: vignettes, landscapes, minute portraits of writers, Mallarmé for example.

My father used to say that his writing was so tiny in his youth that people often could not read his notes or letters.

A book containing his early poems and sonnets has been preserved. The tiny, clearly spaced figures run like an ornamental script, like a spider's web across the paper...

... Rodchenko was not able to have a secondary education but although not accepted formally as a student, he was allowed to attend the classes at the Kazan School of Art. Having studied there he could only graduate in four subjects from the school of general education (a church-run institution) and on finishing received this testimony:

This certificate is awarded to the son of a peasant, to Alexander Rodchenko, who having joined the course in the department of drawing as a voluntary student in the month of September, has completed the full course of the Kazan Art School in the Fine Art department exemplarily and made good progress in drawing and painting but could not enjoy the rights extended to those who have completed the course of the above-mentioned school as he had not taken a course of General Education and does not have proof of having completed such a course at another institution of General Education. In witness of this stand, this official seal and signature.

...Rodchenko moved to Moscow in 1915 and lived with V.F. Stepanova in V.V. Kandinsky's apartment on Dolgy Lane for some time. Kandinsky had a huge apartment. His mother and father lived on the first floor. There was a piano in the sitting room. Rodchenko loved music and would sometimes improvise at the piano although he did not know a note of music.

In 1922 my father was given a studio on Myasnitskaya Street (now Kirov Street) by Vkhutemas. V.F. Stepanova wrote:

"In the middle of the studio stands a long shelf for books. It divides the part used as a studio from the room where we live. Technical books, books on radio engineering, periodicals.

Folders of work, boxes of photographs and unsorted material rolled up in paper. This is the photograph archive bought at Sovkino last year for six roubles. This was all in a damp cellar, the bulb fused and they were finally put into sacks in darkness....

The laboratory is made out of cardboard on a wooden frame. The partition leading out into the studio is pasted over with posters from Dobrolet and Kino-Glaz.

Rulers, instruments, wire, saws and other things hang on the walls.

In the laboratory everything is painted black. A table with flaps and drawers, an enlarger, various chemicals, utensils, scales..."

In 1932, when I was 7, the partitions dividing the room were made of plywood and were painted with white gloss paint. The large room was the studio. The photography workroom was partitioned off in a corner, the space above it was used for storing things. Rolls of paper, constructions, dusty canvases and models of furniture for the theatre made of wooden slats lay there. The plywood next to the ceiling did not fit well and banged in the wind.

My grandmother, Olga Evdokimova, tall and plump in a soft flannel skirt, would often draw for me. She had learnt to read and draw only at the end of her life. In her drawings people were shown in profile with long noses....

In summer runner beans grew on the balcony. My father loved to sunbathe and would lie for a long time on the chaise longue.

Ladovsky, the architect's, balcony was next to the plywood partition. They would chat leaning across the railings. Ladovsky had red hair, light blue eyes and a freckled nose. He talked in a slightly hoarse lisping voice. He would come out on to the balcony in a black cap and red dressing gown. My father and he worked out a new plan of all the rooms and after repairs the apartment was rearranged according to that plan. It has remained that way ever since....

"Expressive Rhythm", gouache, 1943-44

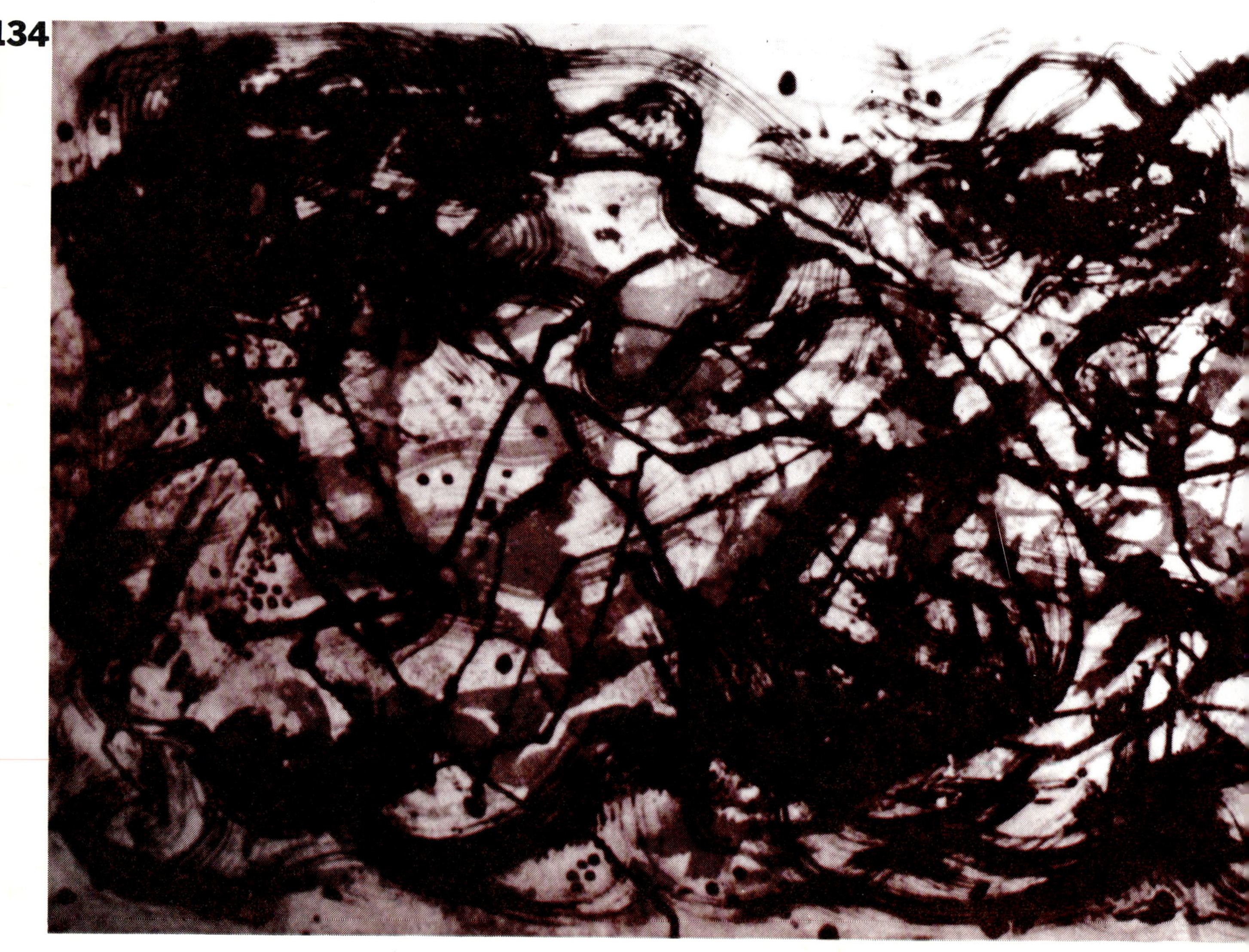

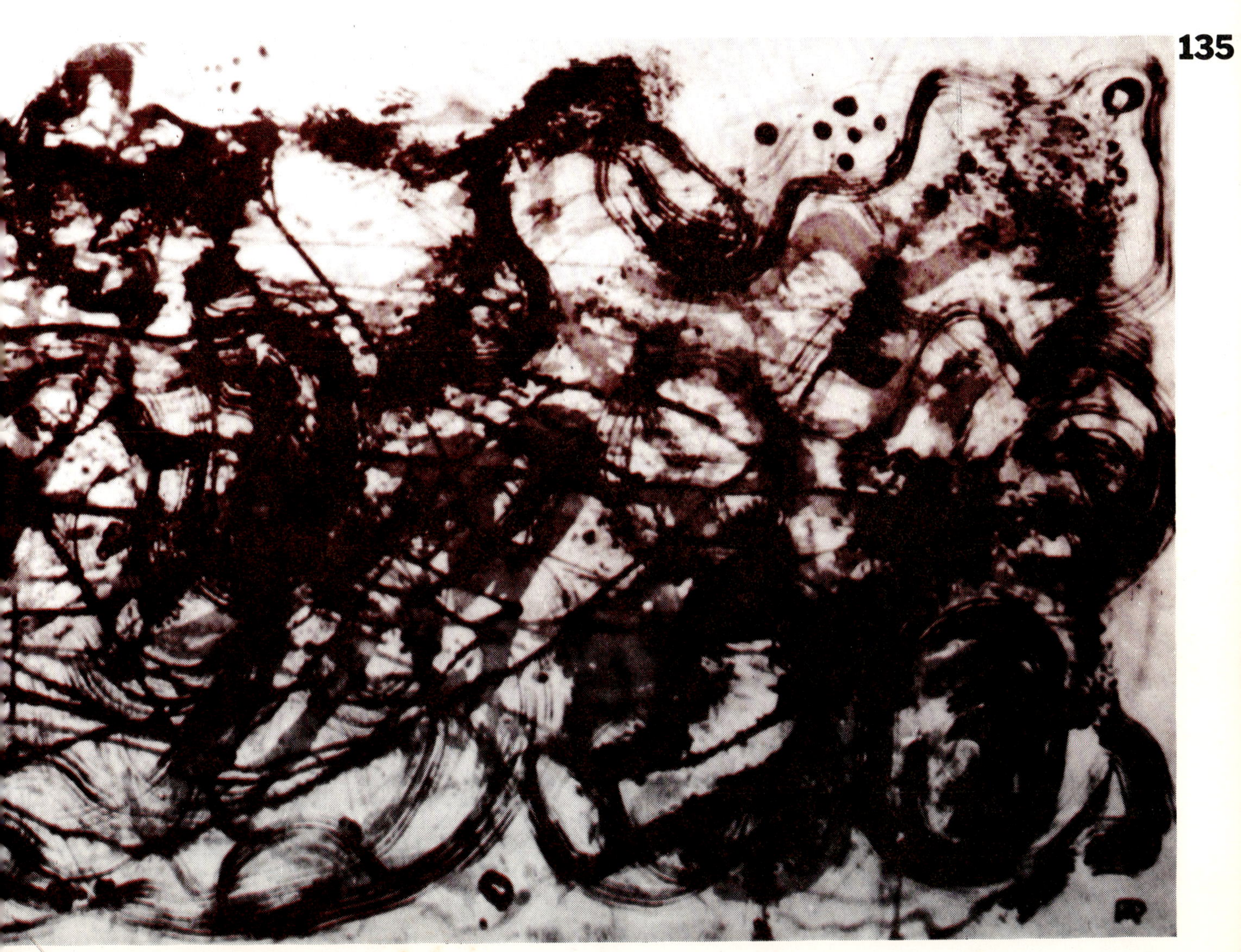

ACKNOWLEDGEMENTS

Many people and organisations through their kindness, co-operation and hard work have contributed to the making of this publication and to the exhibition with which it coincides. I should like to thank everyone who has been involved in the project for their help and commitment.

Special thanks should be given to Varvara Rodchenko, the artist's daughter, and to her son, Alexander Lavrentiev, who have both given their full support to the exhibition from the start. They have willingly provided information and photographs and have both written contributions especially for this catalogue; lastly, they have kindly agreed to lend forty-three works from the Rodchenko Archive to the exhibition.

Generous loans have also been made by George Costakis from his collection and by the Museum of Modern Art, New York, the largest institutional holder of work by Rodchenko in the West.

Others who have kindly loaned work to the exhibition or who have given help in some other way are the Albright Knox Gallery, Buffalo; Arteluche, Rome; La Boetie Inc., New York; The British Library, London; Bruce Fine Art, London; Les Buckingham, Southampton; Galerie Jean Chauvelin, Paris; Il Diaframma, Milan; Galerie Gmurzynska, Colgne; Wilhelm Hack Museum, Ludwigshafen; Annely Juda, London; David King, London; Galerie Liatowitsch, Basle; Professor Lubomir Linhardt, Prague; V. Marcadé, Paris; M. Martin Malburet, Paris; David McKnight, Abingdon; John Milner, Newcastle-upon-Tyne; Andrei Nakov, Paris; Colin Osman, London; Galerie Johanna Ricard, Nuremburg; Staatsgalerie, Stuttgart; Kyril Sokolov, Wooperton; The Society for Cultural Relations with the USSR, London; Gregory Walker, Oxford; the Wallraf-Richartz Museum, Cologne; as well as many who have asked to remain anonymous.

In London the British Council have been most helpful in sponsoring a research trip to the Soviet Union under the Anglo-Soviet cultural exchange scheme with the Ministry of Culture in Moscow. While in Moscow much valuable help has been given by Roland Smith, Cultural Attaché at the British Embassy and by A.G. Khalturin, Director of the Fine Arts Section of the Ministry of Culture of the USSR, and his staff.

Translations of much new material from the Russian have been made especially for this publication by Polly Phipps; Professor John Bowlt and Colin Osman have kindly allowed us to reprint from previously published work. Heide Grieve and Susan Spund made the translations from German and French material respectively. All of the critical essays with the exception of that by Hubertus Gassner have been specially written for this publication.

Ko Frerichs has, with the help of Graham Halstead, made skilful reconstructions of the furniture Rodchenko designed for the Workers' Club exhibited as part of the Soviet contribution to the International Exhibition of Decorative Art in Paris in 1925. Patricia Cowan has been tireless in the typing and retyping of innumerable manuscript and translations. Jaap Bremer with Bert de Graaf have organised the Eindhoven showing of the exhibition.

Lastly the making of this publication would not have been possible in the first place without the support of the Arts Council of Great Britain and the Elephant Trust.

Photographs: La Boetie, Inc., New York; Szymon Bojko, Warsaw; The British Library, London; Bruce Fine Art, London; Jean Chauvelin, Paris; Creative Camera Yearbook, London; Ex Libris, New York; Hubertus Gassner, Hamburg; Galerie Gmurzynska, Cologne; Annely Juda, London; David King, London ; Professor Lubomir Linhardt, Prague; Museum of Modern Art, New York; Colin Osman, London; Rodchenko Archive, Moscow; The Sunday Times, London. Photographs were specially made for the exhibition by Graham Bush, Alexander Lavrentiev and Miles Spackman.

"Non-objective composition: black on black", 1918, in the collection of the Museum of Modern Art, New York is not in the exhibition and does not appear in the catalogue section, its details are as follows: oil on canvas; 81.9 x 79.4cm; gift of the artist through Jay Leyda.

Full details of all other works illustrated can be found cross-referenced in the catalogue section.